Back to Nature

The Arcadian Myth in Urban America

Peter J. Schmitt

Foreword by John R. Stilgoe

THE JOHNS HOPKINS UNIVERSITY PRESS
BALTIMORE AND LONDON

For my wife

© 1969 Oxford University Press, Inc.
Preface, Foreword, and Selected Readings since 1969
© 1990 The Johns Hopkins University Press
All rights reserved
Printed in the United States of America

Originally published in 1969 in a hardcover edition by Oxford University
Press, Inc., with a foreword by Richard C. Wade, general editor,
Urban Life in America series
Johns Hopkins Paperbacks edition, 1990

Published by arrangement with Oxford University Press, Inc.

The Johns Hopkins University Press, 701 West 40th Street,
Baltimore, Maryland 21211
The Johns Hopkins Press Ltd., London

LIBRARY OF CONGRESS CATALOGING-IN-PUBLICATION DATA

Schmitt, Peter J.
  Back to nature : the Arcadian myth in urban America / Peter J.
Schmitt.—Johns Hopkins paperbacks ed.
  p.   cm.
  Reprint. Originally published: New York : Oxford University Press,
1969. Originally published in series: Urban life in America series.
  Includes bibliographical references.
  ISBN 0-8018-4013-9
  1. United States—Civilization—1865–1918. 2. Man—Influence of
environment—United States—History. 3. Landscape assessment—United
States—History. 4. Nature in literature. I. Title.
E169.1.S343   1990
973—dc20   89-43533
                                                                CIP

Cover illustration: "A member of the Pioneer Automobile Party in his
Toledo Car at the rim of the Grand Canyon," 5 February 1902, photographer
unknown. Courtesy of the Library of Congress, copy negative U S Z 62–7119.

Contents

Foreword

Wilderness preservation, wildlife conservation, antipollution legislation, scenic river easements, endangered species acts—such is the casually, almost thoughtlessly accepted vocabulary of late-twentieth-century Americans. Everyone seemingly accepts clean air, fresh water, sparkling clean beaches as proper goals for the Republic. Economic and social policies remain up for grabs, the dangerous stuff of congressional and radio talk-show diatribes, the raw material of Supreme Court decisions. About abortion and affirmative action, Third World brushfire wars and protective trade tariffs, much is said and nothing is quickly accepted, if accepted at all. But saving the whales and the California condor, guaranteeing the survival of West Coast redwoods and East Coast salmon, preserving Mississippi Basin prairie and Rocky Mountain crests, preoccupies not only special interest groups but an ever-widening circle of allied organizations now determined that prudent management of the natural environment, and particularly of the wilderness environment, is a good thing (and a safe thing, politically) to favor. Who, after all, champions pollution, massive forest fires, damming rivers? These days, virtually no one. An argument has carried much of the opposition before it. After centuries of subduing the wilderness continent, of "making land" with broadaxe and grub hoe, few in the United States now dare to suggest that a swamp might be drained.

In *Back to Nature*, Peter J. Schmitt stares back over the curving wake of national thought, almost of national consciousness, marking the era when a concatenation of new ideas first gathered enough force to change popular thinking, and then tracing it—and its

growth in extent and subtlety—toward the present. Here is a significant book, one thrusting far beyond run-of-the-mill analysis of
educated, elite opinion into the complexities of mass circulation
magazines, newspapers, and popular cinema. Here is a book on a
level with Leo Marx's *The Machine in the Garden* and Henry Nash
Smith's *Virgin Land: The American West as Symbol and Myth*, a
work that carries forward the concepts of wilderness introduced
by Roderick Nash's *Wilderness and the American Mind* and expanded in Cecelia Tichi's *New World, New Earth: Environmental
Reform in American Literature from the Puritans through Whit-
man.* But Peter Schmitt makes his greatest contribution by probing
deeply into the turn-of-the-century popular mind, finding riches
like those uncovered in David S. Reynolds's *Beneath the American
Renaissance: The Subversive Imagination in the Age of Emerson
and Melville.* Interdisciplinary in scope and approach, *Back to
Nature* illuminates a profound change in American popular thinking, perhaps the most profound of the twentieth century.

"With the development of industrialism and the concentration
of population in cities, there disappeared both the need and the
place for daily intimacy with the out-of-doors," asserts William
Gould Vinal in his 1940 opus, *Nature Recreation: Group Guidance
for the Out-of-Doors.* "In some schools, nature study degenerated
into an ambitious accumulation of facts chained to the pickled and
desiccated biology of the past." By 1940, Vinal had long been
active in "nature study," pioneering in enterprises analyzed by
Schmitt, especially popular ornithology, summer camps for city
children, and wilderness camping. His efforts, and those of his
colleagues, deserve scrutiny. Spiced as they are with Emersonian
Transcendentalism, revised understanding of Native Americans,
and a fervent desire to reform urban public school curricula, they
offer a thousand insights into the origins of state-supported conservation efforts and, especially, into the popular embracing of
ecology as an important science. Vinal and his early-twentieth-
century contemporaries saw their nature study movement penetrating every facet of American life. "Conservation is not school-
room conversation. It is not evangelism. It is not a subject or a

textbook for recitation," Vinal argued. "It is a way of living, a practical treatment to be accorded the outdoor environment." But Vinal understood—indeed, announced in the very title of his book—the intimate connection of conservation and ecology with recreation, and especially the recreation of city dwellers. In his thinking, the wilderness outdoors exists as a fragile and wonderful playground in which city dwellers may re-create their spirits.

As early as 1884, George Washington Sears had argued the virtues of wilderness camping for the urban masses, and his *Woodcraft*, one of the first American manuals of recreational camping, hints at the antiurbanism that Schmitt so precisely detects in this volume. As the nature study, wilderness recreation movement gathered strength, it focused on the plight of urban residents locked into what it denounced as a degrading physical environment. Sears turned his sentiments into verse:

> For brick and mortar breed filth and crime,
> With a pulse of evil that throbs and beats,
> And men are withered before their prime
> By the curse paved in with the lanes and streets.
>
> And lungs are poisoned and shoulders bowed.
> In the smothering reek of mill and mine
> And death stalks in on the struggling crowd—
> But he shuns the shadow of oak and pine.

Between *Woodcraft* and *Nature Recreation*, roughly the time span of Schmitt's study, love of wilderness became a national love, blossoming in the Boy and Girl Scout movements, in the summer camp movement, in the camping vacation, reshaping the coursework of public schools, fueling parkland acquisition and development, and producing a juvenile and adult American literature of stunning proportions. Titles like *The Motor Boat Club on the Great Lakes* and *The Camp Fire Girls at Pine Tree Camp* endure only on dusty public library shelves and perhaps on fireplace mantels in forest cabins, but adult books like Owen Wister's *The Virginian*, Jack London's *Call of the Wild*, and, perhaps most notably, Gene Stratton Porter's *The Girl of the Limberlost* and *Freckles*—all of them in their time best sellers—remain widely read today. One struggles to think of any "urban novel" that had the popular, if not the artistic, success of these.

And here, perhaps, is the most intriguing dividend of the book that follows. *Back to Nature* offers a sort of trailhead from which to explore the continuing dislike of urban living now suffusing the Republic, a dislike that for many foreigners is now the most salient national characteristic. As Peter Schmitt makes brutally clear, "Retreat to the wilderness was a middle-class response to urban pressures." In the wilderness, in solitude, the twentieth-century American might find his or her spirit renewed in ways no city might match. This book contributes not only to our understanding of the place of wilderness in the popular mind, but to the forces that made early-twentieth-century Americans dissatisfied with the urban lives they had chosen. It offers insights into why urban young people move about attired in wilderness apparel and equipped with backpacks, almost as though they are ready, on a moment's notice, to abandon urban form for the enriching world of nature. Even as it traces the formation of contemporary thinking about wilderness experience and ecological approaches to resource conservation, it hints at the future of the American urban environment.

JOHN R. STILGOE
Robert and Lois Orchard Professor in the History of Landscape
Harvard University

"It was a pleasure and a privilege to walk with him," Emerson said of Henry Thoreau, who wore "straw hat, stout shoes, strong gray trousers" and carried nothing but an old music book in which to press specimens and "diary and pencil, a spy-glass for birds, micro-scope, jack-knife, and twine" in his pockets. In 1862, Thoreau rooted his "sauntering" in "Sainte Terre"—the Holy Earth—in the 54 pages of "Walking." Turning toward forest and sunset, calling West another name for wild, he told his readers, "in Wildness is the preservation of the World."

In 1968, Colin Fletcher quoted both Emerson and Thoreau in *The Complete Walker*. He took 353 pages and 750 index entries to tell Americans what to carry and how to travel. Between Thoreau and Fletcher, the American nature movement developed in all its variety, complexity, and expense. As John Stilgoe has shown in *Borderland*, Americans made separate peace with urban and in-dustrial problems. They moved to suburbs, sent children to camp, formed a national park system, and subscribed to outdoor adven-tures in *Forest and Stream*, *National Geographic*, and "summer numbers" of family magazines.

Ostensibly, city people fled "back to nature." But the image is deceptive; many thought they were going forward, toward an urbane esthetic country people would never know. They found Arcadia at the country club, the dude ranch, and the summer place. They spent money lavishly to live "the Simple Life." Surro-gate adventurers sought distant places with brush and camera, sending back trophy words and images for city people. Gene Strat-ton Porter tramped in muddy boots, but sanitized her Limberlost

for city readers. Twentieth-century tourism harmonized natural
beauty with urban comfort. Americans made armchair adventure
and vacation travel the crowning convenience of city living.

As the years passed, people overcrowded parks and trampled
wild places. Isolated climbers on the faces of Yosemite could look
down on roadways clogged with cars. So many Americans turned
out that outdoor leaders preached minimum impact to save the
countryside. Environmental lawyers wondered whether trees had
legal standing.

Outdoors proved a growth industry in the 1970s. Thoreau's "Simplicity, simplicity, simplicity!" brought more and more nylon, high-
tech gear, and freeze-dried food. By 1984, Colin Fletcher needed
twice as many pages to keep up with new equipment and new
ethics in *The Complete Walker III*. Yet careful observers noted
that many a purchase never left the patio. One *Backpacker* writer
offered to take others' equipment on exotic treks and certify it
"expedition gear." Catalog merchants kept their outdoor labels but
tailored products to an indoor market. Like nature programming
on public television, sumptuous photography in *National Wildlife*
or *Birder's World* captured outdoor thrills in perfect comfort.
First-ever photographs of the azure-rumped tanager fulfilled the
promise of distant mountains and rugged vistas. As Thoreau
mourned so long ago, "We now no longer camp as for a night, but
have settled down." Recent controversies over desert water, Alaskan land, park management, and urban sprawl intensified debate:
What did Nature mean today? Who needed it and why? People
read about environmental ethics, some for the first time.

Thinking about nature came into its own between Thoreau and
Colin Fletcher, as Loren Owings demonstrated in his 324-page
bibliography, *Environmental Values, 1860–1972*. Outdoor writers
now earned their way with book royalties and special assignments.
Anthologies in the 1980s brought together "the new naturalists,"
highlighting a common cadre from Edward Abbey to Ann Zwinger.
In 1986, *Antaeus* asked its writers who preceded them. Stephen
Trimble queried several of his authors for *Words from the Land*.
Inspiration flowed from a narrow cornucopia, from Aldo Leopold

to John Muir and back to Thoreau—a handful of prophets and desert fathers—ascetic origins for today's environmentalism.

Believers thought they stood apart from an asphalt-addicted public. In its "Legacy of Edward Abbey," *Backpacker* said three times that Abbey "preached to the converted"—to the faithful wandering in a wilderness that seemed for some the promised land. When Annie Dillard won a Pulitzer Prize for *Pilgrim at Tinker Creek* and Anne LaBastille published *Beyond Black Bear Lake,* Stephen Trimble wondered why so few women had turned to nature writing, and so recently. Have we lost track? What of an earlier Anna Comstock or Gene Stratton Porter, Kathrene Pinkerton or Sally Carrighar? Who did come before?

Modern America and its crises emerged long ago. What Perry Miller once called "the obsessive American drama"—resolving civilization and wilderness—occupied us for generations. Clearly, stridently, earlier naturists offered valued insights. If today's Deep Ecologists wish to "Live as if Nature Mattered," Liberty Hyde Bailey preached the same message in *The Holy Earth* in 1915. The same Doubleday that named *Foxfire* its all-time best seller also published *Country Life in America* and Gene Stratton Porter's nature novels in Teddy Roosevelt's time. How pervasive back-to-nature thinking has been; how many promoted it with today's fervor long ago. Behind the current "nylon revolution" is a canvas-carrying, smoke-filled, pine tar and pennyroyal past, when environmental ethics found broad popular sympathy. How broad, this book suggests.

P. J. S.

Kalamazoo, Michigan
August 1989

Preface to the First Edition

I am most grateful to Professor Timothy Smith who first started me asking questions, and to The Fund for the Advancement of Education and its committee on the Role of Education in American History for supporting two years of research in an area at first glance so far removed from "educational history." When I first began to explore the effect of urbanization on the traditional agrarian interpretation of "nature" at the turn of the century, I discovered very quickly a large group of men of diverse backgrounds who engaged in public definition of themselves and their relationship to the natural environment. Such men lost no opportunity to declare that urban Americans were desperately in need of outdoor activities. Some felt city dwellers must have contact with natural scenery simply to survive; others seemed to suggest that nature belonged to the urban intellectuals with money and insight enough to appreciate it. Yet all appeared eager to spread their ideas as widely as possible. There developed in the last decades of the nineteenth century a considerable body of "nature writing" that appeared in a wide variety of popular periodicals, technical journals and government documents. By the twentieth century, school administrators, youth workers, city planners, and politicians began to act as though people in cities did require some exposure to the country. If historians are correct in ascribing urban interest in the out-of-doors to lingering nostalgia for independence, self-sufficiency and family farming, the consequences may well be minor. If, on the other hand, city dwellers have replaced Thomas Jefferson's agrarian ideas with a new and urban nature myth, public policies could increasingly reflect it.

I should like to add that this study has grown out of extended reading in the materials of "popular culture" which encompassed something over a thousand books and articles. Documentation in addition to that given in my Notes is available in "Call of the Wild, the Arcadian Myth in Urban America, 1900–1930," Ph.D. dissertation, University of Minnesota, 1966.

I am indebted to the editors of *Forest History* and *The Journal of Popular Culture* for permission to reproduce materials which previously appeared in different form in their pages.

P. J. S.

Kalamazoo, Michigan
August 1969

Introduction

Wild nature has changed almost as much as an image in American rhetoric as it has in its physical features. The first settlers once fought against "barbarism" to preserve what they knew as culture and sophistication. But after the Revolution, Americans fashioned a new identity for themselves. Fortified with European Romanticism, they took nature and not civilization as the common denominator of the new republic. Fourth of July orators proclaimed that American republicans were products, not victims, of the wilderness. Thomas Jefferson wrote that sturdy yeoman farmers, shielded from the artificiality of commerce and city life, lived lives of quiet simplicity as the "chosen people of god."

Jefferson's belief developed into a popular myth: one of those "attitudes" James M. Williams described as "generally prevalent ways of reacting of which people become conscious only incidentally as they try to drill them into their children or as they meet people of contrary attitudes." [1] In 1893, Frederick Jackson Turner worked the agrarian attitude into "The Significance of the Frontier in American History." But Turner spoke to the American Historical Association at a Columbian Exposition which celebrated America's urban and industrial future. Americans might still want their Presidents born on the farm in 1893, but they hardly expected a working farmer.

Turner accepted Jefferson's dichotomy between rural good and urban evil, and he noted with a touch of sadness that frontier agriculture and frontier virtue were giving way to urban com-

[1] James M. Williams, *Our Rural Heritage, the Social Psychology of Rural Development* (New York: Knopf, 1925), p. 10. Permission to quote by courtesy of Appleton-Century-Crofts, Division of Merideth Publishing Company.

plexity.² Later historians, most notably Richard Hofstadter and Henry Nash Smith, continued to interpret the imagery of factory and farm, of city and country, even of sophistication and simplicity, as clearly antithetical. Smith identified "nature" as a source of moral virtue, with agriculture as a way of life. He argued, however, that "the static ideas of virtue and happiness and peace drawn from the bosom of the virgin wilderness . . . proved quite irrelevant for a society committed to the ideas of civilization and progress." Leo Marx declared in *The Machine in the Garden* that America's continuing enthusiasm for the out-of-doors represented a flight from reality into "naïve and anarchic primitivism." George Mowry called this enthusiasm a vitiating "social nostalgia" which "America's ruling economic classes" stimulated because they found "rural virtues" politically useful.³

But so considerable a cross section of urban intellectuals claimed to be "nature lovers" at the turn of the century that "social nostalgia" for a farmer's past may not adequately explain their commitment. Many praised their rural childhood, but few returned to farming; few seemed frustrated in the suburbs because they could not raise chickens. Urban Americans settling in suburban developments and visiting country clubs, summer camps, or national parks had little in common with their country neighbors. They looked at scenery and sportsmanship and country living, in a way, it seemed, that only "city people" could. When city dwellers began to insist on taking over suburban nature for themselves

---

² Frederick Jackson Turner, "The Significance of the Frontier in American History," in *The Frontier in American History* (New York: Henry Holt and Company, 1920); for a penetrating discussion of Turner's melancholy see William Coleman, "Science and Symbol in the Turner Frontier Hypothesis," *American Historical Review*, LXXII (October 1966), pp. 22–50.

³ Henry Nash Smith, *Virgin Land: The American West as Symbol and Myth* (New York: Vintage edition, 1957), p. 135; Leo Marx, *The Machine in the Garden: Technology and the Pastoral Ideal in America* (New York: Galaxy Book edition, 1967), p. 11; George Mowry, *The Urban Nation, 1920–1960* (New York: Hill and Wang, 1965), p. 2. See also Roderick Nash, "The American Cult of the Primitive," *American Quarterly*, XVIII (June 1966), p. 526; and Morton and Lucia White, *The Intellectual versus the City, From Thomas Jefferson to Frank Lloyd Wright* (New York: New American Library edition, 1964), p. 230.

they quarreled with traditionalists who equated country living with a rural society.

Americans turning "back to nature" rather than "back to the land" responded to a philosophy only faintly related to the pattern of thought which Richard Hofstadter and others have called "agrarianism." [4] Simply put, this urban response valued nature's spiritual impact above its economic importance; it might better be called "Arcadian." Those who looked to nature for a living had categorically settled for something less than Arcadia; the man on the street, not the man on the land, might better benefit from "natural" resources. Webster's *Dictionary* cited John Burroughs in 1899 to demonstrate that "Arcadia" as a word meant little more than a "scene of simple pleasure and untroubled quiet." As a place it lay somewhere on the urban fringe, easily accessible and mildly wild, the goal of a "nature movement" led by teachers and preachers, bird-watchers, socialites, scout leaders, city-planners, and inarticulate commuters, all of whom applauded William Smythe when he offered in *City Homes on Country Lanes* "the cream of the country and the cream of the city, leaving the skim-milk for those who like that sort of thing." [5]

However ancient the Arcadian heritage, and however modern its values seem today, men trying to cope with the pressures of urbanization at the turn of the century worked hardest to define

[4] The "back-to-nature" movement differed from the "back-to-the-land" program which sought to place the urban poor on garden patches in the suburbs. Social reformers such as New York lawyer Bolton Hall were sure that all men could be producers with vacant-lot gardens and rural vegetable patches. "Agriculture is unique among occupations," Hall told his audiences, "in that it can be engaged in without one's first attaining any particular experience." Any dunce, he continued, could raise a crop of onions on an acre of land. John Burroughs believed that where there were cows there was Arcadia, but to Bolton Hall the cow was merely "a ruminating machine for producing milk." The industrial metaphor was as disconcerting to nature lovers as Hall's "little lots well-tilled" were foreign to working farmers. See Bolton Hall, *A Little Land and a Living* (New York: Arcadia Press, 1908), pp. 40, 80; John Burroughs, *Signs and Seasons*, Writings of John Burroughs, VII (Boston, New York: Houghton Mifflin, 1904, 1st ed. 1886), p. 254; Bolton Hall, *Three Acres and Liberty* (New York: Macmillan, 1907), p. 10.
[5] William Smythe, *City Homes on Country Lanes* (New York: Macmillan, 1922), p. 60.

the role of nature in an industrial society. Then a whole generation of "literary commuters" took it upon themselves to translate nature into urban terms. Genteel essayists like Andrew Jackson Downing and *Harper's* editor Donald G. Mitchell had written earlier the "life of a cultivated mind in the country," as Downing put it in the 1840's.[6] They suggested urban Americans pattern themselves after the gentry they knew through English literature. From the 1880's on into the 1920's, middle-class journalists tried to combine country life and city culture in essays calculated to appeal to urban readers. These writers were scarcely gentlemen farmers. They were college professors, merchants, clerks, men of distinctly urban interests who tried to make rural America the playground of an urban society. Some, such as Ernest Thompson Seton, felt so strongly the need to reach urban readers that they embellished their writing with literary devices to attract a wider audience. Others, such as John Burroughs, argued that the message was too sacred to manipulate, and thus they began a "nature faker controversy" that embroiled even Theodore Roosevelt. In any event, a philosophy which seems in retrospect appropriate only to *Outing* and *Forest and Stream* blossomed in the *Ladies' Home Journal, Good Housekeeping, Atlantic Monthly,* and *Saturday Evening Post.*

Other nature enthusiasts took Arcadia out of books and tried to locate it in life, first for adults and then, more poignantly perhaps, for children. By the middle of the nineteenth century, garden suburbs, city parks, and country estates began to show the influence of landscape designers. Landscape architects like Andrew Jackson Downing and Frederick Law Olmsted tried to make American nature conform to their reading of Romantics like Uvedale Price and William Gilpin. Still relying on Price and Gilpin, Olmsted and later Charles Eliot carried down to the twentieth century the idea that nature could be made to conform to urban tastes.

[6] Andrew Jackson Downing, *The Architecture of Country Houses* (New York: Appleton, 1850), p. 258.

Landscape designers found a lucrative field in the park movement that swept the cities in the 1880's and 1890's. But others also came to feel that city dwellers must have at least occasional contact with peaceful scenery. Psychologists, sociologists, and educators developed insights into urban behavior that suggested society could not survive without nature. Instinctivists, environmentalists, and crowd psychologists all supposed that man was not made for urban life. Many educators were impressed with G. Stanley Hall's genetic psychology. Hall argued that children must recapitulate human development from primitive rural stages to complex urban life as they matured; denial of this process in the cities bred social immaturity, crime, and chaos. Fresh Air Funds and summer camps for city children multiplied rapidly after the 1880's. The Woodcraft Indians, the Sons of Daniel Boone, the Campfire Girls, and the Boy Scouts offered outdoor exposure to city children. At the end of the nineteenth century more and more educators came to feel the schools must provide the contact with nature that city children lacked. Bluebirds and bean-sprouts had a decidedly rural savor, but "nature-study" was not designed for rural schools, and not intended to make farmers of city children.

Enthusiasts claimed the country was in the midst of a full-scale return to nature. They cited increasing state and national park statistics, the growth of commuter railways, and a variety of other sources to back their contention. Yet it always seemed that Arcadia was easier to find in literature. Twentieth-century readers found a steady stream of nature essays and suburban self-help advice in newspapers and popular magazines. Children in extraordinary numbers enjoyed the outdoor adventures of the Bobbsey Twins and the Rover Boys. Their elders put "nature romances" such as those of Gene Stratton-Porter and Harold Bell Wright on bestseller lists over and over again.

By the 1920's, however, many suburbanites began to discover urban sprawl. Some responded by joining primitivists in a retreat to wilderness areas. Under the enthusiasm of men like Benton MacKaye, others identified with the Regional Planning movement, hoping that engineering could bring about a metropolitan Arcadia. MacKaye conceived of a New England megalopolis bounded by nothing less ambitious than the Appalachian Trail. Conservative planners confined themselves to urging open-space zoning, green-belt developments, and parkway construction. Many of the regional planners reflected a growing belief that the nature movement had lost intensity, even as more and more people looked to outdoor recreation. They and men like them felt they must guard the remnants of natural environment for an urban majority not quite capable of applying Arcadian principles in day-to-day situations.

It would be idle to try to locate beginnings for the Arcadian philosophy in the influence of single individuals or even to suggest that a single individual brought change or direction to the nature movement. Some men gained more prominence than others. *Harper's* editor Donald Mitchell was better known than landscape designer Charles Eliot. Essayist John Burroughs became a legend to those who saw in him the virtues they ascribed to nature itself. But most who contributed to the Arcadian mystique were only modestly known. Just such an individual was Cornell University educator Liberty Hyde Bailey. Bailey felt himself a spokesman for the nature movement, and his writings illustrate something of the interests and fervor of the "nature-lovers." Like most nature writers, in fact like most Americans of his time, Bailey grew up in the country, but he soon decided that "horticulture" offered more than frontier farming. His reputation rests on his career as a teacher of teachers; but, convinced that city dwellers needed outdoor life, he turned in 1901 to editing Doubleday, Page's new suburban journal, *Country Life in America*. Integrating inspiration and do-it-yourself directions for the good life, he made that journal the most popular of all suburban periodicals.

Bird-watching, landscaping, and the new interest in city parks seemed proof to Bailey that urban America heard the call of the wild, but he particularly feared that city children might lose the echo of the country. In 1903 Bailey gathered together materials from his editorials and published *The Nature Study Idea*, a high-water mark in the philosophy of the nature movement. "Of late years," he wrote, "there has been a rapidly growing feeling that we must live closer to nature; and we must perforce begin with the child." [7] Correctly taught in city schools, summer camps and youth groups, in nature essays and wilderness novels, nature lore could transform first the children and then society.

Bailey hardly stood idle waiting for the gospel to trickle through formal educational channels. When the Education Committee of Boston's Twentieth Century Club invited him to lecture in 1905, he spoke on "The Outlook to Nature." The need for "landscape that is easy of access and undefiled" he found "indicated by the rapidly spreading suburban movement, by the vacationing in the country, and by the astonishing multiplication of books about nature." [8] Future Americans, rightly guided, must be neither "country-bred nor city-bred, but suburban-bred, product of neither extreme." Bailey aimed his doctrine at those who went to the country for "more room, less racket, better health, more freedom, and closer relations with sun and wind and sky" and not to take up farming.[9]

Theodore Roosevelt chose Bailey to chair his blue-ribbon "Country Life Commission" that examined agrarian ideals in 1908. The Commission collected information so disturbing that Roosevelt asked to have it printed at once, but embarrassed Congressmen forbade the Commission to continue in any capacity. Agricultural technology had outstripped the art of country living as farmers rushed pell-mell to city ways if not to city jobs. "The backbone of the rural question is at bottom a moral problem," Bailey found. We had failed to teach farmers "to hoe potatoes and to hear the birds sing at the same time." [10]

As the years went by, Bailey looked uneasily at the burgeoning

[7] Liberty Hyde Bailey, *The Nature Study Idea* (New York: Doubleday, Page, 1903), p. 14.

[8] Liberty Hyde Bailey, *The Outlook to Nature* (New York: Macmillan, 1905), p. 8.

[9] *Ibid.*, pp. 95, 97.

[10] Liberty Hyde Bailey, *The Holy Earth* (New York, 1943, 1st ed. 1915), pp. 26, 37.

nature movement. Nature-study answered increasingly to science; summer camping for all its virtues turned to institutional efficiency; popular fiction romanticized nature almost unbearably. In 1915, he published *The Holy Earth* to order Americans back to fundamentals. "Most of us live from the box and the bottle and the tin-can; we are even feeding our cattle from the factory and the bag," he wrote; "no thought of the seasons . . . comes with the trademark or the brand. And so we all live mechanically, from shop to table, without contact, and irreverently." Down through the eons of geologic time the earth was holy; but Bailey noted "how desperately soon may men reduce it all to ruin and to emptiness, and how slatternly may they violate the scenery!" [11]

Yet it seemed to Bailey that "no people should be forbidden the influence of the forest." [12] Nature writing and country-life essays might serve for dreaming, but they were not enough. Americans on the land must hold it in stewardship not only for future generations but for those already living in cities. In the public domain, wild land ought to be "held by the people to be sold in small parcels to those who desire to get out to the backgrounds but who do not want to be farmers. . . ." [13]

Bailey concluded in a later reprint of *The Holy Earth* that critics had passed him by. His essay faded in the bird and flower and forest romances dominating the nature movement. But if he could no longer believe that the nature movement would reform the whole society, Bailey still argued that the minority should impose its will on the majority as a duty to the future. However much we became a nation of cities, we could not escape our need for wild land, "and to keep this land, for ourselves and our successors," he believed, must be "the first responsibility of the race." [14]

Yet by the 1920's, Bailey acknowledged that his hopes had tarnished. The "nature movement" was active enough. Nature writers published as often as ever. Landscape architects still

[11] *Ibid.*, pp. 65, 114.
[12] *Ibid.*, p. 105.
[13] *Ibid.*, p. 44.
[14] Liberty Hyde Bailey, *Universal Service* (New York: Macmillan, 1923), p. 35.

thought of themselves as more evangelists than engineers. Conservation was governmental policy and national park facilities already overcrowded. Nature novels and wilderness movies were immensely popular; but the great vision seemed dissipated even as its influence spread. In 1923 Bailey made his last real effort to rouse the old enthusiasm in a cryptic little volume he called *The Seven Stars,* a search through the hubbub of commerce, where men mistook "noise and tinsel and jingle for happiness." [15] Arcadia, which seemed so near at hand in *The Nature Study Idea,* evaporated as Bailey's hero moved beyond the city to suburbs where nature seemed all but lost in occasional vacant lots. Real country people appeared as indifferent as ever to their surroundings, and the quest continued into the last refuge of the backgrounds. Still, Bailey, like nature writers, landscape architects, and wilderness lovers, convinced himself that he still held the vision, however much others might have strayed, and still must point the way even though he tailored nature worship to the problems of suburban living.

Bailey and others who made public confession of their philosophy supported parks, youth organizations, and other public causes, yet always appeared ready to withdraw to country clubs and private estates. The best-known supporters of the movement (with the exception of John Burroughs) were middle-class promoters of a genteel country life they clearly thought superior to agriculture. They made their ideas known in popular periodicals ranging from the *Atlantic Monthly* and *Saturday Review* to *The Arena* and *Cosmopolitan* and may well have provided the inspiration for a much larger group which did little more than argue that the city was no place to raise a family.

[15] Liberty Hyde Bailey, *The Seven Stars* (New York: Macmillan, 1923), p. 7.

BACK TO NATURE

1

Back to Nature

To those of us who live and work amid the artificiality of
city life there is something irresistibly attractive in the idea of
being close to the heart of nature, wearing old clothes and
living for a time the free and easy life which we like to imagine
was lived before the call of the city became insistent.

Robert Van Court, "Vacation Homes in the Woods,"
Independent, LXXII (June 6, 1912), 1239.

As the nineteenth century came to a close, many people, like
English sparrows, seemed to thrive on city life. Others returned
as failures to the family farm, praising country life; but an increasing number of city dwellers turned "back to nature," rather
than "back to the farm," mainly to escape the minor irritants of
urban life. Poverty, crime, and disease disturbed them less than
did the press of crowds along antiquated sidewalks, the rattle of
iron wheels on cobblestone streets, or soft-coal smog. Such folk
heartily approved the opportunities for social and economic success, the educational and religious benefits, and the cultural
advantages that accompanied urban life. They simply realized,
as every suburban mother knew, that the city is no place to
raise a family.

"Nature lovers," as they called themselves without embarrassment, believed their urban vantage point gave them a special
sensitivity toward the world around them. Long before Jack
London and the twentieth century, sophisticated men had listened to the call of the wild; it had flourished in the urbane
world of the eighteenth century and echoed in the Romantic
thought of the nineteenth. But as the twentieth century ap-

3

proached, the "back-to-nature" movement shifted from being a
luxury of the rich to a preoccupation of an urban middle-class.
Ordinary city dwellers longed for contact with the natural world,
and headed for the wilderness and the suburban backyard.

Sportsmen tried to capture by temporary immersion in wild
nature what wilderness-lover Robert Marshall once called "the
ecstasy in non-intellectual adventure." [1] Others combined country
life and city convenience as commuters. They appropriated open
lands and abandoned farms on the urban fringe to establish their
own domestic landscape. Nostalgia for an agrarian past played
no part in their thinking; inevitably they rejected a mythology
that exalted men who lived off the land. Sportsmen and commuters
both discovered a wall between themselves and their country
neighbors "higher than any class barrier in all civilization," as one
of them put it; they looked upon fields and forests as inspirational
resources for their urban life. [2]

"It is becoming more and more apparent that the ideal life is
that which combines something of the social and intellectual
advantages and physical comforts of the city with the inspiration
and peaceful joys of the country," Cornell educator Liberty Bailey
wrote in 1901. Bailey's "ideal life" assumed a set of values hardly
envisioned in the cluster of attitudes that literary historians have
called the "Agrarian Myth." In the complex of ideas behind
Thomas Jefferson's belief that God's chosen people must be
farmers lay most of the virtues dear to the eighteenth and nineteenth centuries: industry, order and justice, freedom from want
and ambition alike, and homely dignity. Wild nature, in the
agrarian economy, was a gift from Heaven to sustain the progress
of the American people. A natural resource advanced civilization
and enriched the individuals favored with its development. [3]

The American agrarian myth was a response to a complex economic order in which the urge to get ahead dominated pioneer
ethics, but intellectuals like Jefferson soon made it the vocabulary
for a system of nature-centered values descending, with an echo
of the *Georgics*, from European Romantic thought. [4] Romanticism
was a literary cult, committed to a picturesque landscape minis-

tering to men's minds rather than to their bodies. In the absence of country gentlemen and Lake poets who felt no need to make the land yield more than a literary crop, American intellectuals grafted Romantic justification to agrarian economics. But to Lewis Mumford, whose Romanticism was stronger than his interest in agriculture, the gap between nature worship and nineteenth-century farming was "one of the most sardonic jests in history." Farmers made poor Romantics, Mumford found. The sturdy yeoman of the agrarian myth, with his eye on the main chance, was only too ready "to barter all his glorious heritage for gas light and paved streets and starched collars and skyscrapers . . . ." [5]

The European Romantic's distaste for city life was tempered in this country by the need for money to finance the ease of a "country gentleman." American commuters combined Romantic idealism and urban income in a movement that was hardly unsophisticated or anti-intellectual, however much it encouraged "the simple life." A growing literature of country life and natural history written by middle-class intellectuals like John Burroughs, Dallas Sharp, and Liberty Bailey served to guide commuters who extracted the romance from the agrarian tradition, bolstered that romance with their understanding of psychology, and wove, in their own defense, the myth of an Arcadia beyond the trolley line.

Middle-class merchants and professional men had begun to look for a place in the country as soon as railroads radiated outward from major cities in the nineteenth century. Landscape architect Andrew Jackson Downing noted as early as 1848:

> Hundreds and thousands, formerly obliged to live in the crowded streets of cities, now find themselves able to enjoy a country cottage, several miles distant,—the old notions of time and space being half annihilated; and these suburban cottages enable the busy citizen to breathe freely, and keep alive his love for nature, till the time shall come when he shall have wrung out of the nervous hand of commerce enough means to enable him to realize his ideal of the "retired life" of an American landed proprietor.[6]

Beginning in the 1850's, *Harper's* editor Donald G. Mitchell wrote of the "retired life" in half a dozen books of essays. His *Reveries of a Bachelor,* published under the pseudonym of "Ik Marvel" in 1850, pictured a city hero of refinement, dozing and dreaming by the country fireside; it passed through twenty-eight editions as the standard nineteenth-century version of the simple life. Mitchell concluded that agrarian idylls existed only in the language of "a plentiful crop of orators for all the agricultural fairs (most of them city lawyers, not knowing a Devon from a Hereford), who delight in expatiating upon the opportunities for culture afforded by the quiet and serenity of a farm life." It must be "the grossest kind of an untruth," said Mitchell, "to say that the working farmer's life is specially favored in this respect." He went on to describe "the horny hands, the tired body, the hay-dust and the scent of the stables" that accompanied serious farming.[7]

Mitchell, like the nature lovers who followed him, preferred the "imaginative labor of filling out a pleasant rural picture, the brooks murmuring with a contented babble, cattle lazily grouped that need no care, and flowers opening that need no culture." He advertised for "a Farm, of not less than one hundred acres, and within three hours of the city. It must have a running stream, a southern or eastern slope, not less than twenty acres in woods, and a water view." "Edgewood," as he came to call his country place, was near enough to a town of forty thousand to "give a good every-day feeling of companionship with the world, without the world's noises." If his neighbors scoffed at his cottage of native stone or his strand of ivy from Kenilworth Castle, Mitchell felt it was simply that country tastes were too ambitious.[8]

Most working farmers lacked the funds for Arcadian country living, and they also lacked the leisure. Mitchell satisfied himself that:

> If a man perspires largely in a cornfield on a dusty day, and washes hastily in the horsetrough, and eats in shirt-sleeves that date their cleanliness three days back, and loves fat pork and

cabbage "neat," he will not prove the Arcadian companion at
dinner . . . . A long day of close fieldwork leaves one in a very
unfit mood for appreciative study of either poetry or the natural
sciences.[9]

A half-century later, New York journalist Andrew Wheeler
agreed that farmers found little time for reflection when crops
meant money. "There isn't any delicious odour of new-mown hay
in the haying operation," he wrote in 1901: "the Arcadian delights
of it are only apparent to the on-lookers, and, if there is any
satisfaction to the workers themselves, it depends a great deal on
whether hay is worth twelve dollars a ton, and who owns it." [10]
Local farmers hired to perform the necessary chores of country life
often scorned the changes that city people made in traditional
ways of doing things, and could be annoyingly independent. One
commuter confided hiring a "native" gave a man the same friendly
feeling he had toward "a walking stick which he has cut from
one of his own trees." [11]

Journalists like Downing and Mitchell might praise commuting,
and men like John Burroughs and California's John Muir might
even pursue country life back to elemental simplicities, but the
great mass of nature lovers in the nineteenth century only sea-
soned their lives with wildness. Urban gentlemen took to forest
and stream for temporary outings, secure in their belief that they
remained gentlemen, no matter what the semblance of "roughing
it."

As early as 1869, the Reverend William Murray described an
area the size of Connecticut, a wilderness lying at the gates of
New York, in a little volume called *Adventures in the Wilderness
or Camp-Life in the Adirondacks*. "In beauty of scenery, in health-
giving qualities, in the easy and romantic manner of its sporting,"
he wrote, the Adirondacks were a paradise.[12] Murray's book
spurred a rush of city sportsmen to such entry ports as Plattsburg
and St. Regis. The rustic hotels and accessible scenery of the
Adirondacks became a mecca for urban intellectuals. In a period

when expert knowledge of woodcraft was not a mark of the
gentleman, they enjoyed themselves with the carefree inefficiency
Charles Dudley Warner described in his *In the Wilderness.*
Warner, like many of the writers of his time, did not fully com-
prehend the Arcadian impulse. "The instinct of barbarism that
leads people periodically to throw away the habits of civilization,
and seek the freedom and discomfort of the woods, is explicable
enough," he wrote in 1878, "but it is not so easy to understand why
such passion should be strongest in those who are most refined,
and most trained in intellectual and social fastidiousness." [13]

English journalist Henry William Herbert did more than anyone to popularize outdoor recreation in this country. Calling himself "Frank Forester," he began a series of volumes on hunting,
fishing, and dog handling in the 1840's. Herbert's *Field Sports,
Fish and Fishing,* and *Complete Manual for Young Sportsmen*
taught a generation of American sportsmen to dress and speak
and shoot according to the best English models.[14] Aided by Herbert, "gentlemen sportsmen" learned to think of hunting and fishing as part of English "field sports" and to dissociate themselves
from native hunters in every way.

In 1846, William T. Porter, publisher of the sporting paper,
Spirit of the Times, brought out the first American edition of
Peter Hawker's English classic, *Instructions to Young Sportsmen.*
Ten years later, Dr. Elisha Lewis offered his perennially popular
American Sportsman. Around these volumes clustered a host of
lesser works by men like Robert B. Roosevelt, Joseph Long,
Theodore Van Dyke, and William Leffingwell. All carried the same
message: the sportsman was a gentleman in the field, a man to
whom hunting was an exercise in good taste. As Robert Roosevelt
put it, he "makes no profit of his success . . . shoots invariably
upon the wing, and never takes a mean advantage of bird or
man. It is his pride to kill what he does kill elegantly, scientifi-
cally, and mercifully." [15]

In *The American Sportsman,* Elisha Lewis defined the best of
English sporting conversation, offering his readers an obvious
means of distinguishing themselves from the uninitiated. Gentle-

men sportsmen would speak of a "covey" of partridge, a "pack" of grouse, a "wisp" of snipe, and a "wing" of plover. They might sometimes refer to a "flock" of wildfowl, but sophisticated hunters spoke of a "team," a "badelynge," or a "company" of ducks, a "gaggle" of geese, a "gang" of brant, or a "whiteness" of swans. No sporting terms applied to the kills of one, two, or three hundred birds which professional market-shooters sometimes made. Instead, a gentleman counted his birds in pairs: a "brace" of partridge, a "leash" of grouse, a "couple" or a "couple and a half" of woodcock or snipe. Lewis felt that this vocabulary was fully established in the sporting press, and the sportsman who wished to be called a gentleman must respond to it.[16]

Frank Forester offered several suggestions to make it quite certain that city sportsmen would not be taken for country hunters. The gentleman shooter must use a "fowling piece" rather than a rifle for all but the largest game, and he must take his birds on the wing. He could count only the smaller and more delicate birds as "game," since no sportsman hunted for food. The ducks and geese and passenger pigeons so popular with market-shooters appealed less to the gentleman than quail, woodcock, and "bay-snipe," as shorebirds were called. Shorebirds and diminutive sora rail were above all the gentleman's targets. Summer hotels rented blinds in which sportsmen combined a warm-weather outing with an hour's gunning in sophisticated comfort. Each Fall, Elisha Lewis reported, an army of gentlemen took the field against the tiny rail. Poled through reedy tidal marshes, they had but to fire and load, while their guides marked down fallen birds and kept a watchful eye on competition.

The rise of the gentleman sportsman and his Arcadian values brought a decline in the prestige of men who hunted for a living. Professional shooters found "market-hunting" a profitable industry at a time when every cookbook insisted that game dinners were part of gracious living. Working from midsummer to late spring, these men made hunting a steady business. "Battery" blinds hidden on feeding grounds and punt guns which fired as much as four pounds of fine shot enabled them to sell their ducks and geese by the barrel. One New York storage plant offered nearly 42,000 game birds for sale in 1902. When New York outlawed the sale of game in 1911, New York City firms reported 190,000 birds in cold storage.

Men who shot for the market and men who shot for the pot were equally disreputable in the sportsman's code. By the twentieth century, in fact, "pot shot" had entered American slang as an act of cowardice and ill-breeding. Elisha Lewis declared the pot hunter "the most disgusting, the most selfish, the most unmanly, the most heartless" of the hunting fraternity. He killed "without regard to etiquette, humanity, law, or even the common decencies of life," and all because he was hungry. To Robert Roosevelt, men who made a business of hunting were no better than "loafing, disreputable, tavern-haunting poachers." [17]

Sportsman and sentimentalist alike proposed legislation to discourage those who "sordidly shoot for the frying pan," as William Hornaday put it.[18] Restrictive legislation was nothing new in the 1880's and '90's. New York first protected quail, ruffed grouse, and turkey in 1708. Deer were protected in Massachusetts from 1718 to 1720, in Virginia in 1772, and in Vermont from 1865 to 1897. North Carolina agreed that property owners had a right to post their lands against hunters in 1784. But such laws were sporadic and in no way restricted the market on which native hunters depended. By 1900, however, the days of market hunting were numbered. In 1896, the Supreme Court declared that wild game belonged to the state and not to the landowner in *Geer v. Connecticut*. Six western states prohibited the sale of game before 1900, and New York's closing of the nation's largest markets in 1911 paved the way for the final ending of market shooting through the Migratory Bird Treaty Act of 1918. Thus wild game moved from a profitable crop to an aesthetic resource, protected for public enjoyment and the sportsman's pleasure.

While the status of the professional hunter declined, a new folk hero emerged: no longer Cooper's mighty hunter or Thoreau's French-Canadian woodcutter, but "Old John," the guide. Outwardly he shared many traits of the earlier figures. William Mur-

ray found him "bronzed and hardy, fearless of danger, eager to
please, uncontaminated by the vicious habits of civilized life," [19]
but in hiring out for wages he surrendered the freedom of Cooper's "Natty Bumppo." Like innkeepers, guides appreciated the
Arcadian philosophy but made their living by exploiting an em-
ployer's love for nature and so were never true companions, regardless of campfire equality. Since city sportsmen felt no need
to be versed in woodcraft, guides came to be more nearly personal
servants than pathfinders. In the literature of the outdoors, they
were the same repository of knowledge and they ministered to
the same weaknesses in urban man as did the Cooper hero, but
tied to the whims of their "sports" they could rarely show prowess
as hunters or fishermen. Instead they must be versed in boat handling, woods lore and campcraft—skills of servitude left to women
in pioneer times. As one city sportsman noted, the "thorough
woodsman guide cares for your health and does the work of a
valet in a motherly fashion. He carves out the fuel while you
admire him as an athlete and a sculptor. He cooks with the dignity and skill of a laboratory professor . . . ." [20]

As early as the 1850's, city sportsmen united in informal associations to ensure the company of social equals. Hunting clubs
soon appropriated the better shooting grounds on such famous
waters as the Chesapeake Bay and Currituck Sound, offering col-
lectively to members the sport and comfort which none singly
could afford. By the end of the century, the hunting club's suburban equivalent, the "country club," developed from the same desire for an appropriately private, rural landscape. The Brookline
Country Club, for example, was opened in 1882 as an exclusive
private "inn," a midway point for Boston carriage outings. Among
its charter members were such men as landscape architect Frederick Law Olmsted and Charles S. Sargent, director of the Arnold
Arboretum.
    The Brookline Country Club was a horse and hunt club, similar
in this respect to the hunt clubs of New York City. There city
businessmen established such groups as the Meadowbrook Club

and the Rockaway Club in the 1870's to spice the daily routine
of commerce with late-afternoon fox hunting. Like the Queens
County Drag Hounds, these clubs chased scented "drags" that
were pulled over the course ahead of the hounds. Such ritualized
hunting, derided by local people, resulted from no scarcity of
foxes. The foxes were simply not well-regulated enough to start
promptly or to confine themselves to horse country. Furthermore,
businessmen, unable to hunt before three in the afternoon, could
hardly spare the time to find a real fox. They looked for a chase,
guaranteed "to begin promptly, and to end with certainty in time
for dinner." [21]

The fashionable interest in nature that called for the suburban
hunt clubs spelled their decline as it spread to the general population. Real estate developments hampered the Rockaway Club
in particular. "People *will* buy lots and build suburban houses
in its country," Edward Martin noted in 1897. "As hunting cannot
be successfully carried on in a country that is all lawn and kitchen-
gardens," he added, "the Rockaway men feel that the days of
their sport are numbered." [22] Fortunately for country clubs, "golf"
came from Scotland at about the time that suburbia throttled the
fox hunt. In 1892, five years after the St. Andrews Golf Club was
formed in Yonkers, a splinter group of the Brookline club laid
out a primitive six-hole course and campaigned vigorously for support among their fellow members. By 1902, when the Brookline
club doubled the size of its clubhouse as a concession to the game,
there were more than a thousand other golf clubs in the country. [23]

The country club offered polite recreation not otherwise available to harried businessmen. Its amusements, whether golf, pigeon
shooting, or drag hunting, were refined enough to convey a gen-
tility appropriate to the annual dues of the organization. On the
golf links and the jumping courses, urbanites found a purified
and predictable nature both accessible and exclusive. As a convenient compromise with wild nature, the country club promised
at the turn of the century "to be the safety valve of an overworked
nation." [24]

By 1900, outdoor writers called the average sportsman "a plain, unpretentious businessman of sedentary habits," interested enough, but satisfied with a quick canter to the hounds or a few rounds of golf. In spite of Jack London, the call of the wild was hardly atavistic. Going back to nature does not mean "going back to savagery nor to barbarism nor to any pestilential past; it only means opening the doors and windows," Canadian-born Bliss Carman wrote from New York City. "We go back to nature," he added, "every time we take a deep breath and stop worrying." [25] But bird books and wild-flower gardens appeared a bit effeminate to some sportsmen; weekend carriage drives seemed no antidote for the ills of urban society. Such sportsmen found their proper prescription in "the Strenuous Life." If urban America was indeed a sick society, said journalist Emerson Hough, she "found her sickness within doors, through looking at images of a man with a cigarette and a ticker tape, instead of the old figure of a man with a rifle and a hunting shirt." [26] To protect themselves against false gods, these sportsmen took to the woods and periodically lived for a time the primitive life they would not dream of making permanent.

Theodore Roosevelt, hunter, rancher, founder of the "Boone and Crockett Club" of gentlemen hunters, proclaimed "the Strenuous Life." But even Roosevelt understood that the life he enjoyed was strenuous only by comparison to the ordinary routine of middle-class Americans. As he wrote to his friend Henry Needham in 1905:

> I am not an athlete; I am simply a good, ordinary, out-of-doors man. For instance, day before yesterday I took Mrs. Roosevelt on a fifteen-mile row around Lloyd's Neck including a portage. We had our lunch with us—and two or three books! Yesterday I rowed off with my boys and some cousins and their friends and camped out over night, and rowed back this morning . . . . Now these expeditions represent just about the kind of things I do. Instead of rowing it may be riding, or chopping, or walking, or playing tennis, or shooting at a target. But it is always a pastime which any healthy middle-aged man fond of outdoors life, but not in the least an athlete, can indulge in if he chooses.[27]

Hunting and fishing and camping were idle pastimes in the modern world, but they taught the kind of resourcefulness Roosevelt admired. In his own prolific writings, he chose most often to chronicle the "epic" of outdoor life. Wilderness areas were fast disappearing, but Roosevelt still found a place for the sportsman "who, although he loves the great cities, loves even more the fenceless grasslands, and the forest-clad hills." Such a man, he added, would "take books with him as he journeys; for the keenest enjoyment of the wilderness is reserved for him who enjoys also the garnered wisdom of the present and the past." [28]

To many nature lovers in Roosevelt's time, it seemed that the man on the street and his children would soon be able only to read of open range and "forest-clad hills." Just as the urban country club reserved some part of suburban nature for aesthetic enjoyment, so the urban public joined the "conservation" crusade to preserve federal and state lands from economic exploitation. Too many Americans still seemed "filled with zeal to make the world over; to cut down all the woods and drain all the bogs, and fill all the ravines with rubbish; to reduce it all to a neat pattern of cement sidewalks, encircling lawns and cabbage patches." [29] "Preservation" offered a simple solution. Land had been idle as public domain, and it should remain so. Natural resources were spiritual as well as economic and should be kept intact for generations to come. Preservation-minded New Yorkers amended their state constitution in 1895 to ensure that lands acquired for state forests should remain forever wild: not to be "leased, sold or exchanged, or be taken by any corporation, public or private, nor shall the timber thereon be sold, removed or destroyed." [30]

New York's policy was hardly typical. To the head of Roosevelt's Forest Service, Gifford Pinchot, forests were not cathedrals but factories for producing wood; the axe was their destiny. [31] Pinchot bitterly opposed the preservationist philosophy. "Its center of distribution is in the towns or cities, and it is largely concerned with purely sentimental considerations," he told the Board of Regents of the Smithsonian Institute in 1901. Landscape de-

signer Frank A. Waugh noted that "presidents of women's clubs,
parish priests, family doctors, principals of schools, and trolley
car conductors, are spreading the same preposterous notion of
conservation." [32] The Forest Service's "multiple use" policy in
selective logging, grazing and watershed development caused
deep concern among wilderness lovers like Emerson Hough and
John Muir. To Muir and many of his readers, the sheep grazing
in National Forests were so many "hoofed locusts" destroying
wild flowers and grasses that were part of mountain scenery.
Fifty years hence, Emerson Hough warned in 1908, "we shall be
living in crowded concrete houses, and at double the rent we now
pay. We shall make vehicles of steel, use no wood on our farms.
We shall pay ten cents for a newspaper, fifty cents for a magazine, as much for a lead pencil . . . ." [33]

Despite their warnings, preservationists seemed to make little
headway. The Agriculture Department controlled the Forest Service. The fledgling National Parks, which preservationists ardently
supported, were embroiled in constant arguments over resources
insignificant on a national scale but representing untold wealth
to interested individuals. Wild nature suffered on every hand in
the name of progress, which meant, to preservationists, in the
name of private enrichment. The Arcadian dream of peaceful
forests and undefiled rivers could hardly compete with the industrial epic that occupied the nation.

Wild nature seemed increasingly remote to many city dwellers
at the turn of the century, but they could surround themselves
with its symbols. For those who could afford them there were
the lilypads and morning glories of Tiffany art glass and the nature themes woven in oriental carpets. For the less fortunate, the
twining vines of *Art Nouveau* graced lampshades and picture
frames, paper weights and candle sticks, silverware and book-
plates, inkstands and hair brushes. Concert-goers listened to Edward McDowell's *Woodland Sketches* and *New England Idylls*,
the latter composed in McDowell's log-cabin studio near Peter-
boro, New Hampshire. "To a Wild Rose" and "By a Meadow

Brook," like the "Joy of Autumn," "In Deep Woods" and "From
a Log Cabin," seemed perfectly programmed for urban audiences.
Innumerable artists tried to capture nature in murky pastels or
the kind of poetry climaxed by that triumph of sentiment over
style, Joyce Kilmer's "Trees." For those who hesitated to "rough
it" out-of-doors, there were balsam pillows embroidered with
scenes of far-off wilderness and "pillow-tents" that offered outdoor air with indoor comfort.[34] California bungalow designers
even included a thoroughly Arcadian "sleeping porch," a sign of
status which George F. Babbitt proudly claimed.

The pursuit of country happiness was a recognized part of
the city dweller's dream life by the 1890's. Those who communed
with nature at their writing desks flooded newspapers and magazines with Arcadian essays. Country life periodicals that had nothing to do with farming mushroomed overnight. Family magazines
devoted regular columns and feature articles to the simple life
between the city and the farm; the suburban migration was on
its way to becoming a mass movement.[35]

As automobile production zoomed from four thousand in 1900
to four million in 1923, commuters willing to drive themselves
could choose their landscapes by aesthetics instead of time-tables.
"The automobile gives one the country, not merely the suburbs,"
a writer in *Harper's Weekly* announced in 1911; "there is no longer
the necessity of attaching oneself to a railroad station, nor even
to a village." [36] Determined Arcadians sought out the abandoned
farm, there to establish that middle-class equivalent of the English estate, the "country place." The sudden appearance of a
prospective buyer prompted many a local resident to part with a
dying homestead for a few hundred dollars. Farmers whose souls
were already on the way to the city, as John Erskine once put
it,[37] had done their best to keep their houses up to date. Air-tight
stoves replaced the old brick fireplaces, panelled walls were
covered with plaster and paint, and Victorian ornaments hung
from every architectural outcropping. It might be difficult to restore the farm home to its original simplicity; but in any event
the commuter did have rolling acres of farmland. He added

porches and plumbing, while his stables decayed and his pastures ran to daisies and goldenrod. Stony fields and straggling
fences could be artistically pleasing, and as the smell of the
stables faded away, he could imagine himself on equal footing
with English country gentlemen.[38] The five to ten acres of the
commuter's ideal were "just enough to bring him the sweet solace
of the soil without the burdens and cares that come from cultivating many acres for profit." [39] In dilettante fashion he shared
an interest in farm techniques and tools with his country neighbor, but however knowledgeable he might wish to appear, the
commuter was in no sense a farmer. Commuters, like sportsmen,
avoided any identification with "the natives" in their apologia for
country life; Arcadia was not for plowmen.

"Living in the country without being of it," one commuter
suavely announced, meant "allowing the charms of nature to
gratify and illumine, but not to disturb one's cosmopolitan
sense." [40] Coming to the country with what Liberty Bailey called
a "town mind," most commuters were unwilling to forego the
luxuries of city life.[41] Earnest, middle-class and quasi-intellectual,
they thought themselves more, not less, sophisticated than their
friends in town. They insisted on defining "country living" as the
highest expression of cultured society. The "Simple Life," a writer
in the young *House Beautiful* declared, was "a final evolution
reached by a system of unlimited complication." Furthermore, the
same writer continued:

> Every owner of a place in the country inhabits a metropolitan
> Arcadia, or an Arcadian metropolis. Our country houses are
> luxurious in the extreme, and visitors would greatly resent hav-
> ing to do without one of the five hundred luxuries, small and
> large, to which they are inured in town.[42]

Canny realtors encouraged commuters to settle in residential
colonies, secure in the company of social equals. In Kansas City's
thousand-acre "Country Club District," developer J. C. Nichols
offered "spacious ground for permanently protected homes, surrounded with ample space for air and sunshine—among flowers,

grass and shrubbery, all expressive of the owner's ideals of beauty, health and comfort." [43] Long Island promoter Dean Alvord advertised "Belle-Terre," a 1,320-acre estate broken into smaller lots. "Bell-Terre's" forty miles of scenic roads, five miles of shoreline, and 400-acre golf and polo field offered country life without country neighbors. [44] According to another enthusiast, such residential colonies enabled city people of moderate means "to obtain attractive country homes at a modest cost, to get into the genuine unspoiled country, to take their own social life with them, to restore to the land its elemental charm," [45] and to create their own particular kind of Arcadia.

Commuters and sportsmen agreed that men might work or pray or study or enjoy themselves in the city, but they insisted that by all popular standards of human psychology it was dangerous to stay there. The call of the wild was instinctive, many of them believed, and instinctive needs could not be lightly denied. Clark University's G. Stanley Hall upset a generation of school teachers by insisting that city children, unable to "recapitulate" the primitive and pastoral stages of man's development, were certain to grow up socially retarded. "Environmentalists" found the blank walls of tenement air shafts a threat; bits and pieces of natural scenery, however constricted in suburban backyards, were normally elevating and vital to a happy and healthy life. "Crowd" psychologists believed that city life weakened individual integrity and fostered herd impulses; nature offered the solitude where urban man might recover a part of his identity. Even Charles Cooley's sophisticated new "role-selection" theory granted cosmopolitan status to those who wore the clothes and followed the customs of sportsmen or country gentlemen.

"It may be a fad just now to adopt abandoned farms, to attend parlor lectures on birds, and to possess a how-to-know library. It is pathetic to see 'nature study' taught by schoolma'ams who never did and who never will climb a rail fence," Dallas Lore Sharp wrote in 1908; "it is passing sad that the unnatural natural history, the impossible out-of-doors, of some of the recent nature books, should have been created. But fibs and failures and impossibilities aside, there still remains the thing itself,—the widespread turning to nature, and the deep, vital need to turn." [46] More and more Americans convinced themselves that they were naturists, claiming closer friends among the woodchucks and warblers than among their country neighbors, and taking as their standard the gospel of the holy earth.

2

The Literary Commuter

And this our life, exempt from public haunts and those swift currents that carry the city dweller resistlessly into the movie show, leaves us caught in the quiet eddy of little unimportant things—digging among the rutabagas, playing the hose at night.

Dallas Lore Sharp, *The Hills of Hingham*
(Boston, New York: Houghton, Mifflin, 1916), p. 121.

Frederick Law Olmsted and Calvert Vaux published their plan for "Riverside," Chicago's first suburban development, in 1868. They noted the drawing power of the metropolis, but they also found a "counter-tide of migration, especially affecting the more intelligent and more fortunate classes." It seemed to Olmsted and Vaux that "the most attractive, the most refined and the most soundly wholesome forms of domestic life" were to be found in residential suburbs.[1] But realists soon concluded that suburbs too often copied their mother cities. Urban gridirons destroyed the spirit of the country as new houses rose side by side on twenty-five foot lots in the midst of empty fields where there was no more of nature than straggling Chinese elms along a curbstone.[2] Children might see the forest in a hedgerow and the prairie in a vacant lot, but to adults, life in the suburban countryside was sometimes less romantic. Even with rapid transit, factory and office workers left early and returned late, sleeping peacefully in the country air, but spending their waking hours in going and coming. "The suburban husband and father is almost entirely a Sunday institution," a writer in *Harper's Bazaar* concluded in 1900.[3] Suburban life could discourage "the young wife in lonelyville," Grace Goodwin told the *Good Houskeeping* audience in 1909. "The busy men," she added, "leave on early trains, and are at once plunged in the rush of their accustomed life among their usual associates," but for the wife left "standing behind the struggling young vines of her brand new piazza," the day was sometimes dreary.[4]

That the image of carefree and romantic happiness made any headway against the realities of suburban life is due in large measure to "literary commuters," those idealists whose essays laid the spiritual foundation for an age of suburbs. In the first years of the twentieth century the number of such professional idealists seemed legion. They wrote for magazines and newspapers across the country, and as fast as they could collect their work they published volumes of essays—some good, some bad, but all glorifying the wild land beyond the trolley line. The literary commuter responded to nature "more ingeniously, more movingly, and much more interestingly" than his rural neighbors because, said one reviewer, he "brought to the country a mind saturated with the city." [5] Preacher, teacher, or professional man, he was at home with ideas and emotions, but unable in most cases to wield the magic wand of wealth. He attempted to overcome his lack of money by refining his way of life and, in his essays at least, by instilling spirituality into the smallest suburban tasks. Men like Dallas Sharp, Walter Eaton and Ray Stannard Baker managed thus to play a highly sophisticated role, radiating an appearance of rural insouciance in a complex and urban age.

"It is an inconvenient world, the distant, darkened, unmapped country of the Commuter," Dallas Sharp wrote in 1911, after nine years of meeting the 8:35 train for Boston; "only God and the Commuter know how to get there, and they alone know why they stay." [6] An ex-Methodist minister teaching English at Boston University, Sharp was perhaps the best known commuter in the country. He set forth in twenty-two volumes of essays a formula for happiness compounded of a small farm of an acre or more, a small income of a thousand or more, and a small family of four or more. Rural life, he declared, must offer "some of the necessities that are lacking in the city—wide distances and silent places, and woods and stumps where you can sit down and feel that you are greater than anything in sight." [7] His fourteen acres of rocks and stumps and woodchucks in suburban Hingham gave Sharp the compromise between the wilderness of his imagination and the conveniences his family required. College teaching brought him the income and the culture he needed. Evenings, weekends and summers he rambled over his acres, learning what he could of the wild life around him, and fashioned his observations into chatty and often humorous essays that brought him a national reputation through the pages of *The Atlantic Monthly.*

Yet for all his interest in nature, Sharp was neither scientist nor transcendental philosopher. He was a cultured, middle-class family man, a commuter happily integrating his philosophy and his family into an Arcadian design. Thoreau, "sweating among the stumps and woodchucks, for a bean crop netting him eight dollars, seventy one and one-half cents," was most disturbing. "A family man," Sharp concluded, "cannot contemplate that piddling patch with any patience." [8] Sharp idealized the "door-yard universe" in which all things related to himself and his family in the subdued nature of back pasture and woodlot.[9] For him the nature movement did not begin with men like Wilson and Audubon, who mastered the wilderness, but with Emerson and Bryant, who traveled near at home and not alone. "It was not to the woods they took us," he wrote, "but to nature; not a-hunting after new species in the name of science, but for new inspirations, new estimates of life, new health for mind and spirit." Sharp believed the commuter must stay "contentedly within the sound of the dinner horn, glad of the companionship of his bluebirds, chipmunks and pine trees." Let the philosopher "live at home with his wife and children like the rest of us, work in the city for his living, hoe in his garden for his recreation," to avoid the strain of too much thinking; [10] nature was best won by the friendly contact of many hours when the commuter, unlike his rural neighbor, could turn to the fields untroubled with thoughts of gain.

Sharp had come to the country, he wrote half humorously, to

redeem his neighbors. Farmers around him had no conception of
the beauties of nature. "Their feeling for the skunk was typical,"
he wrote in one essay for *The Atlantic:* "they hated the skunk
with a perfect hatred, a hatred implacable, illogical, and un-
poetical, it seemed to me, for it was born of their chicken-breed-
ing." Newly arrived from Boston, Sharp was sure that "life ought
to mean more than turnips, more than hay, more than hens to
these rural people." [11] Yet when he came to raising chickens himself, he learned to balance his own worship with rural economics.

Sharp rode the crest of, as one writer observed, "a definite call
'back to nature,'" that brought with it a new interest in "sports
and landscape gardening, voyages of discovery, arctic expeditions,
and nature poetry and nature study, a hundred or more magazines
of outdoor life, and countless books to remind us of the delights
of living in the open . . . ." [12] Yet despite their popularity, Sharp
and the other literary commuters deferred to a most unlikely
competitor—a government clerk turned truck gardener and wood-
chuck trapper by the name of John Burroughs.

Burroughs worked in the Treasury Office during the Civil War
but left Washington in 1873, moving with his family to a nine-
acre farm on the Hudson River, some eighty miles from New
York. There he set about growing grapes and writing essays
"whose matter," Dallas Sharp concluded, "is nature, whose moral
is human, whose manner is strictly literary." [13] The grapes pros-
pered under hired care, but Burroughs, harried by the bustle on
the Hudson and by an unsympathetic wife, did not. When the
chance came in 1895 to buy a bit of land which was a mile from
his home and "shut off from the vain and noisy world of railroads,
steamboats, and yachts," he wasted no time in building a retreat
called "Slabsides." [14] There he made the chipmunks and songbirds
in his dooryard seem familiar friends to a generation of nature
lovers. He might awe inexperienced readers with botanical and
ornithological virtuosity, but the veery and the thrush, the Maryland yellowthroat and the hepatica carried special connotations to
readers who knew them well. In the next three decades, nearly
seven thousand visitors, including Theodore Roosevelt, signed

his guest book. To his biographer Clara Barrus, the white bearded prophet of the out-of-doors seemed in 1914 "as contented and serene a man as can be found in this complicated world of today." Burroughs's life was so in tune with nature, she wrote, that he could follow the vesper sparrow's song with his own response, carrying a Victrola out to the stone wall to play Brahms's "Cradle Song" or Schubert's "Serenade" for visitors "hushed into humble gratitude for our share in this quiet life." [15]

If urbanization encroached on wild nature, Burroughs's essays, like William Hamilton Gibson's Sharp Eyes and Eye Spy, invited nature lovers to look more closely at what was left. In more than one case, a later nature writer confessed, "Burroughs and Hamilton Gibson were as a pair of rose-coloured glasses" for their readers who "learned at once to differentiate and to beautify everyday things . . . ." [16] But early nature lovers were no transcendentalists. They made Thoreau rather than Emerson their hero; as one editor noted, "in spite of his transcendentalism, he could yet write delightfully." No overthinking there; for all his literary allusions, Thoreau seemed the simple soul at home in the fields and at war with the city. Nevertheless, the average reader found his expectations confirmed more easily in Burroughs's forty volumes. "Burroughs brings us home in time for tea," Dallas Sharp once wrote, while "Thoreau leaves us tangled up in the briars." At its best, he continued, Thoreau's writing was "sheet-lightning, electrifying, purifying, but not altogether conducive to peace," and peace was greatly prized at the turn of the century. [17] Samuel Schmucker, who taught the art of nature-study at West Chester State Normal School, told his students that the sage of Walden offered "a stained-glass window" through which his readers might see nature colored by transcendental meditation. "With Burroughs," Schmucker declared, "we are looking through a window of plate glass and we forget completely the window, which is warding off the raw and blustering air . . . ." [18] Burroughs's first essay, "Expression," appeared in the Atlantic Monthly in 1860. It was redolent with Emersonian thinking, but he soon found transcendentalism too unstable. "I must get this Emersonian musk out of my garments at all hazards," he wrote with rare humor, concluding, "to bury my garments in the earth and see what my native soil would do toward drawing it out." [19] So he turned to the rural memories of his childhood and wrote of stone walls and sugar time, of haymaking and his favorite "rural divinity," the cow on a country pasture.

Though Burroughs chided sentimentalists who viewed the out-of-doors "from parlor windows and through gilt-edged poems," the way of the plow was no salvation. Nature belonged to poets and artists and men of genius by whom "the sentimentalist is cured, and the hairy and taciturn frontiersman has had experience to some purpose." [20] His contemporaries felt that nature belonged to Burroughs. His ability to broadcast "the simple life" in the sheltered and sunny pages of his essays endeared him to readers who would not think of sharing the monastic simplicity of "Slab-sides." Theodore Roosevelt called him "a permanent asset of American life," and Henry Ford claimed his books would be read when "the Bible was forgotten." [21] But a good deal of the worship accorded Burroughs in his old age stemmed from nature lovers who imagined he shared all the virtues of his subject. In actual fact, Burroughs's woodland was a bit too wild for most of his readers. His books were fine for fireside evenings and children's nature-study, but few cared to follow in his steps. Urban Americans were willing to sever only the most irritating of their ties with city life.

Walter Prichard Eaton, who was a drama critic and a lecturer at Princeton, offered a simpler escape. Writing from "Twin Fires," his restored farmhouse near Sheffield, Massachusetts, Eaton found a steady market for his nature essays and for his impossibly sentimental novels of Boy Scouts, of birdhouse-makers, and of young lovers combining courtship and carpentry on the abandoned farms of the Berkshires. Though he lacked something of Bur-roughs's sincerity and Sharp's ability to laugh at himself, Eaton did have an eye for the unusual. This made his essays, as Robert Frost once put it, "full of things I wish I had thought of first." [22] Eaton put together nearly a dozen popular volumes of country-life adventures describing the far Rockies, the Berkshire fields, or hiking trips along abandoned roads in search of colonial ruins. The New York, New Haven and Hartford Railroad commissioned him to write a series of booklets on the pleasures of Cape Cod, Nantucket, Martha's Vineyard, and Rhode Island. *Collier's* editor Mark Sullivan wrote in 1917, telling Eaton that he would "accept sight unseen at any price you name, any story you write." [23]

Even as sophisticated a journalist as Ray Stannard Baker took to the dual life of city and country. Baker earned a national reputation for reform journalism. But more popular than Baker himself was his semi-autobiographical hero, "David Grayson." Originally a pen name which Baker used to publish sentimental nature essays side by side with his muckraking articles, "David Grayson" emerged as a folk hero. The mythical Grayson matched a popular conception of the literary commuter. Born in the country, he worked in the city at the hectic pace so popular in country life accounts until a physical breakdown brought a prescription for long walks and rural scenery. Grayson found the delights of a simple life uncluttered by thoughts of money on his farm near "Hempfield." In a series of articles later collected in *Adventures in Contentment, Great Possessions* and eight other volumes, Baker persuasively sounded the call of the country with a warning that simplicity came only to those who could afford it.

Like John Burroughs a generation earlier, Sharp, Eaton, and Baker published a steady stream of essays. Eaton and Baker turned to romantic fiction from time to time, and Sharp tried his hand at children's readers, but all continued to praise the simple life of the American commuter. Others who contributed to the literature of commuting did so only occasionally. Such was Mrs. Frances K. Hutchinson, who began her chronicle in 1907 with *Our Country Home: How We Transformed a Wisconsin Woodland.* [24]

Mrs. Hutchinson, a Chicago socialite, wrote of the rewards and the ironies in confronting nature with unlimited funds. The Hutchinsons discovered a piece of "real American forest" on Wisconsin's Lake Geneva in 1902. They talked of "a small and simple abode where the birds may nest close to our windows," but social pretensions, faults in the building site and the disposition of thirty cords of firewood all compromised the original plan. The main building, designed "to look like a house dropped down in the woods, rather by chance," grew to a one-hundred-and-twenty-foot English half-timbered mansion with a Norman tower, in a style which Mrs. Hutchinson chose to call "Early English domestic ecclesiastical architecture." A 33,000-gallon water reservoir and a seventy-five foot woodshed served the household and 15,000 loads of dirt smoothed a terrace overlooking the lake. Two carefully felled trees, arranged with block and tackle to simulate a natural windfall, became the wild grape arbor, and an artesian well, an imported boulder, and a cement-lined hollow formed a rock garden that was "absolutely a part of the wilderness." [25] Country life, Mrs. Hutchinson concluded, "has revealed to us the charm of solitude, and it has given to us the opportunity to become better acquainted with our kind" through the selective social life that only a house in the country can provide. [26]

The charms of solitude attracted others who preferred to court the public from a distance. Artist, author, and boy's club leader Ernest Thompson Seton lived at "Wyndygoul," a 200-acre farm in Connecticut. There his "Woodcraft Indians" floated in birch-bark canoes on an artificial lake and played at ceremonial rites among the pines while a full grown peacock looked on. Dorothy Canfield Fisher spent her time on a farm in Vermont "to avoid being trampled underfoot by the herd." For Booth Tarkington, "the house that Penrod built" was a summer retreat at Kennebunkport. [27] In 1904, Upton Sinclair built his own country home some three miles from the Princeton library as he prepared to expose the brutality of life in Chicago. There he managed an inexpensive if Spartan cottage of varnished pine, which cost, he gleefully told the readers of Country Life in America, $156.

Popular novelist Thomas Dixon published "From the Horrors of City Life: The Experience of a Dweller in Flats, in Boarding Houses, in Nineteen Feet of Baked Mud, and in Suburban Homes,

Who (the Illusion of City Life Gone) at Last Found Happiness
in a Country Home." Dixon's particular Arcadia was a mile of
waterfront in tidewater Virginia. His fifteen-acre lawn sloped
gently from the house to the beach, where a motor launch, two
sailboats, three rowboats and an ocean-going schooner rode at
anchor. Twelve fireplaces met his need for quiet musing.[28]
Theodore Thomas's twenty-five acre mountain home in New
Hampshire typified the intellectual's country retreat, where nature was tamed, not to produce crops, but to make it more spiritually wild. The brushy, boulder-strewn mountainside offered only
the beginnings of a "wild, free and natural" landscape. Thomas,
who conducted the Chicago Symphony during the winter, spent
his vacation time improving his property—until new avenues
swept "broadly over accommodating clearings; wayward paths
meandered alluringly through the woods"; and "highest triumph
of all—the rank, ugly swamp was metamorphosed into a charming
pond, with brook and waterfall." He had to deepen the pond and
rebuild the dam three times before water would lie where none
had been before, but gradually "the unkempt aspect of the land
was softened to a graceful wildness," worthy, Mrs. Thomas wrote,
of a Beethoven piece.[29]

"The last decade has marked what might be called the rise of
the American country place," the young *House Beautiful* magazine announced in 1901; and with this rise came a number of
periodicals catering to sophisticated suburbanites.[30] *Countryside,
Country Calendar*, J. Horace McFarland's *Suburban Life*, and
Country Life in America among others joined *House Beautiful* in
offering commuters the technical advice and inspiration to cope
with suburban house lots and the sagging floors and cracking
plaster in abandoned farmhouses. *Good Housekeeping, Saturday
Evening Post, The Woman's Home Companion, Ladies' Home
Journal* and virtually every popular family magazine contributed
regular columns or feature articles to the nature movement.
Poetaster Maurice Thompson, who held that mankind had but
two worthwhile dreams, "one religious, the other in some form

arcadian," [31] wrote mellifluently for the *Independent* magazine
from 1889 to 1900. The Reverend E. P. Powell succeeded Thompson, doing his editorial work from a country home in upstate
New York. "Inside half a century," Powell predicted, "suburbanism will cover half the country." [32] He tried hard to educate
his readers to beautiful suburban living. In his book *The Country
Home*, as in its predecessor *How I Cultivated the Beautiful and
Made Money At It*, he told the budget-minded, "there is money
in the beautiful," but the whole of his book described the beautiful life awaiting city workmen with scarcely a dozen lines devoted to making money. [33] In 1901 *Collier's Weekly* brought
Caspar Whitney's popular but bankrupt *Outing* into its pages
as "Outdoor America," calling it "the response of the national
weekly to the outdoorward movement." In 1917, *Independent*
magazine absorbed the *Countryside Magazine* and continued it
as a monthly feature "for those whose interests lie between the
city and the farm." [34]

Ever-popular articles like Frank Olmsted's "A Country Home
for Eight Hundred and Twenty Dollars: How We Bought a Farm
of Forty-two Acres for Three Hundred and Fifty Dollars, and Re-
built the Old Farmhouse with Our Own Hands," [35] gave hope to
many commuters whose love of nature outweighed their income.
But the country life audience delighted most of all in reading
about the splendors of the rich. Jay Cooke had his island in Lake
Erie, the Vanderbilts their forest in North Carolina, and Theodore
Roosevelt his Sagamore Hill. Newport boasted seaside "cottages"
and Mount Desert Island in Maine its rustic retreats, including
that of Harvard's President, Charles Eliot. Railroad men, steel
men, financiers and statesmen, all had castles in the country;
country-life magazines with limited access to the retreats of the
rich persistently outlined in story and picture the lands where, as
Leonidas Hubbard put it, "the millionaire may temporarily become the man with the hoe." [36]

In addition to functioning as clearing houses for information
and inspiration, country-life magazines advertised city conveniences appropriate for suburban homes. A portion of this ad-

vertising space was given over to the exchange of country homes. The largest estates appeared in three- and four-page advertisements which delighted less-ambitious commuters secure in their suburban cottages. Pittsburgh businessman Joseph Vandergrift announced his "Vancroft," a 600-acre estate somewhat damaged by fire, to readers of *Country Life in America* in 1904. He thought of his land as a great island of cultured privacy. Far removed from "perpetual picnicking or refined roughing it," his home combined forty buildings serviced by a $50,000 macadam driveway. Interior appointments included a dining area finished in imitation birchbark, a library concealed by curtains of studded elephant skin, a stuffed owl with electric eyes overlooking the billiard room, and the head of the world's largest buffalo hanging in the den.

A writer in *Outlook* magazine noted in 1903 that "no sign of the times is more significant of the change in American habits than the number of volumes on flowers, trees, shrubs, birds, which are constantly coming from the press." [37] No publishing house more enthusiastically backed the nature movement with business acumen and advertising skill than the one that Frank Doubleday, Walter Hines Page and Sydney Lanier founded in 1900. Doubleday, Page and Company based its success on the illustrated news magazine, *World's Work*, but turned almost at once to publishing a stream of well-advertised nature fiction, nature lore and praise for country life that included nine readable volumes by Neltje Blanchan, Doubleday's wife. *Country Life in America*, which the new company launched in 1901 with Liberty Bailey as editor, soon became the most popular of suburban periodicals. Tapping a market of country commuters and city dreamers, it pictured a life where scenery was more important than soil in what Bailey called "the spirit of pleasant inquiry, of intellectual enthusiasm, of moral uplift." [38]

In 1910, Doubleday, Page and Company followed its own advice and moved to Garden City, Long Island, an established suburb forty minutes from Penn Station that seemed to offer the best compromise between country life and good business. The first major publishing house to leave Manhattan, it became in many ways a symbol in its own mythology. Theodore Roosevelt, favoring "everything that gives more chance for fresh air to the men, the women, and above all, to the children," laid the corner-stone for the new plant.[39] When completed, it occupied the center of a thirty-acre tract, a showpiece of ornamental landscaping which the company was fond of using to illustrate its concern for nature. Setting out "to foster a love of the wide outdoors, the home of health and broad horizons" and "to minister to all the needs and enthusiasms and joys of those who live in the country and love it," the company doubled its business from 1910 to 1913.[40]

By the First World War, the literature of commuting had reached a peak. The country-life movement as the commuter knew it was older than his own generation. Popular nature writers published in what seemed to confirmed urbanites an alarming profusion. Occasionally those who opposed the call of the wild launched bitter attacks on literary commuting. *Outlook's* Lyman Abbott and Edwin Slosson, literary editor of *Independent*, classed nature essays with such barbarizing influences as deckle-edged paper, worm-holed furniture, coarse cloth, jazz music and foot-ball. Nature was "our treacherous and unsleeping foe, ever to be watched and feared and circumvented," warned Slosson, but he represented a minority view.[41]

Journalist Walter Dyer, converted to country life by Ray Stan-nard Baker, found himself at the end of ten years "a rather curious sort of person in an unaccountable environment, seeking persistently, if somewhat blindly, for contentment and satisfac-tion." [42] Yet he, like other nature writers, was convinced that contentment, satisfaction and commuting were bound together. Despite long hours of travel, more and more people turned to a country life tempered with city conveniences. "The country stands far ahead of the city," one happy family concluded, "especially when one has, as we have at Huntington, waterworks, illuminat-ing gas, an ice plant, trolley, electric light and good schools." [43]

By 1925, environmentalists like Harlan Douglass concluded that "a crowded world must be either suburban or savage." The agrarian sanctity of the single-family dwelling had barely survived apartment-house life by the nineteen twenties in the suburbs. Even moderate zoning like that in Paterson, New Jersey, authorized fifty-five to one hundred and ten families per acre—a far cry from the five to ten acre ideal of the commuter's family. Whether or not environmentalism meant much to sociologists, it impressed the literary commuter. "It is easier to be good," Dallas Sharp concluded, "in an environment of largeness, beauty, and peace." [44] Suburbia seemed very good to Sharp, who sucked the nectar of country life without the farmer's concern for survival.

The peculiar Arcadia that inspired literary commuters met with a polite reception from the world at large. "The week-end habit is one of the most remarkable features of modern life," the *New Statesman* concluded in 1917. "There is no enthusiasm prevalent today which has better vocal expression among writers and is more adapted by those whom they lead," the British journal noted in the midst of the World War, "than what publishers, and occasionally railroad companies call 'the cult of the country.'" The *New Statesman* found the literary commuter a familiar figure: "a man who dumbly but obstinately believes the nature of life and the nature of books are one and the same and withdraws to the country." [45] Once there he sowed his spiritual crop amidst the thistles and goldenrod and harvested literary nature according to his ability. With half-truthful, half-imaginative praise of country life, such literary commuters created a full-blown mythology and an emotional vocabulary which ordinary suburbanites made part of their perception of reality.

3

Birds in the Bush

Unlike most movements, this is an absolutely new one in the history of the world . . . . The popular enthusiasm for out-of-door life generally and for the birds particularly . . . is one of the signs of our times.

Neltje Blanchan, *Birds Worth Knowing*
(Garden City: Doubleday, Page, 1917), p. 3.

Nature writers combined both science and sentiment in their essays. They tried from an urban vantage point to give natural objects aesthetic and spiritual connotations. Wild birds came to have a larger and larger place in their vocabulary. Even Philip Hicks concluded in his scholarly study of the natural history essay that "their beauty, their friendliness, their human traits and ways, combine to endow them with a charm superior to that of any other of nature's children." [1] Edith Patch began her *Bird Stories* in the "Little Gateways to Science" series by telling her readers that a little black-capped preacher lived "in the heart of Christmastree Land." Her readers might smile at the minister who called himself "Chick D. D.," but they must never laugh. His very proper sermon was all about "peace and good-will and love and helping the world and being happy"; and he proved his points by the life he lived. "It is written in books that, in all the years, not one crime, not even one bad habit is known of any bird who has called himself 'Chick, D. D.,'" Dr. Patch concluded, "and because no one can watch the black-capped sprite without catching, for a moment at least, a message of cheer and courage and service, does he not rightly name himself a minister?" [2] For a

brief period before bird watching became a subject for satire and
ornithologists ceased to communicate with the public, scientists
and sentimentalists approached American birds with common
concerns and a common language.

Early ornithologists like Alexander Wilson and John James
Audubon had given names to previously unknown species. Later
writers could only begin to use bird life as emblems of wild
nature when they had established a common vocabulary. In the
nineteenth century, most Americans recognized only the com-
monest birds they shot for food. Those too small for sport went
unnamed if not unseen. Country people followed whims of local
nomenclature, and, however realistically derived from sound, size,
color, or distinguishing habit, regional names only confused a
national audience. The mallard, for example, was called the Wild
duck, Stock duck, English duck, French duck, or Gray duck.
Golden plover, known both for annual migrations from the far
north to Argentina, and in the game markets for tasty flesh, had
twenty-six names in the field. Seven were refinements on "plover,"
but others ranged from Muddy-belly, Toad-head, and Hawk's
eye to Frost bird and Prairie pigeon.[3]

The Ornithologist's Union, organized in 1883, set out almost immediately to reduce this profusion to a national language. Beginning in 1886, its committee on nomenclature published periodic
check lists to familiarize the public with the official names for
American birds. Sportsmen and nature writers soon found it a
matter of pride, almost a moral obligation, to know the "proper"
names of their bird neighbors.[4] With the aid of these check lists,
nature writers developed a system of meaningful correlatives
through which they could establish a descriptive rapport with
their readers. The call of the Maryland yellowthroat, the flash of
the Yellow-breasted chat in a hazel thicket or the drumming of a
Ruffed grouse established emotional and topographical allusions
impossible a generation earlier.

In the twentieth century, nature lovers developed a voracious
appetite for bird lore. Colored bird pictures even entered the
medium of advertising. As premiums with Church and Dwight's

"Arm and Hammer Baking Soda," modestly accurate representa-
tions of more than one hundred and sixty woodland and water
birds reached into homes where little else resembling bird life
ever penetrated. Churchmen found something frightening in the
thought that man had so far lost touch with God's handiwork
that he no longer knew what to call those creatures he had been
given the responsibility to name. A meticulous awareness of
nature was also important to the polite transcendentalists reading modern reprints of Emerson and Thoreau. By 1930, ornithologists had tabulated life histories for virtually every species in the
country; nature writers relied on these histories as an aid to or a
substitute for their own observations.

However united by interest and sympathy, ornithologists and
amateurs did differ. Ornithologists did not always see analogies
between the human and the bird world as clearly as the sentimentalists. Since these analogies could be interpreted more easily
in literature than in life, nature writers came to function for the
bird watcher as literary commuters did for the suburbanite.

"You must have the bird in your heart before you can find it in
the bush," John Burroughs told his readers, and he proposed that
the bird in the heart and the bird in the bush be one and the
same. The titles of eighteen of his books reflected Burroughs' avid
reporting of American bird life. He had served an apprenticeship
to ornithology, and he wrote of little known birds of pasture and
woodland—thrushes, finches, warblers, woodpeckers—but his readers were undeterred. They bought well over a million copies of
these titles between 1880 and 1933.[5] Other writers with less
ability also interpreted the world of birds in books. Mabel Osgood
Wright collaborated with a respected ornithologist, Elliot Coues,
to produce *Citizen Bird: Scenes from Bird Life in Plain English
for Beginners* in 1897.[6] Illustrated by young Louis Agassiz Fuertes,
it depicted city children learning scientific terminology on an
abandoned farm in New England. Similar volumes like Neltje
Blanchan's popular *Bird Neighbors*, Jenny Stickney's *Bird World*,
Sara Prueser's *Our Dooryard Friends*, Gilbert Trafton's *Bird
Friends*, and S. Louise Patteson's *How to Have Bird Neighbors*

established a relationship between men and birds which became part of the bird watcher's ideology.[7] One satirist decided in 1913 that in fact "some of our most violent Nature-lovers watch birds exclusively in books," [8] yet bird watchers saw no inconsistency. Many admitted their contacts with wild nature were sometimes uninspiring; its features were generally a bit too shaggy and its spiritual content too uncertain. Moreover, its potential was obscured by flies and dust and other distractions. The nature writer's gift of vision often seemed more worthwhile than the scene itself. "A bird in a poem is worth almost as much to a child as a bird in a bush, perhaps more," Dallas Sharp concluded. "I have learned many facts in the fields," he added, "but how many of my feelings have come to me out of books!" [9]

From books, then, as well as from observation, turn-of-the-century bird watchers came to believe in a system of "Christian ornithology" by which they gave a moral interpretation to the habits of birds. Both scientists and sentimentalists believed that men could interpret ethical lessons from the lives of birds. Sophisticated nature writers sometimes attributed spiritual qualities to birds and animals as a literary device, but their audience found such analogies entirely believable. Thus in the Arcadian world, the goose came to stand for wanderlust, the mourning dove for romantic affliction, robins and phoebes for domesticity, chickadees for cheerfulness, bluejays for saucy vandalism, song sparrows for innocence, hawks for cruelty and owls for silent wings of fate. The song of the shy and solitary thrush was the voice of the wilderness, detached and spiritual because the bird itself was rarely seen by ordinary men.[10]

Animal orators like Thornton Burgess's "Peter Rabbit" and Felix Salten's "Bambi" were patently humanized; but ornithological science suggested that birds somehow really did possess traits which, by analogy, could instruct mankind. Edith Patch's *Bird Stories* went through seven printings in the 1920's. It typified the coloring which Christian ornithology gave to introductory science. Her stories were grounded firmly in accurate observation and were painfully sincere. "Chick D. D." was not a real minister, her young readers learned. He had not gone to the schools of men, but he was a "bird-of-the-happy-heart," living "so wisely that he can teach us how to be happier, too." [11] She introduced to city children birds of the wilderness—chickadees, nuthatches, redpolls in the winter woods, sandpipers on the shore and loons in the northern lakes. Scientific observation yielded touching parables of childish virtues. The little sea gull struggling to break out of his prison found at last that it was no thicker than an eggshell, and her readers learned that "there are few places so tight that we can't get out of them if we go about it the right way, and make the best of what power we have." From "Peter Piper," city children discovered that obedience and trust were prime forces in the world of sandpipers, where life itself depended on adult judgment. Sandpiper children, they learned, obeyed their parents without question, playing happily together or apart. They lived amidst the beauties of wild nature because they, unlike "children of men," felt no need to harvest the flowers that grew along the shore. [12]

Ornithologists and nature-study experts both agreed that there were "good" and "bad" birds, and they judged them by standards of Victorian morality. "Good" birds had pleasant if not musically significant songs and attractive plumage. They ate weed seeds and insects, but not grain. In large part they built handsome and intricate nests, mated once a year and did not disturb other nesting birds. If they did not mate for life or return to the same nesting area year after year, they at least preserved an appearance of family unity through the nesting season. Their habits were at least well-bred, and they displayed virtues which the nature lover admired: domesticity and paternal joy in the wrens, industry among the nuthatches and woodpeckers, dignity and devotion in the herons, bravery in the kingbird, modesty among thrushes.

"Bad" birds and animals were to be punished because, judged by human standards, they committed crimes: in a world of seed-eaters, bad birds fed on meat. Hawks and owls killed the weak and helpless, the mothers and the young. The shrike, whose claws were too weak to clutch its prey, was called the "Butcher-bird" for impaling its food on thorns. The bluejay, like the red squirrel, robbed other birds' nests. Cowbirds built no nests at all, but laid their eggs in the nests of smaller birds.

Above all others, English sparrows must be condemned. The bird watcher's hatred of the English sparrow exceeded even his dislike of cats and squirrels. It was a European bird, artificially introduced by man; it was alien and un-American. Its song was harsh, and its sooty plumage gave the impression that it rarely bathed. Feeding on the dung of grain-fed horses, it was, unlike other birds, "a bird of the street" and fulfilled every connotation of such a label in Victorian society.[13] Raucous and combative by nature it seemed to squabble constantly; it drove native birds away from food and nesting sites and harried smaller birds unmercifully. It nested not once but four to six times a year in unsightly bundles of twigs and debris, and its mating habits seemed barbarically primitive. It seemed to Ernest Thompson Seton that male sparrows made love with all the finesse of a lynching party, congregated in noisy flocks, fouled roosting places, and generally behaved in Cockney fashion.[14] "The kingdom of ornithology is divided into two departments—real birds and English sparrows," wrote New York City's fisherman-preacher, Henry Van Dyke. "English sparrows are not real birds," he added; "they are little beasts."[15]

Strangely enough, the object of these attacks was properly neither English nor a sparrow. Originally a European house finch, it was introduced into New York City's Greenwood Cemetery in 1852. As urban noises drove native birds away, civic-minded nature lovers imported breeding pairs of these "sparrows" to combat "the caterpillar nuisance."[16] English sparrows came to Portland, Maine, in 1854; in 1860, twelve were freed in New York's Madison Square. More arrived in Central Park in 1864, and in 1866, two hundred were introduced into Union Park. New Haven released forty pairs a year later. The city of Philadelphia imported a thousand birds in 1869, and they were introduced in Cleveland and Cincinnati the same year. Colonized in more than a hundred cities and towns, English sparrows established themselves in thirty-five states and five territories by 1886.

In an era when native birds provided one of the few remaining links with wild nature, English sparrows were urban birds. As they multiplied beyond their food supply, however, they spread outward along highways and rail lines where grain had dropped from passing cars, defiling the countryside in an ornithological suburbanism with parallels which were all too clear. Ornamental elms still suffered from the canker worm and caterpillar, and government ornithologists reported some seventy different native birds molested by sparrows as they searched for food and nesting sites. In 1889, the U.S. Bureau of the Biological Survey devoted its first bulletin entirely to "The English Sparrow in North America." After four hundred and five pages of testimony, compiler Walter Barrows concluded, with the weight of the Federal government behind him, that these foreigners were "a curse of such virulence" that they should be systematically and completely destroyed. Barrows's recommendations were harsh and abrupt. Protective laws should be repealed and new legislation substituted. "Killing of the English sparrow at all seasons of the year, and the destruction of its nests, eggs, and young" ought to be legalized. It should be made a misdemeanor punishable by fine or imprisonment "(a) . . . to intentionally give food or shelter to the English sparrow, except with a view to its ultimate destruction; (b) to introduce or aid in introducing it into new localities; (c) to interfere with persons, means or appliances engaged in, or designed for, its destruction or the destruction of its nests, eggs or young." [17] Furthermore, it should be made a crime to kill the shrike, the sparrow hawk, screech owls, bluejays or grackles, since these birds preyed on English sparrows.

Said to be "much superior to quail," sparrows sold for a dollar a hundred in the game markets of the 1880's. According to Barrows's report, W. T. Hill, professional sparrow trapper for the city of Indianapolis, personally captured some forty thousand birds in 1886 and 1887, delivering many to the firing squads of local shooting clubs.[18] Nature writers repeatedly boasted of their

efforts to exterminate their own share. In winter they spread
feed in long narrow lanes until sparrows congregated in large
flocks. They then fired shotguns down these lanes until the
sparrows failed to return. Other writers preferred grain soaked
in cyanide, strychnine or both; still others recommended nets to
be dropped on feeding platforms. Nature-study expert Gilbert Trafton suggested a variety of methods in his *Bird Friends*. Poison and
shotgun traps were sometimes feasible, but in the suburbs com-
mercially available sparrow traps were more efficient. Such traps
imprisoned unwary sparrows in wire mazes as they followed
baited trails. At least one writer recommended emptying sparrow
traps into the fire door of the cookstove, but Trafton suggested for
family use a trap which delivered the sparrow into a central
receptacle from which it could be quietly dropped into a pail of
water. Those who felt that traps and poison were not proper for
families with small children advocated supplying the sparrows
with easily opened nesting houses, then destroying eggs as they
were laid.

Bird watchers and ornithologists spent almost as much energy
protecting deserving birds from man. Militant preservationists ob-
jected strongly to the annual harvest of game birds for the market
and to the killing of songbirds by "Italians" whose eating habits
were not yet Americanized. They found the trade in feathers for
women's hats particularly offensive. Feather merchants played an
important part in the fashion world at the turn of the century.
From world wide sources they provided the millinery trade with
decorative plumage varying from hummingbird feathers to egret
and ostrich plumes.[19] The trade in duck and goose down for pillows and comforters rarely aroused the bird watcher's anger, but
the use of plumes and even of stuffed birds on women's hats led
preservationists to present a frightening array of photographs and
statistics in opposition. They found all the evils of the trade in the
annual "aigrette" harvest. Aigrettes formed part of the mating
plumage of the snowy egret, a large and dignified member of the
heron family. The feathers were "ripe" only in late spring or early
summer, when egrets congregated in nesting colonies. Preservation-

ists said that plume hunters attacked these nesting colonies with all
the brutality of frontier massacres. Nature lovers felt a sentimental outrage as they visualized parent birds killed in defense
of their nests, their feathers plucked, their offspring starving. The
General Federation of Women's Clubs in Pennsylvania and New
Jersey soon forbade their members to wear aigrettes in any form.
In 1909, however, poachers harvested three hundred thousand
sea birds for their feathers in the newly established federal bird
refuge at Laysan Island in the Pacific. Highly colored reports of
the "Laysan massacre" gave added sense of urgency to those
who believed that federal and state governments were responsible
for protecting bird life.

In a period which many people saw as the age of extermination, the death of the last surviving passenger pigeon came with
special shock in 1914. Once the most populous bird in the world,
it symbolized natural abundance wasted. Extermination seemed
unimportant to some—buffalo were hides and tongues and pigeons
so much meat. But more and more people watched uneasily as
the buffalo dwindled to fewer than a thousand and the passenger
pigeon disappeared. In the spring of 1910, one of the chief
figures in the nature-study movement, Clifton Hodge of Clark
University, brought the immensity of extinction to school children
through the *Nature-Study Review*. In a massive but pathetic
effort "to decide whether the finest race of pigeons the world
has ever seen is extinct or not," he promised a reward which
grew eventually to more than four thousand dollars to anyone
discovering a surviving pair. School children across the country
scoured former nesting sites, but no one claimed the reward.

Sportsmen also posed ethical problems to serious bird watchers.
According to the best estimates in 1911, three million hunters took
to the field each season. In 1912, they bought nearly seven hundred and seventy-five million shotgun shells. Pressure on wildlife
seemed intense, particularly when six million hunters took the
field in 1920. The Biological Survey first officially defined "game"
birds in 1916. Included were bobolinks, catbirds, chickadees,
cuckoos, flickers, flycatchers, grosbeaks, hummingbirds, kinglets,

martins, meadowlarks, nighthawks, nuthatches, orioles, robins, shrikes, swallows, swifts, tanagers, titmice, thrushes, vireos, warblers, waxwings, whippoorwills, woodpeckers and wrens. Bird watchers viewed this broad definition with some dismay. Sponsored at first by a handful of naturalists, the movement to educate the public to appreciate bird life gathered more and more impetus as it spread to women's clubs, church groups and school children. Leaders of organizations dedicated to preserving what seemed to them to be the nation's heritage encouraged massive enlistments of popular sentiment. Some groups seemed too sentimental to be taken seriously, but all mirrored public interest.[20]

The National Association of Audubon Societies was perhaps the most effective of these special-interest groups. Originally founded in 1886 by George Bird Grinnell, the society had faltered and died for lack of purpose. Reorganized in 1896 and enlisted in the cause of bird preservation, it had local societies in thirty-seven states by 1916. By 1906, Society president William Dutcher had secured passage of a model bird-protection law in thirty-two states.[21] In 1911 the National Association began to reach school children through Junior Audubon clubs. Ten-cent membership dues provided educational pamphlets, identification pictures, lapel pins, and for each ten members a regular subscription to *Bird Lore*—all to aid school teachers in presenting the bird study section of the elementary science curriculum. In 1916, the Society reported 205,138 junior members. By 1930, 4,327,477 children had been registered at one time or another, and by 1933, the Society had distributed some fifty-three million bird pictures.

Several similar groups worked to interest younger children in bird life. By far the largest of these, the Liberty Bell Bird Club, was organized in 1913 by *Farm Journal Magazine* of Philadelphia. In 1916, it claimed 706,000 members pledged to study and defend American song birds. Through these groups school children learned to value the wide variety of native birds. They also came to share the paternalism by which nature lovers sought to atone for the past. Children and adults both learned that it was a social responsibility to provide birds with winter food and shelter.

Bird house building programs flourished in crafts classes around the country, and suburban householders derived great pleasure from the wild birds they were able to entice into their yards.

The paternalism motivating the bird watcher's crusade for protective legislation, his birdhouse building and winter bird feeding alarmed some naturalists. To those who took their transcendentalism seriously, there was something disturbing in the sight of purple martins nesting in many-storied apartment houses that resembled gothic mansions or Indian pueblos. Birds were wild; their homes were tree trunk cavities or nests of their own design. Victorian cottages might seem allegorically proper, but even nesting boxes designed to resemble natural tree trunks were somehow artificial. Bird feeding was commendable, but it, too, distorted the natural lives of the birds and clouded the moral allegories in their unfettered activities. *Bird Lore* and similar periodicals delighted in photographs of chickadees that so far forgot themselves as to feed from the palms or lips of men, and of nestlings perching on pencils, cigarettes or children's fingers. But naturalist Stanton Kirkham warned, "you may think when a bird has eaten from your hand that you have at last attained to a certain intimacy; but you have merely brought the bird around to your way, you have not brought yourself to its way." [22]

To many Americans the bird watcher seemed a comical if pathetic figure lavishing his social concern on chickadees and seagulls at the expense of mankind. But he found in wild birds a visual reminder of a way of life and a world unspoiled by man. On the floors of Congress, in school science texts, and even in baking soda boxes, he sought to bring his vision to a public not always aware of his sincerity. The chickadee, the tufted titmouse and the nuthatch might have no souls, but in the eyes of the bird watcher there was in them the same breath of life that invested humanity. That they existed gave them meaning in the hazy theology of the nature movement, and that they had names by which they might be known gave them individuality. Watching their daily activities, the bird watcher saw mirrored his ideas of bravery, cheerfulness, affection, industry and humility. Particularly when these traits were hinted in literature, they had a powerful emotional effect on his conceptions of nature and of life. Those who did indeed have the birds in their hearts found much that was meaningful in the ways of the birds in the bush. In the sight of a chickadee or the song of a sparrow, even in the mention on a printed page, there was much that was sincerely moving. Rarely articulate himself, the bird watcher depended on professional writers like John Burroughs, Mabel Wright and Edith Patch to pass on the vision of the birds to generations to come. In literature, birds emerged with an artistic and a moral purity which both sentimental nature lovers and ornithologists were sure that they possessed in real life.

4

Nature Fakers

> I have in no instance taken liberties with facts, or allowed my imagination to influence me to the extent of giving a false impression or a wrong coloring. I have reaped my harvest more in the woods than in the study; what I have to offer, in fact, is a careful and conscientious record of actual observations and experiences, and is true as it stands written, every word of it.
>
> John Burroughs, *Wake-Robin*
> (Boston, New York: Houghton, Mifflin,
> 1904, 1st ed. 1871), v.

In fusing fact and emotion, nature writers thought of themselves as necessary intermediaries in a communion between nature and their readers, for Arcadia existed as much in an act of will as in objective fact. It was based on the nature lover's faith in a world he saw through the eyes of his favorite authors. If this faith were threatened by obvious insincerity or by the laughter of its critics, the whole mythical structure might crumble.

John Burroughs asked in 1895 whether "such books as mine give a wrong impression of Nature, and lead readers to expect more from a walk or a camp in the woods than they usually get." [1] He spoke rhetorically then, but in a few years his question seemed critically relevant to the whole movement. The nature essay was a literary and not a scientific form. It succeeded only as it subjected natural phenomena to literary techniques. But by 1900, nature writing had entered a phase that disturbed both scientific observers and philosophical naturalists like Burroughs. Claiming that the old accounts of patient and repeated observation lacked impact and excitement, new and untried authors brought to natural history all the conventions of dramatic action. To Burroughs and other watchdogs, sincerity and truth seemed very near to

45

parting company in the works of men they came to call the "nature fakers." As a young man, Burroughs had readily admitted that "literature does not grow wild in the woods." Then every writer had seemed entitled to do "something more than copy Nature." Now he maintained that "no man can invent incidents and traits as interesting as the reality." Those who tried to do so were "bearing false witness against the animals." [2]

Nature fakers went beyond the illusions of art to the illusions of fantasy. Capitalizing on their publishers' desire to please the public, they passed off a combination of folklore, fiction and tall-tale humor on such staid periodicals as *McClure's, The Century, Harper's* and *Country Life in America*. Yet strangely enough, the writers most frequently branded as nature fakers—men like Ernest Thompson Seton, Sir Charles G. D. Roberts and the Reverend William J. Long—offered credentials every bit as good as those of their critics. They loudly proclaimed their love for the wilderness and their desire to communicate it to their audiences. Still they were denounced as miracle workers. Dallas Sharp noted urbanely that they leaned too heavily on "their style and prefaces for their interest—falling back rather hard upon the preface, it must be said, as if somebody had been lying." [3] The form they adopted was as old as civilization—the animal fable. But, to the consternation of scientist and literary naturalist alike, they insisted that the adventures of their animal heroes, however fabulous, were absolutely truthful. In Seton's phrase, they dramatized as fiction "the actual facts of an animal's life and modes of thought." [4]

Ernest Thompson Seton was as popular as John Burroughs, if not as highly regarded. Born in England in 1860, he came to the Ontario wilderness at the age of six. Through his childhood adventures and Beadle's dime novels, he conceived a lifelong love for Indians and untamed nature. As a wildlife artist, he studied for a time in Paris with his friend, Robert Henri, served as a government naturalist in Manitoba and finally moved to New York City in the 1890's. There as an author, lecturer and youth worker, he made a career of bringing "the Woodcraft Way" into American life.

He published the post popular of his fifteen volumes on outdoor life, *Wild Animals I Have Known*, in 1898. A half million copies passed onto American bookshelves by the 1930's, along with nearly two million copies of his other titles. In his first volume Seton established the form which nature fiction was to take for a generation. Avoiding such conventions as talking birds and animals, he enlisted his readers' sympathies by arranging his natural history to point up analogies with human problems. "I have tried to emphasize our kinship with the animals by showing that in them we can find the virtues most admired in Man." He wrote of his heroes in *Wild Animals I Have Known:* "Lobo stands for Dignity and Love-constancy; Silverspot, for Sagacity; Redruff, for Obedience; Bingo, for Fidelity; Vixen and Molly Cottontail for Motherlove; Wahb, for Physical Force; and the Pacing Mustang, for the Love of Liberty." In *Lives of the Hunted* he added "Majesty, Grace, the Power of Wisdom, the Sweet Uses of Adversity, and the two-edged Sorrows of Rebellion" to his catalogue.[5]

Seton's contemporary, Charles G. D. Roberts, was born in 1860, the son of a rural parish canon near Fredericton, New Brunswick. Educated to the classics by his father, Roberts earned a master's degree at the University of New Brunswick and taught English and French literature for a time at King's College, Nova Scotia. In 1896, he followed his cousin Bliss Carman to New York in search of a literary career. Drawing on childhood memories, supplemented by camping vacations with Carman and by library research, he developed a form of nature writing which he called "psychological romance constructed on a framework of natural science." He insisted that motive and not fact was the playground of the literary naturalist; only if he were freed from the tyranny of fact could he probe into animal psychology. Most important, he hoped to offer his readers a "return to nature, without requiring that we at the same time return to barbarism." [6]

Less qualified writers adopted literary techniques that weakened their credibility. They came to rely, for example, on the "composite hero" of romantic novels. To justify extravagance in some of their anecdotes, even Seton and Roberts insisted that "the material of these accounts is true. The chief liberty taken, is in ascribing to one animal the adventures of several." [7] Yet the creation of an animal hero composed of possibilities, however probable, affronted many readers. This was especially true, Mabel Wright noted in 1905, when the creators of these new animal heroes insisted "that the composite be considered as an individual pure and simple, whose comings and goings, and thoughts they have personally (or by proxy) watched and fathomed." [8]

Ever vigilant against exploiters of nature, John Burroughs reacted with unusual vehemence. He insisted that Seton's book should be called "Wild Animals I *Alone* Have Known," for though the stories were "true as romance, true in their artistic effects, true in their power to entertain the young reader," they were unquestionably false as natural history. "Such dogs, wolves, foxes, rabbits, mustangs, crows," Burroughs continued, "no other person in the world has ever known." He acknowledged that Roberts's *Kindred of the Wild* was "in many ways the most brilliant collection of animal stories that has yet appeared." [9] But scrupulous background detail could not hide the fact that Roberts's animals behaved exactly like human beings.

Burroughs's ignorance of the wilderness did not lessen his criticism of Roberts and Seton. "What one observes truly about bird or beast upon his farm of ten acres" [10] served well enough. He would not question Seton's knowledge of wolves, but Old Silverspot, the one-eyed leader of the crows, Burroughs claimed, must behave as crows at Slabsides had always done. Truth in natural history could only be "that which is verifiable; that which others may see under like conditions, or which accords with the observations of others." [11] Unique, isolated, unsupported incidents were not acts of animal heroes but the fancies of incautious observers. Nature in a world of urban chaos still followed predictable laws. The lower animals, however they might mirror humanity's aspirations, were creatures of instinct, and what was true of an individual must also be true of the race. Nature was miracle enough if rightly understood; the larger-than-life hero of the animal romance was inappropriate in a world where the ordinary and the commonplace were already remarkable.

In 1903, Burroughs mounted a serious if somewhat narrow-minded attack on the nature fakers in an article for *The Atlantic Monthly* which he called "Real and Sham Natural History." It was the first in a series of such criticisms over the next decade. But strangely enough, the nature fakers continued to deny any wrong-doing.[12] They insisted their message could not live without literary support; they were equally sure that composite heroes, combining the traits of many individuals, came closer to the whole truth than the fragments in scientific journals.

Seton and Roberts acknowledged in lengthy prefaces if not in their stories the fabrication of composite heroes. Other writers insisted that the exploits they recorded conformed to absolute fact. None set more responsible critics to raging, and none defended himself more adamantly than William J. Long. Like many another nature writer, Long wholeheartedly believed that the wisdom of the wilderness outreached the wisdom of men. The pied piper of the nature-study movement, he offered to take his reader to the "School of the Woods" where he would find "little truly of that which made his heart ache in his own sad world; no tragedies or footlight effects of woes and struggles, but rather a wholesome, cheerful life to make one glad and send him back to his own school with deeper wisdom and renewed courage." [13] Long's credentials seemed impressive. To Burroughs' criticism in *The Atlantic* he replied acidly, if not quite accurately, "for over twenty years, I have gone every season deep into the woods; have lived alone with the animals for months at a time . . . have lain all night in my canoe or slept in the snow alone on their trail, that I might not lose the lesson of their awaking." [14] The adventures of the "Wood Folk at School," he assured his young readers, "passed under my own eyes and were recorded in the woods, from my tent or canoe, just as I saw them." [15]

Long set out quietly enough on his literary career. Born in North Attleborough, Massachusetts, in 1867, he graduated successively from Bridgewater State Normal School, Harvard Uni-

versity, and Andover Theological Seminary. As an Andover Fellow he spent three years studying in European universities, finally
returning to the United States in 1898 with a Ph.D. from Heidel-
burg. He immediately turned to nature writing while serving as
pastor of the Congregationalist church in Stamford, Connecticut.
Drawing chiefly from youthful journals and the corroboration of
guides, hunters and trappers, he published between 1899 and 1906
several articles and thirteen books directed chiefly at school
children.

Long's love of wilderness was unquestionably sincere. Much
that he wrote suffered only from the artificiality of the Indian
names he persisted in giving to his heroes. Yet in a series of letters to men like Burroughs, George Shiras, and William Hornaday, Theodore Roosevelt called Long a "ridiculous creature,"
an "utterly cheap liar," and a "lying scoundrel . . . too shame-
lessly dishonest to mind the scorn of honest men if his infamy
adds to his receipts." [16] On the other hand, Long had equally en-
thusiastic defenders. One of them wrote in 1904:

> One may well wish that every boy and girl in the land might
> become acquainted with Killooleet and Cloud Wings and Huk-
> weem. Children and mere lovers of nature on the one hand, and
> comparative psychologists on the other, owe no small debt to
> men like William J. Long who have the patience and pluck to
> spend years in the wilderness homes of birds and beasts in faith-
> ful observation of their life and habits.[17]

An enthusiast with more credulity than good sense, Long refused to believe in popular theories of instinct psychology. Instead he advanced a brand of comparative psychology which he
called "animal individuality." By what he believed was inductive
reasoning, he found that man and the animals had much in common. Nature writers, adequately to portray these common traits,
must free themselves from the preconceptions of deductive
science. They must, in fact, "struggle against fact and law" to
present nature sympathetically.[18] Because he believed that instinct psychology degraded nature, Long readily accepted any

sign of individuality in animals. Traditional naturalists had seen
only those actions which lowered the individual to the level of
the race. There was no place for heroes in their psychology as
there was in his.

So firmly did Long believe in his position that he presented as
absolutely truthful a series of observations that threw scientists
into an uproar. He told of the muskrat which lost its foot in a
steel trap, then smeared the stump with pitch "from some pine-
tree that had been split or barked close to the ground" to keep it
clean and dry.[19] He told of eider ducks flying to inland ponds to
drown the salt-water mussels that had fastened on their tongues,
and of beaver that raised young otter cubs as slaves. He told of
the orioles which chose to make a home in one particular tree,
but could find no place to hang their nest. They flew to the
ground, arranged a "perfectly measured" triangle of twigs lashed
together with bits of string. They fastened longer pieces of twine
to the ends of the triangle and to a central cord which they raised
to a convenient branch and anchored with a double half-hitch.
Finally they knotted the end of the cord to keep it from ravelling
and proceeded to hang their nest from this platform, the whole
of which, with accompanying depositions from reliable witnesses,
Long had before him as he wrote.[20]

On another occasion Long described a woodcock mending its
broken leg with a cast of clay and straw which dried in the sun
while the bird stood patiently on one leg. When the break had
healed, the woodcock simply waded in shallow water until the
cast would drop away. This tale of "woodcock surgery" followed
by a few months John Burroughs's first attack on nature faking.
Long alleged that it was absolutely true, that he had witnessed
such a feat (though from a distance) some twenty years before,
that he had since killed three woodcocks with signs of previously
broken legs, and that he had the testimony of a variety of sportsmen and game dealers to corroborate his claim.[21] Nevertheless,
reputable naturalists found it difficult to believe that any woodcock could have an understanding, acquired or instinctive, of the

principles of bone setting, of the effect of a hardened cast, or of the properties of clay and straw.[22]

His critics argued that Long's methods were faulty. In the first place he drew supporting evidence from disreputable sources— ordinary people, ill-equipped by training or by intention to accurately witness natural history. As Burroughs put it, the real truths of nature did not come from writers of romance, "nor from the casual, untrained observers, who are sure to interpret the lives of the wood-folk in terms of their own motives and experience, nor from Indians, trappers, or backwoodsmen, who give such free rein to their fancies and superstitions." [23] While hesitating to call him a deliberate liar, Frank Chapman, editor of the *Auk* and of the Audubon Society's *Bird Lore,* judiciously concluded that Long, at his young age, had already "placed upon record more remarkable statements" about the wildlife of New England and New Brunswick than all previous authorities taken together.[24] Long replied, "if scientists and comparative psychologists are honestly looking for new facts in the animal world, I have enough to fill several regular editions of *Science.*" [25]

Long's persistent denial of authority finally brought Theodore Roosevelt's anger into the open. He had privately fumed over almost everything Long had written since 1903, but when *Everybody's Magazine* approached him in 1907, he granted an interview as an expert naturalist in his own right. The President detailed the grounds on which nature fakers in general and Long in particular had failed the nature movement: by arousing the criticism of men outside the movement, they neutralized the missionary work of more reputable nature writers.[26] Roosevelt refused to accept any of "the illusions of art" in a field so serious as nature-study. He was deeply concerned, and his friend George Shiras was "almost raging," over Long's reference to "the long white fangs that could reach a deer's heart in a single snap," of Wayseeses, great white wolf of the North.[27] Such a statement called into question Long's whole attitude toward truth and nature, since, as Roosevelt pointed out on competent authority from Shiras, a wolf's teeth would have to be five to six inches long to reach the heart of a deer or a caribou. When Long told of a Labrador wolf's gift of a red squirrel to the leader of the starving pack, Roosevelt was quick to argue there were no red squirrels in Labrador.[28]

Long's lack of professional perspective and his naive reliance upon untrained interpreters infuriated his critics, but the issue went beyond professional accuracy to the relationship between naturalists and their public. Scientists and nature writers agreed that whatever value nature might have for mankind rested on a foundation of fact. Any transcendental significance depended, therefore, on minutely accurate observation. The whole Arcadian mythology previously rested on the belief that nature actually existed as it was described. Yet even while nature fakers opened the Arcadian myth to ridicule, most still concluded with Long that "Nature reveals not only herself, but some beautiful and forgotten part of a man's own soul, when she finds him responsive in the wilderness." [29]

In popularizing the wilderness to an urban public, however, nature fakers concluded that their readers need not subject themselves to nature. Each must only project his own personality onto the world around him—"must look in his heart, not in the psychologies or natural histories, if he would understand half of what the Wood Folk are doing." [30] No immersion in the reality, no apprenticeship with How-To-Know books was any longer necessary. Long's readers simply read themselves into the role of animal hero after the manner of all fiction. They saw little beyond a pleasurable adventure and gained nothing that they did not already know. By dramatizing the unique and wonderful, nature fakers further cut off their audience from comparable experiences. They made the wilderness a cloak for their inventions, turning it into a world of mystery and enchantment which ordinary suburbanites could not hope to discover for themselves.

Appealing to the love of adventure in an audience which found the facts of natural history a little dull and naturalists a little timid, Long interpreted the meaning of wildness, willingly sifting the evidence of other naturalists, but offering little proof of his own statements because, as he announced simply, "I am accustomed to being believed when I speak." [31] His ever widening audience seemed to appreciate the ready and painless entrance into the wilderness which he offered with literary rather than scientific skill. "I have been greatly shocked by the number of persons who have come to believe in that prince of natural history fakers," William Hornaday wrote to Roosevelt in the Spring of 1907. "All this would be highly amusing," he added, "if it were not so pitifully serious to the children of the public schools, who are using Long's books, and who are taught to believe that what they say is true." [32]

None of Long's critics offered a more reasoned criticism than a writer in the Boston *Evening Transcript*, who characterized him as a man who could be "absolutely honest, and yet not quite telling the truth." [33] He took himself and his convictions very seriously, easily over-valued superficial conclusions, and, no matter how much he knew, was still given to ill-considered illustrations. In short, Long was temperamentally unfit for scientific investigation, a man in whom "imagination was all but reality," who believed in innocence, and uncritically expected it in others.

Seton, Roberts and Long believed in the Arcadian myth as strongly as Burroughs and the literary commuters did. They hoped to be its oracles. In their hands, however, the myth very nearly became more important than the truth. With the demand for nature essays "coming from every class in the community," wrote Mabel Wright in 1903, "the supply must be equally catholic. The idealist may not tolerate the work of the mere reporter . . . neither will the shop girl riding out on her wheel of a Sunday be anything but repelled if forced to read Thoreau's meditations by Walden pond." [34] Reasonable critics like Dallas Sharp, who politely wished that Long at least had not seen "quite so much with his own eyes," [35] acknowledged that nature fakers awakened an audience which traditional naturalists might never have reached.

Men like Burroughs found it difficult to accept the adulation which nature fakers inspired, not so much for nature as for themselves as interpreters. Such adulation led a writer in the *Connecticut Magazine* to conclude, with unintended irony, "not one observer in a hundred would ever have put himself in the place where Dr. Long has been to watch his animals, and not one in a thousand would have the patience or courage to stay there." [36] To Burroughs, on the other hand, Long's books were those "of a man who has really never been to the woods, but who sits in his study and soaks up these yarns from things he has read in *Forest and Stream,* or in other sporting journals." [37] Burroughs remained adamant. Purity in the nature essay could not be sacrificed to popularity. Only if the Arcadian world were founded on fact could it have any permanent meaning. As he wrote to Lyman Abbott, editor of *Outlook* and one of Long's publishers, "Mr. Long may find in the croaking of the frogs a key to the riddle of the universe if he can and be entirely within his rights; all I demand of him is that he be sound upon his frogs. I will not even accept a toad." [38]

5

"This Elegant Art"

In the United States, nature and domestic life are better than
society and the manners of towns. Hence all sensible men gladly
escape, earlier or later, and partially or wholly, from the tur-
moil of the cities. Hence the dignity and value of country life
is every day augmenting. And hence the enjoyment of landscape or ornamental gardening—which, when in pure taste, may
properly be called *a more refined kind of nature,*—is every day
becoming more and more widely diffused.

Andrew Jackson Downing, "Hints to Rural Improvers,"
Horticulture (July, 1848).

Arcadia existed largely in the literary record. City dwellers recognized it only when they perceived their lives through literary
patterns and symbols established by nature writers. A quite different group of professionals, whose prestige rested increasingly
on the existence of the myth, tried to reconcile discrepancies between the literary Arcadia and the suburban estate. These were
the landscape architects. Outside of the pulpit, no American profession began with such Romantic materials drawn so exclusively
from the past. Landscape architecture, "this elegant art," as
Andrew Jackson Downing had called it in 1841, was the hand-
maid of Classic and Renaissance architecture and a dignified
companion to the arts and letters in Romantic thought. But not
until an urban society stylized nature in its parks and estates did
landscape architects achieve in this country the stature they com-
manded in Europe.[1]

In the colonial period, formal gardens served as architectural
devices extending floor plans into an intermediate zone where
geometric patterns symbolized the "humanization" of nature.
Symmetrical mazes of shrubbery and decorative walkways offered
Tidewater aristocracy and New England gentry a defense against

56

barbarism. Within the boxwood hedges and mulberry plantings they could gracefully retire from a bitter struggle against the wild countryside.[2] But the landscaped garden of the twentieth century was no island of civilization in a wilderness world. Rather, it stood in contrast to the mechanized world as an island of nature, "a relief from the too insistently man-made surroundings of civilized life," as Frederick Law Olmsted, Jr., wrote in 1923.[3]

Landscape architects were clearly the interpreters of natural rather than classical beauty. They were consulted whenever a man desired to "lose his consciousness of self" [4] without sacrificing his cosmopolitan sense. The means by which they achieved the simplicity of the informal garden were as complex as the nature essayist's literary techniques. Their manicured landscapes reflected rigid standards of Romantic beauty. By drawing their principles from eighteenth-century sources, they hoped to minister all the more powerfully to the twentieth century. Frederick Law Olmsted's apprentices faithfully studied such eighteenth-century Romantics as William Gilpin and Sir Uvedale Price; Boston's Charles Eliot was sure that the age of creative landscape theory extended only from 1770 to 1834.[5]

From Uvedale Price and William Gilpin, Olmsted's apprentices found that they must learn the principles of natural beauty, not by studying wild nature, but by studying its summation in landscape painting. From art, Price wrote, "we may learn to enlarge, refine, and correct our ideas of nature" according to the best models. There was, he noted, "a wide difference between looking at nature merely with a view to making pictures, and looking at pictures with a view to improving our ideas of nature." [6] In *An Essay on the Picturesque as Compared with the Sublime and the Beautiful*, he analyzed at some length the beauties of crag and gorge, bramble patch and forest oak, returning always to the importance of artistic composition. If the garden designer could learn from the painter, "not his power of imitation, but of distinguishing and feeling the effects and combinations of form, colour, and light and shadow," Price concluded, "it would hardly be too much to assert that a new appearance of things, a new

world would suddenly be opened to him." Eighteenth-century designers, working for general effects on country estates, primarily
mastered such land forms as rocks, water, and trees. Smaller
elements like flower beds were pretty enough, William Gilpin
wrote in his *Remarks on Forest Scenery, and Other Woodland
Views,* but they were "not adapted to form the arrangement of
composition in landscape." Price was willing to admit that "picturesque beauty must in many cases be sacrificed to neatness,"
but it was a sacrifice "which should not wantonly be made." By at-
tending to principles and not to particulars, landscape architects
should be able to imitate "many of the circumstances which give
variety and spirit to a wild spot," even in the smallest gardens.[7]
With the painter's "distant vista," his principles of repetition,
sequence and balance, and even certain of his framing techniques,
landscape designers turned their gardens into picture galleries.
Walkways were no longer decorative in themselves. They shrank
to winding paths, unobtrusively leading the observer from one
composition of foliage and flowers to another. Yet these single
compositions had always to be subdued in favor of overall effects.
The informal garden was a shrine to the unstudied simplicity of
God's creation. Landscape architects must so delicately intepret
their designs that nature would seem self-revealed in her most
inspiring form. If the resulting landscape suggested the style of
Poussin or Claude Lorrain or Salvator Rosa, the enjoyment of the
scene was increased by admiration of the artist's good taste.

Imaginative architects embellished their compositions with artistic and literary symbolism partly to reveal the "spiritual" nature of the site, and partly to reflect their particular tastes or those
of their clients. This was the age of weeping willows, rocky
grottoes and ruined hermitages with artificial tombs. Dying or
blasted trees reminded viewers that life and beauty were transitory. Such trees were also major compositional elements, and
their proper placement a matter of great concern. In the middle
distance, a mature tree with dying branches symbolized mortality
and broke the horizon line without seriously intruding in the
whole design. Storm-blasted trees recorded an historical moment.

As a broken-off trunk in the foreground such a tree might be a "framing" device to place individual compositions within the larger design. As modern landscape architects would continue to do, Gilpin referred all questions of taste to the examples of landscape painting. "We need only appeal to the works of Salvator Rosa," he noted, "for the use and beauty of the *withered top,* and *curtailed trunk.*" [8] Eighteenth-century Romantic aesthetics hardly seemed up-to-date preparation for the modern world, but they provided the standards and techniques which twentieth-century architects imposed on the American landscape.

Mrs. Schuyler Van Rensselaer recognized "hardly more than half a dozen professionals of repute" in 1893,[9] but landscape designers imprinted their particular view of nature on American culture with disproportionate force. They were members of a close-knit craft. Training, outlook and public responsibility varied little within the new discipline, which Frederick Law Olmsted humbly claimed to have fathered.

From the acceptance of "Greensward," the design he submitted with Calvert Vaux for Central Park in 1858, until his retirement in 1895, Olmsted participated directly or indirectly in nearly every major project which could influence urban standards of natural beauty. He advised the landscaping of Prospect Park in Brooklyn, South Park in Chicago, and several other city parks. He worked on the Arnold Arboretum in Boston, the National Zoological Park and the Capitol grounds in Washington, D.C., and he designed specifications for suburban developments at Riverside, near Chicago, at Brookline, Trenton and Denver, as well as offering advice to summer colonies at Long Island's Montauk, Chautauqua Point, and Newport, Rhode Island. He laid out the university campus at Berkeley and worked on designs for Harvard, Amherst, Yale, Johns Hopkins, Colgate, Smith, Stanford, Columbia and Princeton. Among the private projects passing through his office he handled the Rockefeller grounds and much of the work on the great Vanderbilt estate at Biltmore, North Carolina. Finally, he found time to head the California Governor's Commission on Yosemite Park in 1865, to found the *Nation* with

Charles Eliot Norton, to battle for years to preserve Niagara Falls
from industrial power development, and to advise the landscaping
of the Columbian Exposition in Chicago. Through a peculiarly
successful system of apprenticeship, he perpetuated his view of
landscape design well into the twentieth century. As he wrote
to a friend at the close of his career, "I am sure that the result of
what I have done is to be of much more consequence than any
one else but myself supposes. As I travel, I see traces of influences
spreading from it that no one else would detect." [10]

The modern profession emerged rather slowly from the Olmsted offices. The American Society of Landscape Architects
formed in 1899, the same year that Harvard University introduced the first full course in "Landscape Design." In 1902, both
of Harvard's instructors, Frederick Law Olmsted, Jr., and Arthur
Shurtleff, were graduates of the Olmsted firm, and shared with
other members of the profession the Romantic aestheticism.
Frank A. Waugh advised his students in *The Natural Style in
Landscape Gardening* to prepare themselves by studying nature
writing, music, poetry and painting. They were to look continually "for the spiritual significance of the landscape," which
yielded such qualities as Life, Power, Beauty, Peace, Joy, Mystery
and the Holy Spirit.[11]

Textbook writer Henry Vincent Hubbard found much Romantic
vocabulary obsolete, but not the principles of Romantic design
and the spiritualization of natural forms. "As in a stanza of
poetry," Hubbard wrote, the elements employed in landscape
design "should be in themselves beautiful, their arrangement in
composition should be pleasing, their significance should be
worthy, and the sequence of association aroused by their symbolism should be harmonious." He unintentionally revealed the
extent to which the modern Arcadian tradition confused the
Romantic aestheticism with the real world. Architects, he suggested, no longer needed to study landscape painting, because
the natural forms themselves revealed the same standards on
careful scrutiny. Nevertheless, landscape designers were not to

imitate nature. They were to realize the beauty that unadorned nature could only suggest.[12]

Though Hubbard confidently expected his audience to accept landscape design as a worthwhile refinement on natural beauty, earlier architects met with a good deal of public apathy. One of the most important designers to come through Olmsted's office was Charles W. Eliot, Jr., son of Harvard's President Eliot. Eliot spent two years in Europe studying Romantic examples of landscape gardening and landscape art, "that he might learn," his father wrote, "what sort of scenes the masters of landscape painting had thought it worthwhile to depict." [13] Then, in 1888, he opened his own office in Boston. He soon found that the more he mastered the elements of the natural style, the more he succeeded in eliminating any sign of his own contribution to the finished landscape. To counteract this peculiar self-effacement, Eliot, like Olmsted, felt a "professional duty" to publish his designs and the principles behind them, in order that the public should understand precisely what he had done. Confident in their Romantic philosophy, men like Olmsted and Eliot saw themselves as educators teaching with shovel and pen a new meaning for nature in urban society.

Eighteenth-century landscape gardeners worked in the narrow world of the landed gentry, making nature beautiful to a clientele which already shared many of the Romantic assumptions. They worked with a repertory of artificial lakes and streams, groves of trees and distant vistas. But modern landscape designers were less concerned with refining the taste of the rich than with reintroducing nature to the middle class. In doing so they faced a double task—interpreting the beauty of nature and educating the public to appreciate their skill. "Modern crowding into cities results in a counter invasion of the country," Charles Eliot wrote in 1889, "and it is just here that the special modern need of an art and profession of landscape gardening is first felt. How can we add roads, and many or large buildings, to natural landscape," he added, "without destroying the very thing in search of which we left the city?" [14] It was no easy task to restore natural scenery to suburban developments indiscriminately dropped on the blank page of a farmer's field. New houses, fresh from builders' plan books, rode the landscape like empty ships, and vestiges of wild nature along fence rows and roadsides disappeared in the subdivision to city lots.

Amateurs, further, undertook their own landscaping with no understanding of Romantic traditions. "What shall I plant is the question usually asked," wrote Herbert Kellaway, "and not where or how to make pleasing groupings or picture-like arrangements." [15] Even in attempting informal gardens the public revealed the same will to dominate, to erase the connotations of wild nature, that had marked the classical style. This was the era of the "pattern bed," with bright-colored flowers marshalled together to imitate rowboats, arm chairs, garden gates and even human beings. Kellaway found that landscape gardening meant no more to many people than "a red painted pot filled with flowers hanging on a three-forked stick, or a piece of sewer pipe for an ornament, or an old boat filled with earth in which are geraniums and nasturtiums." [16] All understanding of symbolism seemed bound up in souvenir rock gardens, borders of bridal veil spirea, and in that national emblem, the lilac bush.

Yet the Romantic aesthetic gained wider acceptance as more and more people came to share something of the Arcadian dream. Suburbanites dissatisfied with barren lots and commuters who found the landscape of their abandoned farms lacking the inspiration promised by their favorite authors put new faith in "landscaping." The manicured "pastures" in English deer parks depicted by John Constable and his followers appeared most suited to abandoned farms and suburban estates. Abandoned farms approached this ideal as they slowly reverted back to wilderness, but more than one commuter watched his pastures grow shaggier with cockleburrs and brush, scrub pine and oak, until they lost their original appeal. As Beauty with the Beast, the Arcadian ideal went hand in hand with the axe and hoe. In the rather unsentimental mechanics of Romantic design, individual trees had no value save for their function in the overall composition. Land-

scape architects were far more interested in defining the landscape to suit their own ideas than in preserving any transcendental
value in undisturbed nature.

Nowhere was the work of axe and hoe more evident than in the
landscaping of suburban estates. Abandoned farms were preselected for their scenery, but the suburban estate was more often
an accident of convenience. Nonetheless, taste and money could
do much to incorporate the groves and waterways and distant
vistas of the Romantic garden into suburban lawns. Charles S.
Sargent managed one of the better examples of suburban landscaping on his estate in Brookline, Massachusetts. Sargent headed
the Arnold Arboretum, helped to instigate Boston's park system,
and passed as a sophisticated student of landscape design. Traveling with him on a Forestry Commission survey in 1898, John Muir
came upon Sargent standing on a mountaintop in the Appalachians
"like a critic of the universe, as if to say, 'Come Nature, bring on
the best you have. I'm from BOSTON!'" [17] On his hundred and
fifty acres of meadow and woodland in Brookline, Sargent worked
hard to present the "best" that nature, under the supervision of
the landscape architect, could offer.

His estate, just four miles from Boston's statehouse, was like all
real suburban places, "rural in aspect, but urban in convenience,—
private, green, and peaceful in itself, yet close in touch with the
true self of the town," Mrs. Schuyler Van Rensselaer wrote in
1897. She was sure that suburban living demanded "a kind of
beauty which, while it looks spontaneous, is really civilized, refined, and delicately finished." Sargent's grounds appealed to her
chiefly because "the seemingly wild, the rich and polished gar-
denesque, and the simply pastoral pictures" he had composed
seemed "so skillfully separated and inframed in foliage." [18] Another critic suggested that "beauty of so suave and perfect a sort
as this is never a natural product . . . . Nature suggests the ideal
beauty, and the artist realizes it." [19] A great deal of time and effort went into the semblance of "serenity and repose" which
seemed characteristic of the whole estate. As Wilhelm Miller
wrote for *Country Life in America*, "these pastoral scenes, which

to my mind are the chief glory of the place, are the work of the axe. To make these vistas, ten trees have fallen for one that was left." [20] Miller liked best the simplicity and lack of pretension, the "seclusion without exclusion" that marked Sargent's magnificent isolation, though he was located in the heart of a thriving suburb.

The Sargent estate displayed one of the few modern innovations in landscape design—the naturalized domestic flowers which one writer called "the most inspiring floricultural idea of the past quarter century." [21] Daffodil, tulip, iris, or crocus bulbs running wild over suburban lawns gave both the effect of natural wild meadows and a flamboyant disregard for cost. Unfortunately, as Mrs. Frances K. Hutchinson discovered when she had twelve thousand crocus bulbs broadcast on the shore of Wisconsin's Lake Geneva, squirrels and chipmunks viewed the overturning of nature's balance as a personal providence. In two years they ate eleven thousand eight hundred of the bulbs.[22]

Such wholesale effects were hardly proper to the suburban backyard, and there the Arcadian commuter felt the loss of nature most keenly. The typical suburban lot had no natural features and little hint of any "character." Buildings dominated not only the lot itself but the view in all directions. The sprawling effects of Romantic design seemed out of place, and even in the rare case where the lot was set among trees, there could be none of the variety that was so much a part of Romantic aesthetics. In fact, any natural feature was incompatible with postage-stamp landscaping. Nature writers hopefully maintained that true nature lovers could be recognized by "certain qualities of mind and heart rather than the number of acres" in their gardens.[23] They set out bravely to import wild flowers into their backyard beds, and to build concrete ponds for their carp and gold fish. Great rolling landscapes had no place in suburbia. "The shadow of a blackberry-vine as it trails over a gray rock," must give the suburbanite, Mrs. Van Rensselaer wrote, "as delightful an emotion as the sight of a great mountain." [24]

Landscape designers fell back on an abstract arrangement of free-flowing lawns and undulating flower beds in which conventional color hues and shrubbery forms provided the emotional connotations of the country estate. They experimented with landscape "gaiety" in the rippling motions and light-and-shadow patterns of spirea, weeping willow, birch and poplar, but most of all they came to rely on grassy lawns, which shared the sophistication if not the expanse of landscaped greens. "After falling for a while under the spell of their gentle and quiet pastoral charm," said Samuel Parsons hopefully, "one will feel that the very heart of the landscape picture lies within the tender green space, the delicate refined quality of which has, just because it is refined, escaped observation." [25] In suburban landscaping, the "natural style" finally became a desperate effort to hide the house with vines and shrubs, or failing that, to attach it to the soil by foundation groupings of flowers and evergreens that mimicked the encroachment of nature along old stone fences.

Formal gardens remained in the repertory of the landscape architect, and, because of the covert quality of naturalistic design, the public at large assumed such gardens were his stock in trade. But formal gardening had fallen into such disfavor among nature lovers and architects themselves that the rise of the profession actually paralleled the spread of natural design. The principles of the profession were as Romantic as they were venerable. Dedicated, as President Charles Eliot of Harvard wrote in 1914, "to the creation, preservation, and enlargement of opportunities for human enjoyment of mountains and valleys, hills and plains, forests and flowers, ponds and water courses, spring blossoms and autumn tints, and the wild life of birds and other animals in their natural haunts," [26] the landscape architect's ideals seemed to outdistance his commissions. Yet in those city parks and country estates where his designs could mature unmolested, he, more than any other believer in the Arcadian myth, managed to mold the natural world according to his own image.

6

"Keep Off the Grass"

The occasionally so pressing want of that quiet and peculiar
refreshment which comes from contemplation of scenery—the
want of which the rich satisfy by fleeing from town at certain
seasons, but which the poor (who are trespassers in the country) can seldom fill—is only to be met by the country park.

Charles W. Eliot, Jr., "Parks and Squares of United States
Cities," *Garden and Forest*, I (October, 1888).

In America, professional architects were hard put to find the
sophisticated audience that approved of Romantic aesthetics in
England. Rather than confine themselves to designing suburban
estates, they advanced their services, as A. J. Downing put it, for
"refining, elevating, and affording enjoyment to the people at
large," [1] in the brief but far-reaching movement for landscaped
public parks. Under the leadership of men like Frederick Law
Olmsted and Charles Eliot, the new profession broke its old-
world alliance with the landed gentry and hitched its fortunes to
the city to promote, as Eliot declared, "the comfort, convenience,
and health of urban populations, which have scanty access to
rural scenery, and urgently need to have their hurrying, workaday lives refreshed and calmed by the beautiful and reposeful
sights and sounds which nature, aided by the landscape art, can
abundantly provide." [2] Should "the forces which push men into
the arms of ignorance, sin and death, be allowed a free field in
our cities," Eliot asked the Advance Club of Providence in 1891,
or should there be parks and open spaces to redeem the city with
"all that mingling of the natural and the human which we call
landscape?" [3]

"Reservations of scenery are the cathedrals of the modern world," Eliot told the Boston Metropolitan Park Commission in 1896,[4] but city dwellers were not always willing to admit to any particular inspiration in their city parks. The first really widespread affirmation of landscape architecture came in America's contribution to Romanticism: as early as the 1830's, John Jay Smith's Laurel Hill in Philadelphia and Mount Auburn Cemetery near Boston brought nature into the Romantic melancholy of the graveyard. These were followed in 1855 by Adolph Strauch's Spring Grove in Cincinnati as the first of the park-like "rural" cemeteries. William Cullen Bryant's view of nature was enshrined in Greenwood in New York, Walnut Hills at Cincinnati, Lake Forest and Riverside at Chicago, Lakewood in Minneapolis, Forest Lawn in Los Angeles, and Cypress Lawn in San Francisco. In 1892, unable to find a sufficiently rural landscape in San Francisco, The Cypress Lawn Cemetery Association bought eighty acres ten miles distant, along with a special "funeral car" for the electric railway. As Americans somehow confused peace and security with rural scenery and perpetual care, the landscaped cemetery became the first popular monument to the Arcadian myth.

Old-fashioned attitudes toward death and burial were conditioned by crowded old-world graveyards like those in London, where, as one writer put it, corpses are "buried in standing postures because no room is left to lay them down." [5] In many such graveyards, the dead were periodically removed to make room for more, and in other cases, whole cemeteries were leveled as building sites. The American cemetery seemed by contrast "a special kind of park with a peculiar dignity and sacredness," [6] which offered visible signs of grace and immortality with the changing seasons. Romantic melancholy inspired the first "rural" cemeteries, but "no one would now make the cemetery dreary by confining the planting to spruces and weeping willows," Ossian Simonds wrote in 1920. "On the contrary," he added, "every effort is devoted to securing bright cheerful effects by the selection of all kinds of happy-looking plants." [7]

Lavish crypts and stately monuments were only signs of worldly pomp to nature lovers, whose search for eternity included leveling grave mounds and lowering headstones below the surrounding grass. The best of all monuments was, of course, the natural form: a boulder or a living tree.[8] To forestall the embarrassment of a dying tree, at least one monument maker created a tasteful trunk with twining vines in reinforced cement. Edward Bok of *The Ladies' Home Journal* built an elaborate system of concealed graves on his lot at North Laurel Hill in Philadelphia. He imported a natural boulder from his suburban estate, inscribed it only with his name, and surmounted the whole plot with a pergola to cast out any further suggestion of death.[9] Ossian Simonds insisted that "a cemetery is for the living," a place of refuge, a bird sanctuary and a breathing space. With good fortune and the right kind of planning it "might become as beautiful as the Garden of Eden, or even as Heaven itself is to the minds of the children." [10]

Up to a certain point most Americans agreed with Simonds, but they seemed unwilling to grant the same virtue to nature outside the cemetery wall. They sometimes resorted to city parks in astonishing numbers; yet they knew only vaguely that the landscaped park was supposed to provide for passive contemplation of restful scenery—for that mental isolation which geologist Nathaniel Shaler called "the calm, affectionate forthgoing to the environment." [11]

Though landscape architects remained committed to the spiritual necessity of scenic parks, they soon learned that delicate compositions so effective on country estates simply did not survive in public parks. They accepted the limitations of "trampling" with the crowd psychologists' fatalism. The "wilderness" motif was the first to falter. "If the interesting cliffs and boulders and gnarled trees may be looked at and not overrun, such a place of scenery may be a very desirable portion of a park," Henry Hubbard told his students, but "if its Romantic ruggedness is likely to become disheveled shabbiness under the feet of the crowd, then some less interesting but more permanent character might well be chosen." [12]

The tree-dotted meadow so typical of the English countryside seemed most suited to public parks. Its grassy openings were hardy and easy to care for. Its alternating clumps of trees framed a variety of compositions, increased the feeling of spaciousness and at the same time absorbed large numbers of people. To Hubbard it had the precise appearance of "a landscape plainly once the work of man, but so far received back by nature that man's interference is no longer an incongruity, but rather an added pleasure of association." [13] This pastoral convention met the needs of the urban park so well that it was even imposed on lands that were little suited to it.

The rocky rectangle of New York's Central Park was just such a case—one half mile wide and more than two miles long, it contained 843 acres of picturesque gullies and rubbish heaps. Early attempts to turn it into farm land had already failed when in 1858 Frederick Law Olmsted set to work to make it conform to the plan he titled "Greensward." As one park advocate noted thirty years later:

> The triumph of its designers' skill lies in the fact that a narrow strip of land, broken and folded into ridges of rock, has been turned into a series of tree-bordered meadows, each one giving glimpses of what promise to be still fairer and more quiet fields beyond. It is this pastoral scenery, and its restful, healing influence upon the minds of those who are worn and wearied with the strained and artificial conditions of city life, which gives the Park its value.[14]

But even the pastoral motif required some preservation. Crowds of people wandering idly about in the middle distance of its vistas effectively destroyed the connotation of the country. Warnings to "Keep Off the Grass" were simply aggressive efforts to preserve the unspoiled look of rural scenery by funneling the public from one vantage point to another along the old pathways of the Romantic garden.

The general public may never have consciously appreciated the "healing influence" of city parks, but by the 1890's nature lovers convinced city planners to mount a park movement of national proportions.[15] Minneapolis owned no park land in 1880 but had 1,400 acres by 1890. Cleveland expanded its park system from 93 acres in 1890 to 1,500 in 1905. Los Angeles had 6 acres in 1880 and 3,700 in 1905; and New York City, a leader in the movement, enlarged its parks from 1,500 acres in 1880 to more than 10,000 acres in 1926. Boston's Metropolitan Park system included 11,000 acres in 1926, and Cleveland's some 10,000. No matter how justified by the propaganda of the landscape architects, by rising property values, public works programs or local graft, the city park movement represented an economic tribute of massive proportions to Romantic idealism. Between 1858 and 1873, New York City spent nearly fourteen million dollars on Central Park. The Boston system swallowed more than twenty-five million dollars in its first thirty years. Kansas City spent eleven million in twenty years, and Cleveland ten and a half million between 1874 and 1924. Frederick Law Olmsted, Jr., and city planner John Nolen concluded in 1906 that "the cost, both directly in money and indirectly through interference with the street system and with the normal commercial development of the land," was unusually great in any major park system. Only a real need for scenes "of a kind thoroughly contrasting with city life and immeasurably sequestered from all its sights and sounds" could justify the expense.[16]

The ideological argument for city parks presumed a moral value in natural beauty. The same motive lay behind the primitive urban renewal efforts sponsored by such groups as J. Horace McFarland's American Civic Association. Formed in 1904 through a merger of the American Park and Outdoor Art Association and McFarland's American League for Civic Improvement, the new group sponsored "the promotion of city, town and neighborhood improvement, the preservation and development of landscape and the advancement of outdoor art."[17] Its "City Beautiful" campaign aimed to replace the ugly residue of urban development with parks and playgrounds as emblems of progress. In McFarland's own town, the "Harrisburg Plan" to cover up the ugliness of the city got underway in 1901. Architect Warren Manning designed the Pennsylvania capitol's parks as "resting places where nervous and tired people, the sick, and mothers with children can secure a complete change of scene, freedom from noise, boisterous games, and the constant passing of people." In 1906, the first real victory for the Harrisburg Plan came when "Wetzel's Swamp," through which forty per cent of the city's sewage once seeped, was officially dedicated as "Wildwood Park." [18]

Similar efforts to replace public eyesores with parks and playgrounds spread across the country. New York City's "Mulberry Park" rose from the rubble of a tenement block. Washington spread its two-thousand-acre Rock Creek Park over a shantytown dumping ground. When the rubbish had been cleared away and the narrow valley landscaped as a bridle-path wilderness, men of wealth appropriated building lots along its boundaries. The resulting increase in tax revenue had a powerful economic appeal. Following landscape architect George Kessler's comprehensive plan, Kansas City acquired some two thousand acres of park land and eleven of a projected twenty-seven miles of parkway between 1893 and 1905. New York City's park system was one of the largest in the country, but it was overshadowed as a model by Boston's "Metropolitan Plan" which Charles Eliot had begun as early as 1890. Competent observers called it "the most comprehensive, complete and admirable of American park systems." By 1905, it comprised some fifteen thousand acres of city parks and outlying reservations under the jurisdiction of thirty-nine separate municipalities, but all located within twelve miles of the Massachusetts Statehouse.

Out of Blue Hills and Middlesex Fells came the rudiments of the "county park" system, in which rural parks were managed for surrounding cities. New Jersey's Essex County began such a system in 1895, stimulated both by the success of the Boston plan and by growing demands from Newark residents. Hudson County, adjoining Essex, maintained its own system in 1903; and in 1915,

Cook and DuPage Counties began to acquire "Forest Reserves" around metropolitan Chicago. Forest Reserves provided a belt of urbanized wilderness around the city, regulating urban expansion as well as protecting water resources. By 1925, Denver owned some ten thousand acres in outlying reservations. The Westchester County system, begun in 1922, comprised over sixteen thousand acres in 1928; but Cook County's system was by far the largest, with more than thirty-one thousand acres, chiefly in the Chicago and Des Plaines River valleys.

By 1928, New York City residents could travel to six hundred and fifty-five thousand acres of forest reserve within two hundred miles; but most New Yorkers turned to a finger-like reservation, in some places as narrow as two hundred feet, which ran for twelve and a half miles along the Hudson River in New Jersey—Palisades Interstate Park. Originally planned in 1895 to stop traprock quarrying along the riverbank, it became one of the most intensively managed recreational areas in the country. Combined with ten thousand acres which Mrs. Mary Harriman donated as "Harriman Park," the whole system totaled forty-five thousand acres. At a cost of twenty-five million dollars, the Park Commission developed a riverside walking path the full length of the park, family camping grounds, four bathing beaches and sixty rustic rental units which city welfare organizations used to house some seven thousand city children each week in the summer season.

Automobile travel turned many of the old boulevard carriage drives into mass transit arteries. They offered wide traffic lanes, freedom from intersections, and few pedestrians. To many city planners the parkway system appeared to solve urban transit problems, but parkways appealed to landscape architects as well. Designers included them frequently in the metropolitan park system and declared roadside scenery as important as traffic control. Parkway growth was necessarily slow and expensive. The Bronx River Parkway in Westchester County, for example, had been first recommended in 1906 as a means of sewage control on the Bronx River. Twenty years later it was fifteen and a half miles long, with landscaped footpaths as well as rapid traffic lanes.[19]

Harvard's President Eliot suggested in 1914 that "the evils which attend the growth of modern cities and the factory system are too great for the human body to endure" without the consolation of natural scenery.[20] The parks themselves existed because a minority of architects and nature lovers believed they met a subconscious need. Pragmatic planners proposed other uses for patently vacant land. In the years before 1918, park enthusiasts beat off attempts to include in New York's Central Park a 100,000-seat public theater, a stadium arena on the shores of the water reservoir, a street railway, a merchandise display building, an exhibition hall, a cathedral, an academy of design, a playfield for noisy sports, and a permanent circus. After 1918, they defeated proposals for a fine arts center, a subway, a 30,000-car garage, and a metropolitan airfield. But "the green pastures and still waters, the restful and life-giving glance of nature"[21] could not withstand a new kind of social reformer who brought child's play to city parks.

The playground movement altered the whole concept of park design. To landscape architects like Eliot and Olmsted, city parks were "appropriated for the recreation of the people by means of their rural, sylvan, and natural scenery and character."[22] To playground psychologists like Joseph Lee, Luther Gulick and Henry Curtis, rural landscapes ministered only to the overwrought nerves of business barons and their middle-class clerks. Such people had no right to impose their aesthetics on factory workers and the children of the poor. However much landscaped parks brought peace of mind to harried businessmen, the monotony of factory work produced a torpor far more serious. Machine operators exerted themselves hardly more than invalids; one reformer noted that poor children could legally exercise little more than their thumbs in a game of marbles. Factory workers needed the freedom of vigorous movement far more than they needed tranquility and rural scenery. "Keep Off the Grass" warnings, reformers declared, were despotic restrictions which kept the poor from their games so the rich could have scenery.

Joseph Lee complained that landscaped parks were the front parlors of the city. To those who accepted urbanism as a way of life and not an unfortunate accident, it was the empty landscape and not the crowded street that was unnatural. Love of solitude signified a social maladjustment, akin to high fences and gate keepers. "The crowd comes largely to see the crowd. That is the sight best worth seeing," Lee concluded. "There is no use trying to treat a place in the middle of a crowded city on the wilderness motif," he wrote in 1906, "it is going to be smudged and smirched in any case. The thing to do is to frankly recognize that its beauty, if it is to have any, must be civic beauty." [23] Parks were not for the re-creation of lost identity, he argued, but for play. He went on to warn that "the boy without a playground is father to the man without a job." [24] Lee was sure that the fifty-court tennis field in Boston's Franklin Park was a monument of civic beauty; bars of netting, gridironed foul lines and frantic players "added as much to the beauty of the park as anything else it contained." [25]

Emphasizing freedom from physical restraint in rural life, the playground movement began harmlessly enough in "sand-gardens" for young children. This spread out from Boston during the 1880's.[26] Though sand gardens drove the entering wedge in the use of parks as playgrounds, the first real playfield opened in 1893 on a vacant lot in Chicago. Chicago philanthropist William Kent donated the land and Jane Addams' Hull House managed the project. In the beginning, one kindergarten teacher and a policeman served as staff. By 1899, thirteen cities had supervised play areas; by 1906, some thirty-eight. By 1917, five hundred and four cities had regularly supervised playgrounds.

Though at first playgrounds simply substituted the physical pleasures of the country for the spiritual, the play motif was itself urbanized as the movement gained professional standing. "It is not merely play that our cities and our children need," Luther H. Gulick, President of the newly formed Playground Association, told its members in 1907; "they need the kind of play that makes for wholesome moral and ethical life." [27] Professional recreation leaders brought social awareness into child's play, stressing cooperation and obedience to higher authority. Playground directors made group membership a sign of status, and the individual child at play disappeared in a whirlwind of directed activity. "Games" and "contests" with rules and leaders seemed most appropriate. "Supervision not only trebles the attendance of the playground, but makes it a school of character and of all the social virtues," wrote Henry Curtis.[28] As in Boston and Rochester, supervised playgrounds soon passed logically from park-board control to the jurisdiction of city departments of education. City parks were, in the eyes of reformers, simply enclosed space within which children could evolve urban social patterns without distraction.

Play was no longer a means of exercise but an end in itself, a science conforming to the needs of an urban culture. The rural image of informal outdoor exercise gave way to an urban ideal for town and country alike. In the 1920's, the National Recreation Association found rural play patterns woefully inadequate. Country children had nowhere to go but the open fields and nothing but their own inventiveness to guide them. In 1929, the Association published a rural recreation handbook to bring the social games of an urban society to those who still lived in the country. Ignoring solitary activities, the handbook concentrated entirely on active, if not to say frenzied, social recreation. Volley ball, handball, pompom pullaway and tag, as well as such dancing songs as "The Farmer in the Dell," were appropriate rural amusements, as were bean bag games, horizontal bars and teeter-totters. Ping-Pong was "a splendid game for family use." [29]

Sociologist Graham Taylor noted in 1907 that the Playground Association offered the beginnings of a tightly knit organization which could impose its playground philosophy nationwide. Speaking at the first national convention, he prophesied much from the great thunderstorm that closed the meeting. Four thousand spectators scattered for cover, but a hundred girls from Ogden Park, impervious to the forces of nature, doggedly continued their demonstration of Indian Club exercises to the end. The game and its leaders had become so important that even the outdoor park gave way to indoor "recreation centers." Chicago's South Park Board had spent $6,500,000 on ten such centers by 1907, and allocated another $3,000,000 for the same purpose. By 1930, the National Recreation Association announced, "probably no other city in the United States provides so many elaborate and varied facilities for indoor recreation." [30]

As late as 1923, Frederick Olmsted, Jr., could still argue, though ineffectively, for "consistently naturalistic landscapes" [31] which would neutralize the impact of urbanization. Playground leaders had asked for only a portion of the larger parks. Ninety-five per cent of Central Park, for example, remained theoretically rural. But as the playground spokesmen drove for recognition they destroyed the appeal that landscape designers had tried so hard to justify. Men like Joseph Lee and Luther Gulick insisted that warnings to "Keep Off the Grass" had less to do with the aesthetics of rural scenery than with wealth and special privilege. Parks, they said, were for ordinary people with ordinary expectations.

7

Arcadia Comes to School

> Parents and all who have the priceless treasure of childhood
> entrusted to their care should make it a glorious labor of love
> to drive out the false, the artificial and the morally enervating
> influences that invade the child-mind, by flooding its imagina-
> tion with the light, the beauty and the wonder of Nature.
>
> Benjamin O. Flower, "The Great Mother as an Educator:
> Or the Child in Nature's Workshop," *Arena*, xxxviii
> (September, 1907), 311.

One of the better ways to unravel a myth is to examine its transmission to children. However esoteric the Arcadian ideology may
have been, American nature lovers lost no time in adapting it to
children's minds. Their effort owed much of its force and not a
little of its poignancy to the uneasy fear that children could not
grow up properly in an urban world. "The child is a born naturalist," Colonel Francis Parker told the National Education Association in 1889. But Parker had only to look about his own Chicago to see that city children were isolated from the natural world
as few had ever been before.[1] Tree-lined city streets existed
chiefly in the predictions of Arbor Day enthusiasts. Wildlife was
limited to English sparrows and alley cats; and the country, like
Heaven, seemed far away to the very young.

No study of children and urbanization disturbed American educators as much as G. Stanley Hall's examination of "The Content
of Children's Minds on Entering School." In the Fall of 1880, Hall
tested the awareness of nature and country life that two hundred
children brought to the first grade from middle-class homes in
Boston. He hoped to evaluate object-lesson techniques and textbook assumptions, but he uncovered among these city children a

77

frightening ignorance of the simplest nature lore. Ninety per cent
of his group had no understanding of an elm tree or a field of
wheat or the origin of cotton or leather. Eighty per cent could not
identify the common trees of pasture and woodlot. Sixty per cent
had no concept of a beehive, a crow, a bluebird, an ant, a squirrel,
a robin, or of growing potatoes, strawberries, clover, beans, blue-
berries, blackberries, corn, chestnut trees, of seed-time or harvest.
The seasons of the year meant nothing to seventy-five per cent,
and nearly sixty-five per cent had never been swimming. City
children imagined a world in which spools of thread grew on
bushes, meat was dug from the ground, and cows were the size
of mice, a world in which potatoes were plucked from trees,
butter came from buttercups, oats grew on oaks, stones were
made of brick and cows said "bow wow." Yet Hall noted with
unusual humor, "nearly a dozen volunteered the statement that
good people when they die go to the country—even from Boston." [2]

Hall thought classroom nature-study might help city children
recover some acquaintance with the country. "As our methods of
teaching grow more natural," he concluded bluntly, "we realize
that city life is unnatural, and that those who grow up without
knowing the country are defrauded of that without which childhood can never be complete or normal." [3] Progressive educators
reading Friedrich Froebel discovered that nature lore should be
central to all schooling. How could city children understand such
folk expressions as "piggish," or "social butterfly," "wise old owl,"
"early bird," or "slow as an ox," when they had never seen a
pig or a butterfly or a bird? In addition, nature-study offered children a watered-down version of biology, geology, chemistry and
physics in an era when "science" seemed more and more important.

Much of the value that Hall and other educators came to attach to nature education stemmed from their interest in the
"recapitulation" theory of genetic psychology. Hall firmly believed
that, just as the human embryo evolved through a series of stages,
so the human psyche must recapitulate the cultural epochs of
human history. "The prehistoric period must and will recapitulate

itself in every young life," he told the National Education Association in 1904.[4] "In play every mood and movement is instinct with heredity," he wrote in *Adolescence;* "thus we rehearse the activities of our ancestors, back we know not how far, and repeat their life work in summative and adumbrated ways."[5] To genetic psychologists like Hall, Western Civilization drew its heritage not only from the Golden Age of a Greek and Roman past or from the Anglo-Saxon influence but also from the Bronze Age, the Stone Age, and even the arboreal and piscatorial past. Evidences of swimming motions in infants, swaying in standing adults, leg-swinging and love of water in any form seemed the remnant activities of fishy ancestors. Did men fear high winds, thunder and lightning; did they rock their children to sleep? The explanation seemed obvious to genetic psychologists, who could question even the origins of "Rockabye Baby in the Treetops." "Child's play" was serious business then. It was a recapitulation.[6] Were children "lifting, digging, striking, throwing, running and leaping, swimming, pushing, pulling, climbing, rubbing, or grinding, shouting"?[7] Did they play at animals and take instinctively to trees and tree houses at ten or twelve, or spend their time at hunting, fishing, playing "Indians," building huts or digging in the ground? Look to their ancestors.

City children lost all manner of vestigial activities, hunting and fishing, climbing and swimming and exploring—"the ancestral experiences and occupations of the race."[8] To Hall the consequences were all the more frightening because they were levied on future generations. Civilization might well short-circuit itself if nature and the "ancestral experiences" were lost to its children. "Never has youth been exposed to such dangers of both perversion and arrest as in our own land and day," Hall wrote in 1904; "hoodlumism, juvenile crime, and secret vice seem not only increasing, but develop in earlier years."[9] Children, denied their natural maturity, roamed the streets in primitive and warlike gangs. If the child was born a savage, as Francis Parker told the National Education Association in 1889, and if he did "recapitulate" in some generalized way the cultural epochs through which

civilization passed, as Hall and playground psychologist Luther
Gulick insisted in the 1890's, then he must be given the chance to
redeem himself.[10]

Under proper guidance, Hall wrote, what he called the psychological measles that were "now suppressed, perverted, or de-
layed to crop out in menacing forms later, would be developed in
their season, so that we should be immune to them in maturer
years." Children needed playgrounds where sympathetic leaders
helped them prepare for city life. They needed leisure reading
geared to their development: animal stories for the young, Indian
and caveman literature for growing boys, occupational fiction for
adolescents. They needed tribal allegiance in some more appropriate form than the spontaneous play group or juvenile gang.
They needed athletic games and social dancing to discipline their
primitive urges. Most of all they needed an introduction to the
out-of-doors. Hall concluded that "in our urbanized hot-house
life, that tends to ripen everything before its time, we must teach
nature, although the very phrase is ominous." He urged educators to "perpetually incite" urban children to explore "field, forest,
hill, shore, the water, flowers, animals, the true homes of childhood in this wild, undomesticated state from which modern conditions have kidnapped and transported him." [11]

Ideally, of course, nature-study counteracted what Hall called
"excessive confinement, sedentary attitudes and institutionalizing
influences in the school." [12] It aimed to extend the spontaneous
preliterate exploration of young children through the elementary
grades. Yet how could this spontaneous exploration, with its seem-
ing denial of booklearning and formal discipline, be integrated
into the pattern of classroom life? Urban education must continue
to be confined, sedentary and institutionalized; simple logistics
made a kind of martial order inevitable. Professional teachers saw
little purpose in sending children to explore the sidewalks, street
corners and tenement alleyways. Moreover, they knew the value
of sound textbooks and tested lesson plans. In practice, most of
them followed traditional teaching patterns. Textbooks standardized the aims and methods of the new movement, and only

through textbooks in many cases could city teachers offer their pupils the idealized sensitivity to common things that nature-study was supposed to provide.[13]

Early writers worked hard to fashion a textbook which combined a denial of booklearning with the directions necessary to bring about some spontaneous substitute. They valiantly abandoned the vocabulary of the scientist, but they could not escape his methods. In *The Common Objects of the Country*, already in its fourteenth edition by 1892, the Reverend J. G. Wood noted that "nearly everyone who has taken a country walk has seen Woolly Bears, and hardly anyone knows what is meant by 'chilognathiform.'" He determined to treat the subject "for the benefit of the many, even in the risk of incurring the contempt of the few," [14] but he directed his simple vocabulary almost entirely to a technical and anatomical study of insect life.

Wilbur Jackman insisted that adult knowledge could not be meaningfully impressed on childish minds. Sharing Francis Parker's faith in the "divinity of the child," he threatened to substitute chaos for the ordered transmission of textbook learning. Jackman worked out his methods under Parker at the Cook County Normal School, publishing his popular but baffling *Nature Study for the Common Schools* in 1892. He resolved the dichotomy between booklearning and direct experience by arranging an ingenious series of problems and related questions without answers which forced both pupils and teachers to "learn by doing." But these ideas were too revolutionary for most practical educators. In his 1898 volume, *Nature Study for Grammar Grades*, Jackman retreated to such comfortably abstract problems as computing the leaf content of a single tree, furnace control and similar experiments.

In *Common Things with Common Eyes*, Barney Standish kept his readers' exploration at second hand, carefully shielding teachers from dangerous spontaneity by relying upon the traditional recitation method. Standish suggested that instructors conceal their own ignorance by paraphrasing the unassimilated personal observation, common knowledge and simple ecology which he combined in a "chart" and a series of test questions. The chart, in addition to being decorative, took nature-study away from the distractions of the out-of-doors to make it a "regular, rather than a chance exercise." Standish advised teachers to "review constantly, having the chart and questions before the class at each recitation, and near enough so they may be plainly seen." Teachers were to "insist upon every pupil being able to take the 'pointer' at any recitation and to name the objects on the chart, giving the 'Short Description' in full, and an intelligent answer to each of the accompanying questions." For the nature-poet's favorite honey bee, children were to chant,

> a true insect, passing through four stages of development; the egg, the larva, the pupa, and the true insect. It has two pairs of wings and three pairs of legs, a long tongue, strong jaws, and a sting. The body is divided into three parts: the head, the thorax and the third part.[15]

Dietrich Lange reminded teachers of country walks and the sentimental nostalgia induced by such lesson units as "About Our Homes in Fall," and "In the Meadow." But city children were not to share these emotions; they must first serve an apprenticeship on the intricacies of identification. Teachers could best conduct their bird study with "good pictures or mounted birds . . . to impress shape and color upon the children's minds; where this material cannot be had, close outdoor observations must suffice . . . ." For the wild hazelnut, so important to William Wordsworth's poetic description of "Nutting," Lange suggested that children memorize,

> shrub, three to ten feet high; bark brownish-gray; forming copses along edges of woods, along fences, and wherever trees and shrubs grow; staminate catkins exposed during winter. Compare the catkins of birches, alders, hazel, and ironwood.[16]

Textbook writers like Standish and Lange tried to translate traditional science into the vocabulary of children. If they distrusted the result, they subtitled their manuals for teachers and normal schools, where such simplification seemed eminently successful.

Later educators turned from the austere to the openly inspirational. In *How to Study Nature in Elementary Schools*, John
Wilson declared that teachers in beginning grades "should direct attention to the goodness and beauty in nature, so as to
sweeten the life and enlarge the thought of the child," [17] even, as
it sometimes proved, at the expense of scientific accuracy. Similarly, Charles Scott argued that "the most common plants—the
bean and pea and dandelion, the plaintain and burdock and thistle
—the trees and buds and leaves, the birds and insects and fishes,
the stones at our feet, are full of grace if we will but look for
them." Literature, not science, cultivated "the higher nature of the
child, aesthetic, ethical, and spiritual." [18] Nature-study must not
proceed from the simple to the complex, from cell to plant, or
petal to flower; children could not analyze components or recon-
struct dissected fragments. Scientific analysis of the hazelnut com-
municated little to children who had never been nutting.

Many urban educators, therefore, began to substitute literary
nature for the direct experiences city children could not enjoy.
Ernest Thompson Seton's *Wild Animals I Have Known* or William
Long's *School of the Woods* freed city teachers from the need to
find hazel bushes in Brooklyn or to transmute the bluebirds and
chickadees of the textbooks into English sparrows and pigeons.
"It is interesting to note how the popular teaching mind seizes
upon some one prominent factor, pampers it, nourishes it, ac-
centuates it until it completely dominates and distorts the situation," wrote the University of Chicago's Ira Meyer in 1910. "In
the present instance," he added, "the emotional stood in the fore-
ground, caught the attention of teachers, and animal stories became the rage of the season." [19] Dramatics ruled traditional
science in much of literary nature-study. Personification and other
anthropomorphisms helped to bring the Arcadian tradition to
school children, and tender parables of Jenny Daisy and Susy
Squirrel might have taught good character, but literary nature-
study was hardly an accurate introduction to the city park.

Yet nature-study philosophers found pedagogical value in
schools of the woods. "There can be no objection to the poetic

interpretation of nature," Liberty Bailey wrote in *The Nature Study Idea;* "it is only essential that the observation be correct and the inference reasonable." [20] Bailey, for all his sentiment, allowed no backsliding in his followers. He declared there could be "no textbook of nature study," adding that "when one studies a book he does not study nature." Teachers falling back on college science in the nature-study hour abandoned their responsibility. "We must reach the people; but we can reach them only by looking from their point of view," he concluded unswervingly; "we are to teach it for living and for loving—and this is nature-study. On these points I make no compromise." [21]

Bailey underestimated urbanization's effect on childhood, as well as on pedagogy. He supposed it was vital to bring country nature to city children whatever the cost, but city teachers found his suggestions frustrating. Many of them chose as their text, instead, Clifton F. Hodge's *Nature Study and Life,* published at G. Stanley Hall's Clark University in 1902. Like Bailey, Hodge offered nature-study as "the sheet anchor of elementary education" to protect city children "against idleness and waste of time, evil and temptation of every sort." It was, according to his cloudy but popular definition, "learning those things in nature that are best worth knowing to the end of doing those things that make life best worth the living." [22] Unlike Bailey, however, Hodge thought it wisest to concentrate on attainable ideals—to accompany his inspiration with detailed lesson plans and suggestions for methods and materials that were equally adaptable to New York, Kansas City, Los Angeles or Keokuk.

Nature-study as Parker, Jackman, and Bailey imagined it might well appeal "to the aesthetic, the imaginative and the spiritual in the child." It might well lift him "above the brain racking problems of cube root and complex fractions" into a "diviner atmosphere, throbbing with impulses and wooings and suggestions," [23] but many educators were convinced that it must also provide city children with the character to withstand urban life. "The times have changed and very little of the old environment is left," Mary Dickerson wrote with some uneasiness. The "earnest, self-reliant and highminded" frontiersmen were gone, and in their place were "city children of today," many of whom might "become the very opposites of their fore-fathers." [24] In rural and even suburban areas, nature-study and object-lesson methods were still feasible. Colonel Francis Parker brought the farm into rural education by offering geography in the division of the fields, geology in the actions of the brook and the nature of field stone, plant life and zoology through crops and livestock, measurement and arithmetic from the daily tasks of farm life.[25] In 1905, Mrs. Lida McMurray published a little volume called *Nature Study Lessons for Primary Grades*. It was easily the best of nature-study textbooks, but it attracted little attention. She had planned her "lessons" for teachers "dealing with children in the midst of nature"; [26] nature-study had clearly to be tailored to an urban environment if it was to meet the needs of the twentieth century.

8

Bluebirds and Bean Sprouts

> More than any other recent movement, it will reach the
> masses and revive them. In time it will transform our ideals
> and then transform our methods. Nature study stands for di-
> rectness and naturalness. It is astonishing, when one comes to
> think of it, how indirect and how unrelated to the lives of
> pupils much of our education has been.
>
> Liberty Hyde Bailey, *The Nature Study Idea*
> (New York: Doubleday, Page, 1903), p. 18.

Well-to-do families might send their children to suburban "country day" schools or perhaps to an "outdoor school" like the Evans
School for Boys in Arizona, where a Cambridge scholar tutored
Eastern boys "living each in his own cabin, keeping horses, and
making camping trips." [1] "Traveling" schools like Paul Ransom's
Adirondack-Florida School or The Snyder Outdoor School for
Boys offered year-round outdoor life. Snyder's students studied in
the Blue Ridge Mountains in the fall and spring and wintered on
an island near Fort Myers, Florida. They spent mornings at
lessons and their afternoons hunting deer and partridge, trout
fishing, mountain climbing or ocean sailing. Public school administrators finding the beginnings of cultural collapse in children
whose contact with the earth was limited to street sweepings in
the gutter could hardly take their children to the country in such
fashion. Instead, they introduced "nature-study" programs in one
school curriculum after another. For forty years or more, teachers,
superintendents and normal school instructors strove to impose
the Arcadian myth on urban society by training children in the
ways of the woods.

The disparity between the "meaning" of nature and city chil-

86

dren's opportunity to explore it posed continuing problems. "The intelligent observation of nature seems very desirable," one team of educators concluded, "but to secure it under the ordinary limitations of the schools has proved to be one of the most elusive tasks that teachers have ever undertaken." [2] Not so much that training was unavailable; books on the subject seemed almost more numerous than good teachers. Most educators agreed on the need to rescue children from "the narrowing and artificial tendencies of modern life." They had supplied, in fact, "plenty of undigested inspiration on the subject, but not very much execution." The whole problem seemed to be "that the 'authorities' have failed to show inexperienced teachers just how to begin, just how, step by step, to give their first lessons."

In 1905, Maurice Bigelow of the Teachers' College, Columbia University, began a monthly journal which he called *The Nature-Study Review*. Under a succession of editors from various colleges and universities, it served for nearly twenty years as a symposium for leaders of the movement. Surveying teaching and training programs around the country, Bigelow concluded almost at once that nature-study could "no longer safely be left to teachers who depend upon 'loving' nature instead of upon a thorough training in subject matter and methods." [3] Yet Bigelow also argued that scientific methods were out of place. He declared in 1907 that "science even stated in words of one syllable is not for children, because for them we have something better in nature-study." [4] As another educator put it, "true nature-study [had suffered most] from the scientific octopus, which has reached its —ology tentacles down into the common schools." [5] Science seemed to Clifton Hodge "a sort of military ration of a special few," but nature-study was "the daily bread of all alike." [6] The emotional commitment simply would not die. Nature-study was to "create a passionate love for the things in God's great school," wrote Samuel Schmucker, Professor of Biological Science at the West Chester State Normal School.[7] Cornell's redoubtable Anna B. Comstock insisted that "in this God's beautiful world, there is everything waiting to heal lacerated nerves, to strengthen tired muscles, to please and content the soul that is torn to shreds with duty and care." She encouraged the faltering to remember that "nature-study in the schoolroom is not a trouble; it is a sweet, fresh breath of air blown across the heat of radiators and the noisome odor of over-crowded small humanity." [8]

Nature-study instructors came bearing goods from afar. Longing for a bit of wild nature, they assumed that children shared their interest. Dallas Sharp willingly described a woodland world few city readers ever saw, although he argued that nature-study was "not a hunt for the extraordinary or the marvelous at all." [9] Sharp came halfway—as far as city parks or even cemeteries, but he delighted most of all in trying to make his own Hingham wood-lot believable to city children. His *Ways of the Woods* was required reading for eighth-grade students in New York. In it Sharp accounted for the domestic habits of the muskrat, chickadee and chipmunk and described a hunt for tracks after the first snowfall.[10] But no manner of textbook and no amount of training seemed to prepare the urban teacher for her pupils' ignorance of the blue jay, the phoebe, the hepatica or the arbutus. Occasional street-car field trips might have sufficed for suburban children, but they were impractical in the heart of New York City. Even donations from more favored areas—the first steps in social charity for suburban children—hardly substituted for "real" nature. Stanley Coulter insisted that true nature-study "dignifies the commonplace and clothes with interest the child's immediate surroundings." Yet he was equally convinced "that the teacher in the densely populated areas of great cities works at a disadvantage." [11] No matter how much he applauded object-lesson learning, too many objects in city life simply couldn't be dignified. "Commonplace" soon came to mean "country" in the nature-study vocabulary. The city child's ordinary environment provided the justification not the materials for nature-study.

One educator concluded a carefully reasoned analysis of children's thinking by suggesting that "love of an object does not come into a child's heart so much from the beauty or wonder of the object as from association of this object with some loved person, or some place or time that gives pleasure." If children did find familiar things most meaningful, then "association" ought to play an important part in the choice of nature materials. The same educator warned, "we must remember this law of association in the primary grades or we shall find ourselves not only failing to make the children love nature, but taking definite steps toward making them dislike it." [12] G. Stanley Hall's simple faith in exposure to country experience and the missionary zeal with which early nature-study advocates arranged for field trips, pestered museums for stuffed specimens and travelling displays, and sought out charitable contributions from suburban schools reflected a fear of the city which urban children did not feel.

"The city teacher, penned up between brick walls, with a brewery on her right and a livery-stable on her left, high buildings in the rear and a noisy street in front, must make collections," Frank Owen Payne counseled in 1895, "in the far-away country, at the seaside, among the mountains, or anywhere, out of the hurlyburly of her daily life." [13] But a decade or more of teaching with dead twigs, pussy willows, and abandoned bird nests led men like Maurice Bigelow to give up the search. "Is it true that the majority of young children are spontaneously interested in *study* of living things, that they are by nature naturalists?" Bigelow asked in 1907.[14] G. Stanley Hall and Francis Parker might both be wrong. Perhaps in the artificial and inanimate world of urban childhood, nature must itself become artificial and inanimate. Experiments in the chemistry and physics of everyday life might reach children in a way that bluebirds and bean sprouts did not. "Science" might after all be defined not as "organized knowledge" too advanced for childish minds, but as "problem-solving." The experiment, with its simple beginning, its ordered progression and the elements of suspense and surprise in its conclusion, might well appeal to children's love of mystery and excitement.

Artificial injection of sentiment and explicit deprecation of city life seemed suddenly out-dated to Bigelow, and other teachers rushed to employ the trick psychology of elementary laboratory science. Green pastures and Arcadian cows had little to do with

John Brittain's lesson on milk. Instead, his second-year students relied on "a sample of milk sugar, a little extract of rennet, hydrochloric acid, vinegar, litmus paper, a muslin strainer, tumblers, bottles, spoons, enamelled cups," and a "spirit lamp." [15] The increasingly popular "Stockton Plan" included "lessons on air, water, evaporation and condensation, steam, air and water currents, light, heat, sound, electricity, minerals, including the useful metals, soils and soil formation, and other topics," [16] all of which produced unusual, observable, and immediate results.

Litmus-paper and vacuum-pump nature-study did little to glorify outdoor life. Nature-study instructors casting about for something which city and country had in common discovered the weather. Weather observations, one instructor noted, utilized barometer and rain gauge, hygrometer, magnetic needle, maximum and minimum thermometer, a weather vane, a centigrade thermometer, and a small windmill—most of which provided work for manual training classes and all of which required definition, explanation and experiment. [17]

But many educators thought such experiments and observations lacked the sentimental association with nature and the outdoor exercise that ought to be a part of every child's upbringing. They admitted that wild nature might be inaccessible in metropolitan areas, but the miracle of growth remained wherever there was a spot of earth. With sometimes pathetically limited resources, city teachers turned to "school-gardening" to make their young charges "stronger, more intelligent, nobler, truer men and women." [18] If children could not learn from the bluebird and the wren, perhaps in the garden they could discover the virtues that urban society admired. Bringing the country into the school yard had reassuring precedents: Comenius had cultivated the school garden for its beauty, Pestalozzi for its training in industry, and Froebel for its system. Gardening brought children out of cramped and regimented classrooms. It beautified school grounds with ornamental plantings and brought the miracle of seedtime and harvest to children who only knew that spring arrived when swinging doors came back to corner saloons. [19]

But school gardening offered more than mystic communion with seeds and soil. Clifton Hodge said it taught industry and provision for the future; it instilled "courage to fight for home, love of country," and civic responsibility. "To allow a child to grow up without planting a seed or rearing a plant is a crime against civilized society," he concluded, "and our armies of tramps and hordes of hoodlums are among the first fruits of an educational system that slights such a matter." [20] There was work to be done in the garden if immigrant youngsters and rootless slum children were to learn the expectations of adult and urban society. "Gardens are made to offer opportunities for forming correct social views," another instructor noted in 1909:

> Early in their garden life, the children are taught to respect those things that belong to their neighbors; to realize that community property belongs to the whole not to a part but that each must offer his support; to understand that the policy which is best for the majority must be supported.[21]

The "Children's School Farm" in New York City's DeWitt Clinton Park was the best-known among the educational gardens. When Mrs. Fannie Parsons undertook to lead the project in 1902, the "farm" occupied a bit of unused land in one of the poorer parts of town. It would eventually join with a playground, a gymnasium and a public bath, but in 1902 it was an undeveloped dumping ground. Even in 1905, a most successful season, it measured only one hundred thirty by two hundred fifty feet. Fenced away from the rest of the world, it formed a community where young hosts and hostesses guided visitors through the garden and the model house, served them tea and explained their daily activities. The land was divided into four hundred and fifty plots, each three feet by six feet, which the young farmers tilled on hands and knees with pointed sticks. Mrs. Parsons believed that the model house and garden program would teach a thousand children each year to accept lessons of "brotherhood, cooperation, self-respect." [22] She compared garden paths to highways and individual plots to house lots in order to teach the responsibilities of property ownership and land improvement. "I did not start a garden simply to grow a few vegetables and flowers," she wrote in her first annual report. Instead, she aimed to teach "some necessary civic virtues: private care of public property, economy, honesty, application, self-government, civic pride, justice, the dignity of labor, and the love of nature." [23]

In 1907, right in the backyard of Clark University, where G. Stanley Hall still dreamed of bringing country life to children, Worcester, Massachusetts, developed its "Garden City" in Dead Cat Dump. The Worcester plan offered respectability in the garden community, while teaching city urchins "that the business of life is work." This "Good Citizens' Factory" was a "city of little gardens, ten by twenty feet, with streets, boulevards, squares, etc., like a miniature city." Each "citizen" paid five cents for his plot. In return he received five packages of seeds, all the produce he could raise, and the chance to participate in the affairs of self-government:

> This city is well-organized with a Mayor, City Council of seven members, Commissioner of Gardens, of Streets, of Tools, Water Commissioner, etc. together with forty Police Officers. The latter were for the purpose of protecting the property from thieves and bums. In the central square waves "Old Glory," reminding the many nationalities of their country and the laws it represents.[24]

Not only parents and school board members, but children themselves seemed impressed by the "business appearance of labor" in school gardening.[25] Measuring and marking plots and preparing and testing soil were manual training. Gardening and retailing the harvest provided, Alice Patterson noted, "the socializing value" of group experience, as well as "respect for the property rights of others, pride in ownership and civic responsibility." [26]

Seventy-eight per cent of the 1,572 city superintendents, reporting to the United States Bureau of Education's "School and Home Gardening Division" in 1916, supported the gardening movement. But the real thrust to the enterprise came in 1918, when Congress sponsored the "United States School Garden Army." One and a half million school children joined the wartime effort to increase food production on sixty thousand acres of backyards and vacant lots. At the same time they took their training "in thrift, industry, service, patriotism, and responsibility." [27] Much of the enthusiasm faded when peace returned.

In 1910, Ira Meyer perceptively analyzed the contradictions in urban nature-study. Rather than a steady progression from the proposals of Francis Parker and Wilbur Jackman, he found recurrent cycles of interest reaching as far back as the first quarter of the nineteenth century. Earlier movements had begun whenever educators observed that the spontaneous interest which their pupils took in the world of nature exerted a physical, mental and moral influence worth cultivating in the schools. The pattern which each of these cycles followed was most disturbing, however. As Meyer bluntly summarized it, "the school attempts to utilize this interest; knowledge is systematized; a textbook is written, teachers are trained through a textbook, they attempt to teach children by the same method, contact with nature is lost, spontaneous interests vanish from the schoolroom, the study becomes a mere matter of memorizing the system, public protest, exit the study either by neglect or expulsion." [28]

Nature-study, like school gardening, never really established itself. In 1930, as in 1900, the movement continued, its rewards still anticipated, its contradictions unresolved. In any given period the problems were the same: methods not clear, teachers untrained, textbooks inadequate. Always a new text, a new dedication or a new pedagogical evaluation promised to turn nature into "a real, bona-fide branch of study in the elementary school," but somehow the movement never quite matured. [29] Sentimental textbooks that treated nature as something far away and wonderful got little sympathy from hard headed farmers or from rural school teachers busy urbanizing their pupils. On the other hand, educators came to realize that the city demanded a great deal from its children which the bluebird and the bean sprout were powerless to effect. The Arcadian myth seemed all but lost in such units as Clifton Hodge's "The House Fly as a Practical Lesson," which stressed efforts to control the spread of disease, or Anna Comstock's "The Bracket Fungus, a Lesson in Civic Duty." [30]

Kate Douglas Wiggin suggested in her *Kindergarten Principles and Practice* that "the opening scenes of the drama of childhood, like those of the drama of the race, should be played in a garden." [31] Other educators were less impressed by the image of Eden than by systematic, orderly rows of plants. However much nature might abhor it, "there is a great moral force in a straight line," wrote Louise Miller, to whom the work of gardening was far more important than growing plants. [32] Experimental nature-study and the laboratory method seemed more real to many educators than Liberty Bailey's "nature-love," particularly in schools where as many as three-fourths of the children had never seen the country. [33]

As long as the natural world was taught to the city child the conundrum remained. Could the love of the out-of-doors be learned in city classrooms? When wild nature existed only in books and classroom lectures, flower-pots and pictures, could city children visualize the Arcadian world? John Burroughs answered with some asperity, "if I wanted to instill the love of nature into a child's heart, I should do it, in the first place, through country life, and in the next place, through the best literature, rather than through classroom investigations, or through books of facts about the mere mechanics of nature." [34] But Burroughs ignored the realities of an urban age. When natural resources and wild lands were dwindling and conservation was the issue of the day, the very existence of the Arcadian myth depended on the sympathy of city dwellers; as Harold Fairbanks wrote in 1920, "it is from the education of the children in right ways of looking at Nature that everything is to be expected in the years to come." [35] For all the expediency of mosquito control, units on the house fly or Comstock's lessons in civic responsibility, there was still need for the simple and sentimental. "Nature" study in some romantic way must still stand for "country" study. In spite of the impersonality and sing-song vocabulary of professional primers, city children still must learn to read the simple lessons of natural life:

> Ann found a hole. It was a little hole. Some ants dug the hole. Some ants ran into the hole. Some ants ran out of the hole. Each ant had six legs. Each ant had two feelers on its head. Each ant waved its feelers.[36]

9

"The Customary Thing"

The child revels in savagery, and if its tribal, predatory, hunting, fishing, fighting, roving, idle, playing proclivities could be indulged in the country and under conditions that now, alas! seem hopelessly ideal, they could conceivably be so organized and directed as to be far more truly humanistic and liberal than all that the best modern school can provide.

G. Stanley Hall, *Adolescence*
(New York: Appleton, 1904), I, x.

Almost unknown in 1900, summer camps were "the customary thing" by 1915, when Porter Sargent described some three hundred for his *Handbook of the Best Private Schools.*[1] Ninety per cent of these camps were in New England, within easy distance of major cities on the Atlantic Coast. Educators and social workers saw them as a way to control moral backsliding during the summer vacation. Parents used them to free themselves from clamoring youngsters or, if they could afford the "right" camp, to give them the chance to move up in the social structure. Children most often viewed organized camping as a chance for simple fun. But nearly everyone agreed with Liberty Bailey that summer camping, "under competent and sympathetic guidance, with firm but kindly discipline and something like Spartan fare," should be a part of every childhood.[2] Together with "Fresh Air Charity" excursions, summer camps did reach a staggering number of children. Their directors faced the problems met in any mass attempt to actualize a myth. Was the country experience as valuable psychologically as physically? Should it be offered to as many children as possible or offered in depth to a fortunate few? Could children in the country be left to their natural instincts, or must they be guided to use their opportunity? And finally, how could the country experience best prepare children to live in the city?

As early as the 1850's, those who could afford it fled to the country in the hot weather. Gradually the summer exodus spread to middle-class families, but the poor and the children of the poor, who were trespassers in the country, stayed behind. Nature-study in the schools gave them a glimpse of the out-of-doors, but little relief from summer heat and humidity. "Children love to roam about in the fields and forests and enjoy the mystery of their numberless discoveries," wrote Brooklyn educator Frederick Holtz. "They like to be on the water or in it," he added; "they like to fish, hunt, and camp. They like to play the primitive life of the Indian or the pioneer." [3] But if their parents could not afford the country place or vacation trip, they idled away their summers in the streets. "Fresh Air Charity" seemed the logical solution.

In the steaming July heat of 1872, *The New York Times* hit upon a program of one day excursion trips for slum children. "This beautiful charity," as Boston's William Cole called it,[4] tugged at the heartstrings of social reformers, who hurried to provide outings ranging from excursions along the Hudson River and afternoons on recreation piers or swimming barges to "Country Week" visits in rural homes. By 1897 seventeen cities offered organized "Fresh Air Relief" for their children. New York had fourteen nonsectarian and nineteen denominational Fresh Air groups and Boston thirty. Such agencies reached an amazing number of people in the 1890's. In 1895, for example, New York City groups alone provided 188,742 individual outings and other cities offered another 356,531.[5]

However, the large numbers of children served by excursions did not seem as dramatic to many sponsors as did the change in those who went to the country for longer periods. The sick seemed healthier, the undernourished heavier, and the delinquent more tractable after ten days in the "Country Week" program. The New York *Tribune's* famous "Fresh Air Fund" began in 1877 as "a simple Christ-like act of charity" on the part of Reverend Willard Parsons and his congregation in tiny Sherman, Pennsylvania.

Parsons felt a personal call to rescue some sixty children from the heat of New York City. He interested the *Evening Post* in widening the operation, and the following summer more than a thousand children visited country homes. In 1882, when the *Tribune* took over the program, fifty-five hundred children participated. The number grew steadily; after 1889, the Fresh Air Fund served more than ten thousand New York children every season. Participants in Country Week programs welcomed "the little strangers reared in poverty" into their own families, fed them a little more than usual, answered a bit more gently such questions as "Mister, do you have to buy gum for all them cows to chew?", and otherwise introduced them firsthand to country life.

Boston's pioneer "Country Week" originated in 1875 when the Reverend William C. Gannett and his sister adopted the idea from a similar charity in Copenhagen. Within ten years, under the direction of the Young Men's Christian Union, two to three thousand children and perhaps three hundred adults participated annually. William Cole, who described the program in 1896, had read G. Stanley Hall's "Contents of Children's Minds on Entering School." He knew the civic implications in permitting children to remain ignorant of country life. Such children, he wrote, "must almost inevitably grow up with twisted and vicious views of life." [6] In 1895, when almost a third of the City Missionary Society's funds went for Fresh Air work and twenty-nine other agencies were engaged in the same field, 789 of 1,300 school children in three of Boston's poorer districts still did not spend a night away from the city, and 262 had never seen the country at all. "The evil which must result to the city from allowing so many of its children to grow up in the narrow confines of courts and alleys without ever a day's experience of the health-giving and purifying influences of the country," Cole wrote, "does not need a prophet to predict." [7]

However private interests exploited the "back to nature" movement, "Country Week" enthusiasm played a significant role in the growth of "summer camping." Porter Sargent's incomplete history showed eighteen camps established in the 1890's and one hundred and six between 1900 and 1910. Some were hardly more than suburban hotels: Toledo's Chamber of Commerce sponsored forty tents on the beach at Lake Erie—twelve feet from the water's edge; the Borough of the Bronx maintained a martial field of family tents spaced fifteen feet apart on Long Island Sound; and a Washington, D.C., transit company ran a commuter camp at the end of its trolley line. Social workers like Arthur Todd, probation officer for the San Francisco Juvenile Court, led camping trips for boys, who hiked from one community to another, sightseeing, playing, and working part-time at harvesting, odd jobs and exhibition baseball. Generally, however, the summer camp was a semipermanent resort where city children enjoyed a ritualistic and circumscribed communion with nature.

Organized camping not only provided fresh air and healthful recreation, but served institutional needs little related to naturestudy. Dartmouth student Ernest Balch founded "Camp Chocorua" in 1881. One of the earliest of all summer camps, it functioned as a "Boys' Republic" where wealthy campers traded indolence at a summer hotel for an island "work camp" to learn the skills of business management. As a concession to roughing it, the boys did their own camp chores, but youthful construction companies also bid for carpentry work, the "Goodwill Contract Company" handled camp laundry, and the "Soda-Water Trust" provided for refreshments. Enterprising campers used a miniature boat-yard to make canoes—status symbols in an island camp—which could be contracted for and sold like other commodities.

Scout leader Dan Beard entered summer camp work in 1912 as director of the new "School of Woodcraft" for younger boys at Culver Military Academy in Indiana. Under his care, thirty-six boys spent eight weeks mastering academic subjects along with camping, swimming, forestry and ornithology. In 1916, Beard left Culver to form his own "Outdoor School" near Hawley, Pennsylvania. Despite its illustrious director, it differed little from hundreds of private recreational camps. Between forty and fifty boys descended on Beard for the eight-week season every summer. He worked hard to attract more campers and corresponded repeatedly with wavering regulars. "Camp out with Dan Beard, the famous scout," he wrote to one young applicant: "learn real woodcraft from a real woodsman in the heart of a real wilderness. Learn the secret joys known only to those who live close to nature." [8] To parents he offered their children health and tractability:

> all the advantages of the big outdoors, the strict discipline and regularity of the military camp, the high aims and ideals of the scout camp, the poetry, adventure and romance of a woodsman's camp, the instructive qualities of a naturalist's camp and the unique novelties and pastimes designed by a famous veteran in the world of American sports. [9]

To war-conscious maiden aunts he offered "a place safe from mobs, riots or aerial or marine attack." [10] He promised that his campers would develop "all the vigor, initiative and huskiness of the roughneck combined with the manners of a gentleman and the ideals of a scout." [11] He based his "Buckskin Regulations" on old-fashioned courtesy, neatness, military discipline and Spartan simplicity. Such home remedies often succeeded. "I am delighted with the improvement in little John," one mother wrote, "he came back so happy and husky and self-reliant and so thoroughly in earnest—he got from the school just what I hoped he'd get and more. I intend to send him every year of his life until he gets too big." [12] He valued character-training more than recreation, but he seemed unaware of new and professional techniques in vogue in the 1920's.

"Camp Ahmek," at Canoe Lake in Ontario, was a far more sophisticated effort "to utilize current principles and procedures of education, psychology, mental hygiene and sociology in the achievement of 'character' outcomes in the lives of boys." [13] Despite this description, Camp Ahmek remained a rustic camp. The "paramount educational asset," its chroniclers wrote, lay in "the naturalness and simplicity of life in the woods in contrast with the complexity and artificiality of civilized city life." Character training entered the woodcraft atmosphere when "normal everyday

experiences and incidents" of life in the woods became "occasions
of earnestness and social importance." Carefully avoiding things
the boys might do at home, Ahmek offered neither athletics nor
movies. The "canoe cruise" instead seemed brimful of educational
potential. It offered adventure and exploration that "modern organized education and even camping have largely eliminated
from the experience of youth." Prestige figures like Ernest
Thompson Seton and Jack Miner gave canoeing and woodcraft
instruction the flavor of the real out-of-doors.

In spite of the efforts of woodsmen like Beard and Seton and
Miner, however, organized camping inevitably compromised the
Arcadian ideal. Spontaneous communion with the out-of-doors
and budding naturalists' patient contemplation were bound at
every turn by the military precision which seemed necessary to
manage two hundred campers and a hundred counselors scattered over the landscape. Even at "Ahmek" exploration gave way
to formal instruction, that familiar means to measure progress
and equalize ability. Professional camp directors argued over the
merits of "rural" and "urban" camp programs. Some favored the
rugged simplicity of wilderness outings and concealed the mechanics of routine beneath a veneer of informality. They rejected
urban amusements in favor of primitive woodcraft activities.
Many directors saw some value in the undirected exploration of
nature that "woodcraft" camps promoted, but larger camps often
turned to "stimulated competition and regimentation," centering
on athletic activities already familiar to incoming campers, since
there was neither time nor personnel to train them for new adventures.[14]

Ritual and regimentation went beyond early rising, daily in-
spection and campcraft lessons. Once campers were conditioned
to centralized direction, the opportunities for social action were
endless. Summer camps offered a captive audience unmatched
even in the public schools. "The organized summer camp,"
Harvard President Charles Eliot told the National Association of
Directors of Girls' Camps in 1922, was "the most important step
in education that America has given the world."[15] "Institutional

camps," controlled by organizations with roots in the city, soon
came to have little sympathy for the "Fresh-Air" and emotional
types of summer camping.

Professional youth workers talked of rescuing children from
parents as well as from the streets. Sociologist Emory Bogardus,
basing his study on the reports of social workers, found that traditional families could no longer bring up children in any proper
fashion. The strange new world, to which children adjusted more
rapidly than their parents, brought a complexity to child-rearing
that only professional social workers understood. Family units,
like summer vacations, seemed increasingly obsolete. Only professional youth workers had the training, dedication and detach-
ment to rear city children. "After a parent has had experience
in raising a hundred children, or better, a thousand, he might be
in a position to make some observations of comprehensive value
—provided he had regard for scientific thinking," Bogardus concluded in his study of *The City Boy and His Problems*.[16]

Schools shored up the home for a part of the year, but the summer was "a period of moral deterioration." The typical American
businessman, "too busy or too indifferent to attempt the training
of his children himself," packed them off to summer hotels or
watering places.[17] Bogardus offered instead the "twenty-four-hour
School" to reclaim children whose home environment was less attractive than the public school system, but most youth leaders
favored the controlled environment of the summer camp. "The
camp must first of all take the boys from their homes for as long
as possible," felt Sidney Peixotto, who operated "Carmel Camp"
as a boys' work-republic where professional youth workers could
bypass family influences.[18]

As summer camping spread across the country, it appealed to
institutions not primarily committed to the out-of-doors. The isolation of camp seemed tailor-made for group experiments. The National Experimental Camp of the Pioneer Youth of America—a
coeducational venture "in personality development and social
living"—operated as a "child-size community." Group activities
and "the uninterrupted contact of staff and camper" provided a

rare opportunity for "the growth of social-mindedness" [19] rather
than for individual communion with nature. Similarly, the
Chicago Public School System gave its backing in 1919 to "Camp
Roosevelt" at Silver Lake in Indiana. Roosevelt provided morning
tutoring and afternoon athletics to six hundred boys in a seven-
week program. The staff included army officers for military instruction, YMCA men for the entertainment, comfort and spiritual
well-being of the boys, and Red Cross personnel for matters of
health and sanitation.

Lacking a firm belief in a particular type of camping and
faced with opposing theories of camp management, institutional
camps frequently vacillated from one program to another, always
seeking the most approved goals. "Scy Camp," the experimental
YMCA camp which Carlos Ward studied in 1935, opened near
Nashville, Tennessee, in 1923, with an award system planned for
the needs of the institution and the imagined interests of the
campers. Of thirty-two award classifications, three dealt with the
out-of-doors. Others included personality analysis, group games,
choosing a vocation, world brotherhood and knowledge of the
Bible. In 1924, however, one of the counselors belonged to Seton's
Woodcraft League. By simple division the campers formed three
"Woodcraft Bands." Organized group activity and intergroup
competition were thus introduced for the first time. In 1925, the
Woodcraft Plan was discontinued in favor of a "project curriculum." The following year the project plan and its award system
were both abandoned as overdirective, and the camp directors
instituted "town-meeting" camper government as a preparation
for life. In 1929, however, the program came full circle as a complete turn over of staff and campers brought to power a Hi-Y
organizer of the academic tradition who felt that self-government was a waste of teaching time. He reinstated awards and
numerical grades, and the campers moved once more along a
prearranged course.

When a million youngsters trekked to more than seven thousand
organized camps in 1929, standardization seemed a necessary
compromise with practical charity. William H. Kilpatrick, study-

ing the summer vacation activities of school children, found a
disturbing emphasis on statistical success in organized camps that
seemed too large, too stereotyped in their activities and too militaristic in their routine.[20] Private camps serving from a dozen to a
hundred boys ranged, Porter Sargent noted, from those specializ-
ing in "roughing-it" with "Indian guides and no rules," to those
offering " 'camp mothers' and compulsory tooth brushes." [21]
Somewhere in this range parents could choose a camp experience
which answered their interpretation of the call of the wild. But
the institution projected onto summer camping the personality it
maintained in ordinary urban activities. Parents sending their
children to institutional camps chose the organization rather than
the camp. In the absence of campers preselected for particular
interests or abilities, such camps could pursue a variety of courses
suited to their own requirements, as well as offer a variety of in-
centives to campers.

Institutions oriented to social betterment brought to camping
the educational ideals of professional social work—sternly reminding themselves that "just living out of doors and having a good
time is not enough." [22] According to Porter Sargent, the camping
experience was to "develop in them social habits," as well as "team
work," and the "ability to get on with others." [23] Wild nature
ceased to be a goal and emerged a fortunate accident isolating
the group from outside influences.

Old-line camp directors argued that "a little roughing it for the
boy is the finest of all experiences." [24] Some institutional camps
were willing to go so far to avoid "the soft, easy, mechanical life"
as to forbid ice cream or movies,[25] but they had neither the
facilities nor the inclination for the rugged outdoor life of canoe
camps and western horse tours. Moreover, Joshua Lieberman
noted, "most of the children who came to camp were totally un-
familiar with nature." To such children "the woods were a barrier rather than an invitation," [26] marking limits beyond which they
could not go. Outdoor life and the "Woodcraft Way" seemed a
mockery to many camp directors whose charges came from
second- and third-generation urban families. They imported so

many urban activities that the rural environment played little or no part in the camper's daily routine.

In contrast to "instinct psychology," the recapitulation theory made primitive camping and woodcraft a vestigial activity—a stage applicable to early adolescence—rather than a permanent urge. Outdoor life for children served to prepare them for adulthood. Hence institutional camps placed basic needs of adult society above the frequently romantic wishes of individual parents. Carlos Ward noted in 1935 that "our changing social order demands a new type of camping." He maintained that "pioneering" or "roughing-it" would have little place in the modern organized camp—particularly since some camp directors, social workers and even parents doubted the value of primitive life for city children who appeared no longer capable of sustained physical activity. Ward found greater and greater emphasis on social adjustment and far less on the strenuous life and woodcraft skills. But regardless of the ends that youth workers might visualize, and regardless of those who maintained that any organized camp violated Arcadian solitude, many of the smaller and more versatile private camps, the canoe camps and the pack trip tours, still approximated the primitive freedom they symbolized. Even though as institutional camps they imprisoned much of their campers' experience with routine, they still preserved some fragment, however tainted, of the outdoor heritage which Americans seemed bound to perpetuate.

10

"Backwoods Brotherhoods"

Some boys cannot go to camp for a summer, while others
cannot even go to camp for one week or two weeks, but there
isn't any boy, no matter in what city he lives or how big it may
be, who cannot go out into God's out-of-doors for a week-end
hiking party or camp.

John L. Alexander, *Boy Scouts*
(n.p.: Minute Tapioca Co., 1911).

According to a popular story among social workers at the turn
of the century, a certain rich man, much impressed with "Fresh-
Air" charity, hired a steamer, gathered several hundred children
from New York slums, and headed up river for "a day in the
woods." Once in the Catskills, he sent the boys ashore to "go in
now and have a glorious time." A short time later he found them
scattered about in the underbrush, smoking cigarettes, shooting
dice, playing cards and waiting to go home. The story carried a
lesson many youth workers discovered for themselves. "It is not
enough to take men out of doors," Ernest Thompson Seton wrote;
"we must also teach them to enjoy it." [1]

Seton, Daniel Beard and a number of other Americans agreed
with Sir Robert Baden-Powell that city children should not be left
to their own devices in the country. Baden-Powell insisted that
his English "Boy Scouts" be trained in the outdoor spirit; "the
key that unlocks this spirit," he wrote, "is the romance of Woodcraft and Nature Lore." [2] In this country, Seton and Beard organized efforts to bring the "Woodcraft Way" back to an urban
world. Seton's "Woodcraft Indians" and Beard's "Sons of Daniel
Boone" were forerunners of a number of "Backwoods Brother-

hoods" dedicated, as Seton put it, to the "revival of Woodcraft as a school for manhood." [3] Most of these early associations operated informally, often through the pages of family magazines whose circulation they helped to boost. *Recreation, Woman's Home Companion* and *Pictorial Review* carried woods lore to larger audiences at less cost than any self-supporting organization. Only when the "Camp Fire Girls" and the "Boy Scouts of America" capitalized on Seton's and Beard's successes did such youth groups begin to carry out their programs independently.

In 1900, Seton bought a group of abandoned farms in Connecticut. There he fenced off a private estate and tried his hand at conservation experiments. He turned youth worker to end the ingenious vandalism of neighborhood boys whose hunting grounds he had preempted. After his careful pitch on Indian lore, the boys chose to make peace and Seton agreed to teach them "the best things of the best Indians." [4] In 1902, he introduced his idea to a national audience in Edward Bok's *Ladies' Home Journal*. His "Woodcraft Indians" were to find "something to do, something to think about, and something to enjoy in the woods, with a view always to character building, for manhood, not scholarship, is the first aim of education." [5] His was "a character-making movement with a blue sky method." It was based on "the simple life of primitive times, divested, however, of the evils that ignorance in those times begot." [6] In his "Woodcraft League," Seton rewarded outdoor skills with a series of "coups," awards for daring, to be given after rigid and realistic tests that ranged from sleeping out of doors for sixty consecutive nights to a thousand miles of canoe paddling. These tests were grouped around such titles as "Canoeman," "Forester," "Hunter" and "Runner," and incorporated in a manual called the *Birch Bark Roll*. After examining things for himself, John Burroughs grudgingly wrote to Theodore Roosevelt in 1906 that Seton had "a big thing in his boys Indian camp . . . well worthy of your attention and encouragement." [7]

Others interested in children criticized more freely. In 1905, Daniel Carter Beard decided that Seton, a Canadian-trained

naturalist with "a literary love for woodcraft," might well organize American boys "into bands of play Indians." [8] Beard had
been reared in Kentucky, however. He preferred Anglo-Saxon
frontiersmen, first with the "Sons of Daniel Boone," which he
promoted through *Woman's Home Companion,* and later with
the "Boy Pioneers" which he organized in *The Pictorial Review.*
Beard's ideas were as simple and romantic as the buckskin
clothing he delighted to wear. Rather than call his boys "runners,"
or "foresters," or "sachems," he substituted "tenderfoot" and
"scout" from the Anglo-Saxon past. Seton's "coups" he changed to
"top-notch" awards for such things as "the Walker making the
best excursion in pure wildness." [9] Where Seton called his manual
the *Birch Bark Roll,* Beard would write the "Buckskin Book." "We
are teaching the gospel of out-door life," he claimed in his *Buckskin Book* for the Boy Pioneers, "and we want all other boys,
whether they belong to our society or not, to learn to love the
great out-door world, and with that love to imbibe a reverence for
real honor and good citizenship." [10]

Concentrating as they did on primitive, barbaric sports such as
canoeing, Seton's Indians seemed, to Beard at least, to ignore the
problems of urban citizenship. Sir Robert Baden-Powell expected
his English "Boy Scouts," on the other hand, to find lessons for
city life in the "school of the woods." [11] Baden-Powell resented
the poor mental and physical conditioning that city boys displayed in military service. He surveyed Seton's Woodcraft Indians
and similar American youth groups and, in 1908, formed the
English Boy Scouts to put "on a positive footing the development, moral and physical, of boys of all creeds and classes, by a
means which should appeal to them while offending as little as
possible the susceptibilities of their elders." [12] He stressed to his
scoutmasters the importance of outdoor activities for city children. "Nature lore, as I have probably insisted only too often,"
he wrote in 1920, "gives the best means of opening out the minds
and thoughts of boys." Through the romance of woodcraft, scouting would create "the Brotherhood of the Backwoods" [13] even in
industrial England.

Along with "romance and adventure," Baden-Powell stressed those "invaluable qualities which go to make up a good citizen equally with a good scout." [14] His emphasis on good citizenship attracted Chicago publisher William D. Boyce, who discovered the movement when a Boy Scout rescued him from a London fog. Boyce returned to the United States determined to establish the organization there. Together with members of such groups as the Camp Fire Club of America and the Young Men's Christian Association, he incorporated the "Boy Scouts of America" on February 8, 1910. The new group was mobilized rapidly, staffed by men like John Alexander and James E. West from the YMCA movement. By October of 1910, twenty-five hundred scoutmasters had enrolled in forty-four states, Puerto Rico and the Philippines. The National Council included an impressive group of men: naturalists Charles Abbott, David Starr Jordan and J. Horace McFarland; youth workers Dan Beard, Ernest Thompson Seton, and Jacob Riis; psychologists Luther Gulick and G. Stanley Hall; and other national figures like Admiral Dewey, Theodore Roosevelt, William Howard Taft, Gifford Pinchot, Henry Van Dyke, Charles Scribner and Hamlin Garland.

"There is a call for the scout movement," read an early Scouting pamphlet, "because the boys in our modern life, and especially in our cities and villages, do not have the chance, as did the boys of the past . . . to become strong, self-reliant, resourceful and helpful, and to get acquainted with nature and outdoor life, without special guidance and training." [15] Using a uniform designed by Beard and a handbook hurriedly rewritten from Seton's *Birch Bark Roll*, the new scoutmasters formed their boys, by the gang concept, into eight-member "patrols" united in "troops." Estimates of participating scouts ranged from 500,000 in 1911 to 300,000 in 1912, and sharply downward to 32,929 when registration procedures went into effect in 1913. A wave of Boy Scout fiction published in 1912 and 1913 helped to increase enrollment to 106,937 the following year; thereafter, some thirty thousand boys joined each year.

The Boy Scouts began almost at once to absorb competing organizations. In 1910, the first *Annual Report* called attention to "the annoyance caused by the existence of other movements whose purposes were not as clearly defined as ours." [16] The "Boy Scouts of the United States," under Peter Bomus, and William Verbeck's "National Boy Scouts" quickly capitulated, followed in turn by the "Boy Brigade," the "Boy Cadets," and Frank Masseck's "Knights of King Arthur." William Randolph Hearst's "American Boy Scouts" stayed aloof until 1912.

Similar groups for girls sprang up immediately. In February of 1912, Dan Beard's sister Lina echoed Beard's interest in the American folk heritage when she led the first meeting of "The Girl Pioneers of America." The next month Mrs. Juliette Low brought Baden-Powell's English "Girl Guides" to Savannah, Georgia, as the forerunner of the "Girl Scouts." Luther Halsey Gulick and his wife called their new organization the "Campfire Girls." Gulick was Director of Child Hygiene for the Russell Sage Foundation, the first President of the Playground Association of America and a friend of G. Stanley Hall. He and his wife had begun a family camp to introduce their daughters and friends to the out-of-doors as early as 1888. In March of 1912, with Mrs. Ernest Thompson Seton, they set out to bring Indian lore to city girls. The image of the maiden tending the campfire, while young scouts tramped the forest, soon attracted forty-seven hundred adult advisers and sixty thousand girls who answered to the romantic "Wohelo" (contrived from the first letters in "Work, Health and Love").[17] The Campfire Girl, with her sensible skirts and school-girl freshness, seemed about to replace the "Gibson Girl" as an American heroine.[18]

But, however attractive outdoor life and domesticated campcraft, the youth organization maintained itself and its reputation through the use of practical techniques of corporate management. The Boy Scouting movement clearly demonstrated this contrast between public image and institutional reality. Competition for financial contributions suggested almost at once that the distinguished "National Council" share control of the organization with a centralized staff of professional executives in order to co-ordinate Scouting policy. In 1911, the central staff established a Scout Supply Service to issue at a small profit uniforms and all manner of peripheral items ranging from clothing accessories to official camping equipment. Soon the literary treatment of the Boy Scout came in for almost as much surveillance as his physical appearance. The Scout handbook, chiefly responsible for the view young scouts had of themselves and their movement, was lavishly edited to conform to the central image. It became one of the ranking best sellers of all time, trailing only the New Testament, the Bible, and Charles Sheldon's *In His Steps* in 1933. Those who favored lighter reading turned to a monthly picture magazine, *Boy's Life*. Authorized in 1913, *Boy's Life* had 76,000 subscribers by 1916 and it sold a cumulative total of 41,000,000 issues by 1937.

Recognizing Scouting's popularity, American publishers rushed into print numberless "Boy Scout" novels varying as widely as imagination and the Scout Oath would permit. But a federal charter in 1916 gave the organization a marketable commodity by establishing their control of the words "Boy Scout." Both advertisers and publishers had to respect this control, and impromptu scouting stories disappeared abruptly. Percy K. Fitzhugh's endless series of Boy Scout novels in turn put scouting in its most advantageous form, largely to counteract the "Tom Swift" stories about industrial wizardry.

Fitzhugh most thoroughly explored the relationship of outdoor adventure to scouting in a series of "Westy Martin" novels. Westy, an introspective lad from New Jersey, imagined the Boy Scouts as heirs of Kit Carson and Daniel Boone. Unwilling to be a "parlor woodsman" or a "back-yard scout," he longed for real wilderness adventures, though he was poorly prepared to survive them. Once he had launched his hero in the wilderness, Fitzhugh unfolded "such adventures as boys do not even read of in these days of football and baseball and boarding schools and Saturday hikes." [19] But Percy Fitzhugh's eighty novels scarcely suggested the complexity of the Scouting image. As late as 1920, while Baden-Powell urged his English Scouts to exchange the

BACK TO NATURE

streets for a "school of the woods," Americans scrutinized the potential of urban Scouting.

Almost immediately, woodcraft-oriented men like Seton and Beard clashed with young YMCA-trained members of the executive staff over the role that "pioneering" and "roughing-it" could play in a movement dedicated to urban social work. The initial conflict evolved around the policy-making activities of the central office staff, and specifically whether YMCA-trained James E. West should be "Executive Secretary" or "Chief Scout Executive." The issue was particularly crucial to Seton, who was the first "Chief Scout," and to Beard, the "Chief Scout Commissioner"; to Beard and Seton any elevation of West meant fundamental policy changes. "All the enthusiasm, all the picturesqueness and all those things which make it interesting are gradually being squeezed out and the whole thing made dry as dust and Academic," Beard wrote to Scout Treasurer George D. Pratt. West seemed business-minded and unimaginative, admirably suited to office work but not trained in "Scout" principles as Campfire Club men like Beard and Pratt himself had been. Beard insisted that "the romantic element, the artistic element, the primal love of nature," [20] which had inspired the Sons of Daniel Boone and the Woodcraft Indians, would disappear in institutional complexity.

Baden-Powell openly derived his English Scouts from American woodcraft models like Seton's Indians.[21] American Scouting, on the other hand, recognized only a direct descent from Baden-Powell through the "Unknown Scout" of the London streets and William Boyce. The American Scout soon came to learn his code of honor from King Arthur and the Magna Carta; Seton, with his Indian influence, was gone from the movement by 1916. Beard insisted he himself rooted Scouting's antecedents in American soil. He asked that troops be named for local pioneers and that Scouting trade Ivanhoe for "Buckskin Knights" like Daniel Boone and Jim Bridger.[22] But "lone Scouts" stood as much chance in the early movement as rough-hewn individualism had before the collective altruism of the Round Table.

The centralized control that appeared so necessary for executive efficiency and financial stability increased in the 1920's. A national staff coordinated not only the literary image of Scouting but many Scouting activities as well. For example, a special Department of Camping established standards for "leadership, equipment, commissary, and sanitary provisions, program and health regulations." [23] It deemphasized patrol and even troop outings by authorizing only approved Scout Camps, to which individuals or patrols might apply; the spontaneity of unsupervised camping gave way to sanitary and educational guarantees. Early scouting literature often portrayed its heroes "heart to heart with nature in constant communion with the woods, the mountains and streams"; but John Alexander argued that camping ought to lead the Scout to "out-door life in order that he may have strength in after days to give the best he has to the city and community in which he lives." [24] The "Merit Badge" system also focused on urban needs. Seton's Woodcraft "coups" dealt exclusively with the "Woodcraft Way," but Scouting merit badges displayed a decidedly "vocational tinge" as early as 1915.[25] They included tests for automobiling, aviation, basketry, business, salesmanship, civics, mechanical drawing, architecture, plumbing, carpentry, electricity, engineering and pharmacy.

Ranking Scouts according to "classes" duplicated in a sense the graded school system. Memorization and rigid examination in somewhat artificial categories were the steps to success. "Uniform, insignia, badges of rank and achievement were means of recognizing growth," Carlos Ward noted in 1935, and "learning by doing" was hardly made easier for the Scout when "most of what he was to do was prescribed for him." [26] As early as 1922, the *Annual Report* demanded "an official ruling" on the way in which Scouts must wear their neckerchiefs and complained of "confusion and detriment to the work of the Boy Scouts of America through a continuance by the Girl Scouts of the use of our name." [27]

The widely quoted slogan, "Outing is three-fourths of Scouting," might be an accurate play on words, but Scout executives knew that "the opportunity to get out in the open and learn things worthwhile" was essentially a false, if popular goal. "Those who really know scouting," continued the *Annual Report* for 1922, "appreciate that these things which win such general approval are simply means to an end . . . ." [28] Arcadian ideals clashed with institutional realities from the earliest Fresh-Air excursions to the latest Scouting handbook, and in most cases, institutions did impose their own goals on children's outdoor recreation. Certainly the successful youth groups turned childish interest in the out-of-doors to far more sophisticated ends than Seton or Beard envisioned. But whatever those ends might be, and whatever the interior struggles in the Scouting movement, the public persisted in seeing the Boy Scout—not ushering at circuses and football games—but staff in hand, surveying the wilderness world with the ghosts of Boone and Crockett at his side.

11

Children's Fiction and the Out-of-doors

Adventures such as herein described may not fall to your lot, oh boy reader, but be assured that whenever you heed the call of the Red Gods and hit the long trail you will find adventure of a degree awaiting you, and you will return stronger physically and mentally for having come in closer contact with the elemental forces which we term nature.

Thornton Burgess, *The Boy Scouts in a Trapper's Camp*
(Philadelphia: Penn Publishing Co., 1915), introduction.

Adults have always taught their ways to children in story form. In the decades after the Civil War, the mercantile parables of Horatio Alger and Oliver Optic stressed industry and commercial aspirations in an urban setting. But in the twentieth century, boys and girls left the city to hunt, fish, hike, and camp in the far-off forests of "outdoor fiction." After 1900, "The Outdoor Chums," "The Ranger Boys," "The Camp Fire Girls," "The Boy Scouts" and other roving bands paraded onto American bookshelves in endless series. Joseph Altsheler revived America's heritage of past adventure; Edward Stratemeyer's staff writers introduced children to industrial technology in "Tom Swift" novels. But no one better registered the changing times than Lillian Garis, who created "the Bobbsey Twins" in 1904. The Bobbsey Twins knew nothing of pluck and peril. They were settled, middle-class and contented —the children of a wealthy lumber dealer in "Lakeport." Their values were those of affluent Americans who had time and money to make a virtue of outdoor life. On occasion, of course, their author sent them to school or to the Great City, but "the Bobbsey Twins" spent most of their time in the country, at the seashore, on a houseboat, on Blueberry Island, in the Great West, at Cedar

Camp or camping out. If the Bobbsey Twins seemed too tame, Mrs. Garis offered "the Outdoor Girls" series in a dozen titles; and in her "Bunny Brown" series, Bunny Brown and his sister Sue found themselves at "Camp Rest-A-While," in the big woods, at a sugar camp, or on the rolling ocean.

Howard Garis, on the other hand, led his readers through "the Curlytops'" country vacations: "Camping Out with Grandpa," having "Fun at the Lumber Camp," or roughing it "In a Summer Camp." His "Buddy" series took little Buddy Martyne and boys of six to ten to the farm, the beach, the forest, the mountains and "On the Trail." [1] Dexter Forrester's "Bungalow Boys" explored the wilderness in a half-dozen volumes, and Milton Richards sent Dick Kent to the Far North in the "Boys of the Royal Mounted Police" series. Claude La Belle and L. P. Wyman put their "Ranger Boys" and "Golden Boys" in the Maine woods, and George Bird Grinnell let young Jack Danvers vacation in the Rockies. Even general adventure series included *The Rover Boys in Camp, Rex Kingdon in the North Woods, The Radio Boys Rescue the Lost Alaska Expedition, The Pony Rider Boys in Alaska,* and *The Motor Boat Club on the Great Lakes.*

Sociologists, child psychologists and social workers in the Progressive era feared nothing so much as premature maturity; the myriad sensations impinging on childish minds in crowded cities seemed to foreshorten natural childhood. Like nature-study in the schools, the outdoors in fiction reinforced elements of childish pleasure and undermined adolescent efforts to imitate adults. The "tenderfoot" in the child's outdoor novel was like Nugent Blundell in *Canoe Boys and Campfires,* "a New York boy, greatly addicted to cream-colored clothes, white vests, patent leather shoes, high collars, gorgeous neckties, kid gloves, and canes." He was seventeen.[2] When the tenderfoot was unfriendly, "The Rival Campers" found that:

> he wore no yachting costume of any kind, nor clothing of any sort fit for roughing it. Instead, he was rather flashily dressed, in clothes more often affected by men of sporting propensities

than youths of any age . . . . In fact his dress and whole demeanor were of one who had a far more intimate knowledge of certain phases of life than he should.[3]

The cure for children made precocious by city life was a carefully controlled exposure to age-old activities in the out-of-doors. The Boy Scouts and Camp Fire Girls, the Girl Scouts and Woodcraft Indians spurred an interest that children's fiction helped to stimulate. When the "Boy Scouts" or the "Camp Fire Girls" went off to the fictional woods, the lakes, the rivers, the mountains, or the seashore—when they were "lost in the north woods," or "in the country" or "on the trail"—juvenile adventures and Scouting principles brought tenderfeet into the ranks of sportsmen and back to the kind of healthy childhood that adults admired.

However varied in title or melodramatic action, children's outdoor fiction followed a common formula. Its heroes were children from wealthy homes, though democratic sentiment required one member of each group to be a ward or a boisterous newsboy. Such heroes were from the city but not at home in it. They spent their free time in field and forest, banded together by a common interest in woodcraft. Captain Quincy Allen's "Outdoor Chums" faced the same question each vacation—"where shall we go for the next outing—because we must get into the woods somehow, and live close to Nature for a spell . . . ."[4] Young Ned Chapman, hero of *Canoe Boys and Campfires*, escaped to the out-of-doors whenever he could. He made himself "an acknowledged authority on everything relating to fishing, hunting, canoeing and boating," though, his author cautiously added, "he did not allow recreation to interfere with his studies."[5] The outdoor adventure was distinctly a vacation activity; it could not interfere with regular preparation for adult and urban life. Walter Prichard Eaton might argue in his "Boy Scout" novels that children could "afford to miss six months of school to learn how to live in the big woods and the wild places"; but when Margaret Vandercook's "Camp Fire Girls" spent six months in the woods, they commuted to school from a forty-five-foot log cabin furnished with piano and library.[6]

Whether hunters and fishermen, campers or nature photographers, the heroes of outdoor fiction stumbled by accident or design into an urban Arcadia. Given unlimited wealth, they conquered their difficulties with ready cash and provided themselves with the multitude of props so necessary to modern Arcadian life. Howard Garis started his boy millionaire on a cross-country camping trip in a custom-made touring car designed especially for outdoor living. Ruel Perley Smith gave his "Rival Campers" a free summer and a forty-foot luxury yacht.[7] The Outdoor Chums could "rough it" in the best tradition by sending their cook and their camping gear ahead while they traveled abandoned logging roads on their motorcycles in "The First Tour of the Rod and Gun Club."[8] Members of the "Black Bear Patrol" kept their own lavish clubroom, where "the walls were hung with guns, automatic revolvers, paddles, fishing outfits, bows, arrows, foils, boxing-gloves, and such trophies as the Boy Scouts had brought from river and forest." As money was no object, they had no difficulty in shipping their speedy motorboat across country from New York so they could loiter in style "for two golden weeks" on the Columbia River.[9]

Children's writers shielded their characters from the worst of raw nature; both rain and mosquitoes were rare. Few suggested any relish in primitive discomfort. "The Meadow-Brook Girls" enjoyed "Fun and Frolic in the Summer Camp," but as even their nickname indicated, they rarely ventured far into the forest.[10] In *The Motor Maids at Sunrise Camp,* young outdoor-minded girls led a "comfortable, beautiful rustic life" in their "thoroughly modern primeval hut"—a log cabin complete with the sure sign of Arcadian aesthetics, a screened-in sleeping porch.[11] In this as in other novels, local people demonstrated that permanent life in the wilds was not inspiring.

Villains in these childish adventures were usually local residents or rival "gangs" from the wrong side of the city. Conventionally ignorant and vicious, they plotted interference ranging from infantile pranks to attempted murder in the typically unmotivated fashion of juvenile melodrama. Some were occasionally won over, as was Pat Malone in *Boy Scouts in a Trapper's Camp,* by Christian morality and Scouting principles; but more often they served as foils to the heroes' superior idealism, imagination or money.[12] Boys like the Outdoor Chums were models of virtue and industry and underwent no transformation in the wilderness. They stood, instead, as symbols of the vigor and morality so prominent in outdoor fiction.

On the other hand, a summer's vacation in the country was quite enough to transform the tenderfoot. Those who most needed transformation acted as Edna did in *The Camp Fire Girls at Pine Tree Camp.* At seventeen "a frivolous, fashionable, money-spoiled child with tastes far beyond her years," she was sent camping with her languid girl friends for the summer.[13] Railing against "fashionable mothers" who "let these pretty, sweet little girls grow into women so early," their guardian determined to introduce them to "genuine childhood" as Camp Fire Girls, though she was concerned that "fashionable clothes" might be "a powerful rival to the Camp Fire Spirit."[14] Edna and her friends shared the failings of all tenderfeet in children's fiction. They blamed "the dreadful weariness of the day upon the forest—not upon themselves. They dream of idle, fashionable crowds at summer resorts, and ignore the wonderful, pine-scented vigor of the forest." In the outdoor world, where life seemed real and earnest, they learned "that this great everyday world is a place of love and beauty and not merely of clothes; that one does not need chiffons and laces and bon-bons and yachts and beaus . . . ."

Outdoor adventure and the Scout Oath worked together in many stories to redeem both reader and tenderfoot. Thornton Burgess designed a "woodcraft camp" for his "Boy Scout" series. This camp appealed to boys like Walter Upton, trained to physical fitness in New York City's gymnasiums and to love of outdoor life in woodcraft novels. There in the forest he and his friends learned "manliness, self-reliance, physical and mental health, strength of character, simplicity of desire and love of nature."[15] In *The Boy Scouts in a Trapper's Camp,* Burgess's middle-class heroes brought Sparrow Muldoon, newsboy and street gamin, into "the great cathedral that God has built for Himself." Two weeks in the woods, "where a man was gauged by his moral strength no less than by his physical strength," changed him completely.[16] In "The Boy Scouts of the Air," "The Banner Boy Scouts" and similar series by men like Ralph Victor, Howard Payson, Walter Prichard Eaton, Herbert Carter, James Otis, Edward Sabin and Alan Douglas, young scouts learned similar lessons. Alan Douglas's volumes on the "Hickory Ridge Boy Scouts" combined nature-study pamphlets on "tracking," "trees," or "fishes," with little novellas which gave his "Wolf Patrol" "splendid opportunities to use their recently acquired knowledge in a practical way." [17]

Nevertheless, such adventure novels failed to expose their young readers to the full force of the wilderness. The "Canoe Boys" on the tributaries of the Susquehanna, or the "Outdoor Chums" at Cabin Point were a long way from the far places of the forest. Accustomed to palatial headquarters in New York the "Black Bear Patrol" chose to camp on the Columbia River partly to avoid the hardships of roughing it. Mountain vacations were arduous for young Scouts, the seashore boring, "and the interior of great forests . . . too often a shut-in place"; a river vacation would give them an opportunity, their author felt, to "join in the amusements of civilization whenever the wilds grow unattractive." [18] Only a few of the children's novelists felt qualified or even motivated to write of real wilderness. Milton Richards sent "Dick Kent" to the Far North, Emerson Hough spun out tales of the "Young Alaskans," and James Hendryx paralleled his wilderness novels for adults with a "Connie Morgan" series for boys. But most children's writers were content simply to get their heroes into the country. Some of those who did set their adventures in the wilderness had little respect for probability. Gordon Stuart nonchalantly let his hero shoot a grizzly bear, carry it down the mountain, and strap it on his pony before he stopped for lunch.[19] In 1906, Roy Rockwood sent his hero by airship to the North Pole; on the way he fought off a horde of eagles

and was saved from sea lions when a herd of polar bears appeared and drove them away.[20]

Those children's authors who did write seriously of the deep
woods felt an almost transcendental responsibility for their material. As early as the 1890's, George Bird Grinnell published his
series of adventures for children. Under such titles as *Jack the
Young Canoeman, Jack in the Rockies, Jack the Young Trapper*,
and *Jack the Young Explorer*, he chronicled the rejuvenation of
fourteen-year-old Jack Danvers, who had grown "slim and pale
and spent most of his time reading, instead of playing out of
doors as all boys should." [21] An explorer, anthropologist and big
game hunter, Grinnell was head of Forest and Stream Publishing
Company, founder of the original Audubon Society and, with
Theodore Roosevelt, organizer of the Boone and Crockett Club.
One of the first to visit Yellowstone Park and later an ardent explorer of the Glacier Park country, he left his name on Grinnell
Mountain, Grinnell Glacier, Grinnell Lake and Grinnell Meadow.
In *Jack the Young Ranchman: or a Boy's Adventures in the
Rockies,* he taught city boys the way of the wilderness on a ranch
owned by "Uncle Will," who summered in the West and wintered
in New York City. Ernest Thompson Seton drew on his training
as a biologist and his own childhood for the immature but accurate Indianisms he put into *Two Little Savages* and *Rolf in the
Woods.* Belmore Browne, writing of the Mount McKinley country from his home in Banff, worked personal experience and
woodcraft skills into such childish adventures as *The Quest of the
Golden Valley* and *The White Blanket: the Story of an Alaska
Winter.*

But the "king-bee story-teller" of them all, as Chelsea Fraser
called him in *Heroes of the Wild,* was the "explorer hero," Dillon
Wallace. Wallace turned to the Labrador country in 1903 with
Leonidas Hubbard of *Outing* magazine in an idealistic and ill-
fated adventure. Lost and starving, Hubbard died and Wallace
barely escaped to lead a second expedition in 1904. After interim
surveys of Mexico and the Far West, he made still a third trip
to Labrador in 1913. A better writer than an explorer, Wallace

promoted the lure of the wilderness in twenty boys' adventure
novels. Over and over again he wove the same formula into his
stories with realistic detail that none of his competitors could
match. Wilderness life taught his heroes more than self-reliance,
simplicity and endurance. It had spiritual values as well. The
people of Labrador "were clean and their vision was clear. Their
view was not cut off or circumscribed by the frivolous and oft-
times vicious amusements that stand as a wall around life's outlook in the town. Their view and their hope were as wide as the
wilderness and the sea, rugged and stern but mighty and majestic
and limitless—God's unspoiled works . . . ." [22]

   Wallace let his tenderfeet work out their salvation in the whole
of the north country. In *The Fur Trail Adventurers* young Phil
Porter went to the wilderness disgraced by a year of college
debauchery. In *The Arctic Stowaways*, the reformed hero was
Harry Metford, once "slight of build, and of nervous tempera-
ment," whose face bore "traces of selfishness, due, perhaps, to
pampering and indulgence." He was clearly "a proud snob," and
to everyone's disgust he smoked. Paul Densmore, outward bound
to Hudson Bay for a summer of shooting in *The Wilderness Castaways*, had been "coddled and indulged and pampered" beyond
his father's endurance. Young Stanley Burton had "made silly,
unmoral movies and tough night clubs his hobby." None of that
was "clean stuff for a young lad," Wallace wrote: "let him feel a
breath of the north wind, and the rain in his face, and the toss of
a canoe in a rapid. Show him how sissy and silly this night club
life is." [23] Such heroes found in outdoor life not only renewed
innocence, but a spur to the kind of ambition which middle-class
Americans honored. Stanley Burton came home determined to
win his own way, independent of his father's wealth. Harry Metford's problems gave Wallace a chance to explain:

> There is nothing like the salt sea air and God's blessed sun-
> shine to clear the brain and revive the spirits. There is noth-
> ing like the deep blue, changeless, but ever changing, sea to
> inspire ambition. The very vastness of the ocean widens one's
> view of life, and impresses upon one the boundless possibilities

> of existence . . . . and no red-blooded man can long live upon
> the sea without imbibing the desire to do great deeds . . . .[24]

Tenderfeet occasionally won through by sheer grit, or with the help of a native youngster, but most often they needed a tutor. Since the children's adventure novel served an urban audience, the ideal tutor was not a sage old woodsman but a sophisticated intellectual who knew the problems of city life. Thornton Burgess made the wilderness spokesman a Dr. Merriam, who introduced his city youngsters to "Woodcraft Camp" by explaining,

> I have lived in many cities, but you see here I am buried in
> the woods and some of my friends wonder why. I'll tell you.
> It is because here I can live simply, unaffectedly, true to myself
> and to God. Here," he swept a hand toward the book-lined
> walls, "are my friends ready to give me of inspiration, comfort,
> advice, knowledge, whatever I demand or may need . . . .
> And then when I step out-of-doors it is directly into the temple
> of God.[25]

In Dillon Wallace's *Troop One of the Labrador,* Dr. Joe, a New York surgeon, came to the North to restore his health and to escape "the noise and scramble, the dirt and smoke and smudge of the city, with its piles upon piles of ugly buildings, and never a breath of such pure air as this to be breathed." [26] In *The Wilderness Castaways,* Wallace sent his millionaire's son, Paul Densmore, and local seaman Dan Rudd, to spend the winter in Labrador as guests of trapper Charlie Amesbury, another refugee from New York who lived in a cozy cabin furnished with white bedspreads, worn copies of the Bible, Shakespeare's plays, Milton's *Paradise Lost,* Wordsworth's poems, a bundle of sheet music and a violin.

Such characters were sympathetic enough, but they functioned only to treat the heroes' maladies. Once brought to their senses, bronzed and hardy, each of the young heroes went back to his rightful place. The Arcadian adventure ended in the city where it began. When he arrived in New York Paul Densmore blurted

to his father, "It's great to be back . . . . If it wasn't so far
from you and Mother I'd like to spend the winters trapping with
Mr. Amesbury. Of course, though, I can't do that." [27] Instead
he went six more years to school, graduated from Princeton and
took over his father's steamship company, a better man for his
sojourn in the wilderness, but one who knew his place. Dan
Rudd, his partner in the wilderness, knew his place as well,
signing on with the company and working his way up to first
mate.

Real children may never have been sufficiently captivated
by adventure stories to pattern their lives after fictional heroes,
but children's writers imagined they were and delighted in putting guide posts into their books for their readers to follow. As
young Ade Durham learned when he set out after Masters of
the Royal Mounted, safety lay "in picking the trail whose beginning you knew was right," and in choosing the wilderness
heroes for company.[28] In children's outdoor fiction, tenderfeet
were skillfully guided to exchange the ways of urban adults for
childhood in Arcadia. The "Canoe Boys," the "Outdoor Chums"
or the "Meadow-Brook Girls" only waited for an opportunity to
parade their woodcraft skills to urban readers. "Boy Scout" and
"Camp Fire Girl" novels overtly pledged the rebirth of their
readers through the Oath and Law which outdoor adventures
only served to underline. In the hands of men whose literary
abilities were little indication of their experience or their sincerity,
stories of the far wilderness were the most realistic anodynes for
urban childhood. The out-of-doors for children was more clearly
a vacation than an escape, a therapy for temporary illness more
than a permanent asylum. Men of Grinnell's and Seton's and
Wallace's stature, who believed as strongly as they did in the
kind of life they wrote about, intended their books to be taken
seriously, however poorly written.

12

The Wilderness Novel

The readers of books, or rather the buyers of current novels, live in the cities; they are hurried, restless people. They long for green fields, clean air, and simple nature, in theory . . . . It only remains, therefore, for the budding novelist to produce the book of the fields, the novel of the country life, something "near to Nature's heart." The reader is politely referred to . . . the books by Stewart Edward White and Jack London, even the Bullen sea stories, for the excuse for their success lies chiefly in the distraction they give the city man—the breath of real life—without inconvenience.

Herbert Stone, "The Art of Writing Novels,"
House Beautiful, XVII (December, 1904), 31.

Edward Weeks of the *Atlantic Monthly* surveyed the "best sellers" of the century in 1933. According to publishers' statistics, five novels issued between 1900 and 1930 had sold more than a million and a half copies each. An amateur nature photographer named Gene Stratton Porter wrote four of them: *Freckles, The Girl of the Limberlost, The Harvester* and *Laddie.* Harold Bell Wright's *The Winning of Barbara Worth* ranked fifth. Next came Owen Wister's *The Virginian* and Jack London's *Call of the Wild.*[1] Even Jack London's novels belonged to the mass of "current literature," where for every primitivist there was an idealist, for every realist a romanticist, for every country hero a city hero, for every story of the present a fable of the past, and for every tale of the poor an adventure of the rich. But current literature, however ephemeral, was "the chronicler or recorder of the present," *Publisher's Weekly* announced in "The Books of 1901." Only through "the books of the hour could readers "keep sharply up to date in all the varying phases of modern thought." [2] The fact that Mrs. Porter, a druggist's wife who called her novels "nature studies coated with fiction," [3] could produce the four best sellers on Weeks' list indicated the extent to which the Arcadian myth had permeated American life.

Wilderness fiction writers spoke of peace and contentment, of fresh air and virgin land and works not made with hands. Unabashedly romantic, each novel fitted like the one before it into a structural and thematic formula that seemed to need no variation. The ideal figures stalking their trails were larger than life, but still believable. Gene Stratton Porter insisted she had "lived mostly in the country and worked in the woods," and she added: "for every bad man and woman I have ever known, I . . . am intimately acquainted with an overwhelming number of thoroughly clean and decent people who still believe in God and cherish high ideals." [4] While Dallas Sharp and the literary commuters put their Arcadia just beyond the suburbs, Gene Stratton Porter, Harold Bell Wright, Stewart Edward White, Mary Waller and James Oliver Curwood took their readers to "the silent places." Their heroes, however, were not primitive woodsmen but sophisticated intellectuals who valued nature's ancient grandeur and a simple life denied to most Americans. [5]

Stewart Edward White, son of a Michigan lumberman, early decided he had found the stuff of an American epic in the romance of logging-camp and river drive. In a series of novels beginning with *The Blazed Trail* in 1902, he tried to turn the pineland forest into an American symbol comparable to the wheat in Frank Norris' *The Octopus,* but he sprawled most often into a muddy recitation of lumbering facts and natural history, as did those who followed him. White's early novels popularized the fictional lumberjack, but they failed to convey the feeling of the "Silent Places" that he would later come to prize. [6]

The "deification of the cutting edge" and the sawmills' "epic chorus" spelled the end of wilderness from Maine to Minnesota. [7] In 1906, Irving Bacheller's best-selling *Silas Strong* countered the logger's epic with Arcadian idealism in a tale of the last logging tract, its stern old guardian, and the young man up from college on a fishing trip. Bacheller's "one high ambition," as he put it, was "to tell the sad story of the wilderness itself—to show, from the woodsman's viewpoint, the play of great forces which have been tearing down his home and turning it into the flesh and blood of cities." Modern society, he wrote, must now "value what remains of the forest above its market-price," must put the wilderness to higher use than feeding "the greed of the saws." [8] Much of the glory of earlier days had disappeared; the green groves were gone from the hills. To White, the "aroma of the open" had become an "essence of fresh sawdust, of new-cut pine, of saw-logs dripping from the water" [9]—better perhaps than the coal smoke of cities, but hardly the smell of real wilderness.

The American frontier was gone, but Alaskan gold and the Canadian Pacific Railway opened a new frontier in the Far North, "the last line of romance on this continent." [10] In January of 1899, an ex-cheechako living in an Oakland tenement began a series of Alaskan tales in the dignified *Overland Monthly* at five to seven dollars a manuscript, payment withheld. With the Malamute Kid's toast "to the man on trail this night; may his grub hold out; may his dogs keep their legs; may his matches never miss fire," Jack London greeted the world in print.[11] London had borrowed a grubstake from his sister to join the Klondike Rush in the summer of 1896. He outpacked the Indians over Chilkoot Pass, wintered on the Stewart River short of Dawson, and returned to San Francisco the following summer. Although he did not reach the gold fields, the Alaskan winter yielded a pocket of fictional ore which London could mine whenever he needed ready cash.

His stories drew fire from wilderness lovers, who claimed he knew next to nothing of the North, and from literary critics, who thought he knew next to nothing about writing. From Gilbert Parker's Canadian romances he learned that "the trail is lonely and the woods are deep and dark" and that the Northland religion was a "faith of food and blanket." But he virtually ignored the drama of the Long Trail, and he treated cold and snow and ice with a nonchalance of the inexperienced rarely matched by other writers.[12] Only once did London raise the wilderness theme to serious art: in 1903 he dashed off "The Call of the Wild" in thirty days and mailed it to *The Saturday Evening Post*. Nature-lovers who had learned from John Muir's "Stickeen" that dogs in the wilderness could be almost human learned from London that humans, stampeding after gold, could be just like dogs. The story of "Buck," the southland St. Bernard "jerked from the heart of civilization and flung into the heart of things primordial," gave London a chance to show the veneer of civilization torn away by the "law of club and fang." As its title suggested, *The Call of the Wild* was a study in instinctivism: Buck returned to the wilderness ways of his ancestors complete with fireside dreams of cave life and long-armed hairy men.[13]

Jack London made the "Trail" grim and forbidding, where "dark spruce forest frowned on either side the frozen waterway" and "vast silence reigned over the land." [14] But others with less experience and many with more found "romance in the long stretch of the great river winding white and silent between its wooded slopes—romance, too, in the wide blue sky, the clean canopy of a man's world whose horizons lay somewhere this side of that other world which it shut out, the world of smoke and noise and corruption." [15] On the Long Trail, the vision of wild nature could redeem readers as well as heroes. The wilderness novelists were often more concerned with the scenery they had experienced or imagined than with their characters.

James Oliver Curwood was chief among the romantic word-painters who made the deep woods into "God's Country." He grew rich on royalties and movie rights from twenty-six wilderness novels, beginning with *The Courage of Captain Plum* in 1908 and ending with *The Black Hunter* in 1926. His novels were translated into French, German, Danish, Swedish, Norwegian, Dutch, Czech, Spanish, Hungarian, Italian and Braille, as he himself translated the wilderness to an urban world. Typical of the wilderness romantics, Curwood was a sophisticated, college-bred conservative, raised through the works of Cooper and Scott to love nature and dislike cities. When he wasn't touring the

Far North, he made his home in little Owosso, Michigan, isolating himself every morning in a miniature Norman castle to write of fur trails and far adventures. For him the wilderness held no terrors. It was a refuge of virtue and content, where his heroes, broken by business and social competition, redeemed themselves against a background of magnificent scenery. The settings of his wilderness novels ranged from Labrador to Alaska and the subjects varied from animal stories to tales of the Mounted Police and caribou ranching. Yet the characters who participated in these melodramas—the hero, the woman, the villain, and the French Canadian were remarkably alike.

Since they invited their readers to project themselves into leading roles, the wilderness novelists described their heroes in the vaguest terms. "His blood was clean, his body knit of fibre woven in God's out-of-doors, his mind fashioned under a clear sky in a land of wide horizons," one writer told his audience. Nothing more than a purposeful stride and a weathered face conveyed all the glamor of the out-of-doors to Gene Stratton Porter. But, however vague the physical features, wilderness heroes had one recognizable characteristic. They turned to the silent woods to find "a life which was not warped by the gilded amenities of the crowded ball-room tonight, by the frenzied dollar fight to-morrow." [16] In Curwood's *God's Country and the Woman*, Philip Weyman claimed "nothing down in that world which you have called civilization—nothing except the husks of murdered hopes— ambitions, and things that were once joys." [17] Even the Curwood Mountie, like David Raine in *The Golden Snare*, escaped from the city for the sake of his soul. But if the wilderness sheltered the sick at heart, it also offered a stern cure for urban profligacy. Gilbert Parker sent Sergeant Fones to the Force in the best English tradition; fat young William Holly became a missionary to the Athabasca Country; and the drunken son of a Kentucky Senator arrived in the North on a dare. Harold Bell Wright sent his weary preacher and silly millionaire to the Ozarks and the West, and young Kirk Brander left his wild ways, his uncle's

house and his allowance to learn "the stern business of making
a man of himself" in the Far North.[18]

To give their heroes an opportunity to redeem themselves and
to provide a melodramatic sense of purpose to their actions,
wilderness writers introduced "the Great Fight." Unlike the
violence of range wars and cattle rustling that turned man
against man in the Western novel, the Great Fight pitted the
hero against his own weakness in the natural world. Gunfights
and brawls in the action Western spoke to primitive passions.
In the "nature novel" the hero struggled with elemental forces—
wind and rain, raging cataracts and blinding snowstorms—to
prove himself. Forcing his canoe across a windswept lake, fleeing a giant forest fire or swimming a rapids to save his lady, the
Curwood hero rejoiced in his own rejuvenation with "pride and
strength, the ring of triumph in his voice." [19] Stewart Edward
White sent his protagonists either on the *"Longue Traverse"* with
only determination for company, or out to get their man in an
epic search across the continent. Charles G. D. Roberts set his
heroes to battling the log jam or the winter trail, or perhaps only
to hiking a day and a half to town for wilderness Christmas gifts.
In every case, the Great Fight reflected the hero's achievement of
wilderness virtue as he accepted whatever challenge his author
prepared. Almost invariably his challenge involved "The Woman."

The wilderness heroine had the virtues of most Romantic
heroines—beauty, chastity, sympathy and understanding—but she
particularly opposed Charles Dana Gibson's aristocrat and the
boyish figures of the nineteen-twenties. She stood for natural
womanhood "glowing with the rich life and strength of the
wilderness," as Harold Bell Wright put it.[20] This goddess-girl
was "slender as a reed, wild, palpitating, beautiful"; to Curwood
"she was life." [21] As "L'Ange," she was idolized by the forest people
for her beauty and her charity, and these people were quick to
defend her from outsiders. Scarcity of women may actually have
produced something of the "passionless love unhinting of sin" that
Curwood and his fellow writers found so appealing. In any event
they underlined "the spirit of chivalrous romance in the north

country," which one of Curwood's heroes called "the one great law of life up here, the worship of woman because she is woman." To trespass this law was to invite "but one punishment . . . the punishment of the people." [22] Even an atavist like London gloried in his heroine's innocence with a puritanism that dismayed his liberal critics. Free, innocent and understanding, the woods girl was the reward of the wilderness, her problems the occasion of the Great Fight and her acceptance the sign of redemption for the hero.

For all his interest in primitive living, Curwood had no intention of abandoning culture and sophistication. His heroine was, with one exception, a child of the North. She belonged, not to the trapper's shack, but to a cultural island, a trader's post or its equivalent which boasted books, fine furniture and a piano. Like London's Vance Corliss in A Daughter of the Snows, the Curwood hero found in his forest lady "the culture he could not do without, and the clean sharp tang of the earth he needed." [23] In North, James B. Hendryx's heroine was born and raised in the wilderness. A better man than most, and beautiful and pure to boot, "she had suffered not one whit in any detail of her education. Her mother had been an apt pupil of a famous old mission school on the MacKenzie." [24] The cultured lady, like the sophisticated hero, escaped the conventions of popular romance; nature writers believed the wilderness really belonged to those sophisticated enough to appreciate it.[25] Like Mary Waller's "Wood-carver of 'Lympus,'" who combined Carlyle and wood-carving for his city friends, Gene Stratton Porter's heroes alienated themselves from ignorant farmers by their books and their love of the forest. "Freckles" studied birds and flowers while guarding his forest from local timber thieves. The "Girl of the Limberlost" pressed moths for scientific collections. The "Harvester" hunted herbs for city hospitals when he wasn't reading Emerson, Thoreau or Maeterlinck. Curwood, like other wilderness writers, had no real grudge against culture or against progress when these were directed for the welfare of "the People." [26] He railed chiefly against social sham and the evils of power divorced from physical strength.

The villains who invaded the Northland brought with them the social and financial dissipation of the big city. Some, like Colby MacDonald in *The Yukon Trail,* represented frontier exploitation, out of place in the conservation era. Others were crafty financiers unaware of wilderness virtue. Such "spoilers" hoped to destroy the land for private gain. Equally important were those who assaulted innocence with worldly ways—those men, in short, who lusted after The Woman.

Curwood's villain was usually brutal, "every line in his ugly face and angular body a line of sin," [27] but occasionally he represented the sophisticated profligacy of the "outside." Jack London sent in Gregory St. Vincent, world traveler, explorer, and hero among women, to woo "the daughter of the snows," but the stamp of sin and passion brought him down.[28] James J. Tynan, in his version of "The Shooting of Dan McGrew," created a villain "soft of speech and with a knack of doing the right thing at the right time," a villain who led his girls "down the crimson path to utter destruction." [29] But men came to the wilderness to worship, not to sin. "Never admire a woman in that way . . . . Never, I say!" one trader warned his English clerk,[30] though warnings were no protection against the sins of society. In Curwood's *Honor of the Big Snows,* an English visitor found the trapper's wife "a flower suddenly come to relieve the tantalizing barrenness of a desert; and with the wiles and ways of civilization he sought to breathe its fragrance." [31] He was strangled by the pure in heart.

The "pure in heart" in the fiction of the Far North was the French Canadian. In Alaskan novels occasional sourdoughs combined Natty Bumppo's wisdom with comic relief, but a hero's stock companion was a French-Canadian woodsman. American affection for this simple "child of nature" dated back to such romantic figures as Francis Parkman's Henry Chatillion, John C. Frémont's Basil Lajeunesse, and Thoreau's Woodchopper. In the moralistic wilderness novel, however, the French Canadian was more than a happy-go-lucky voyageur. As a "brother" to the Anglo-Saxon heroine, or even as a minor figure, he was the heir to old-world chivalry. A man "who had lived always under the stars and the open skies," he was, for Curwood, "not of today, but a hearkening back to that long forgotten yesterday; in his veins ran the blood red and strong of the First Men of the North." [32] He spoke for the wilderness virtues: strength, honesty and sexless loyalty to the Woman. Returning to his place in society, Jack Thornton told trapper Jan Thoreau in *The Honor of the Big Snows,* "We look upon you as wild and savage and with only half a soul—and we are blind. You have taught me more than has ever been preached into me, and this great glorious world of yours is sending me back a better man for having come into it." [33]

The proper balance between urban and wilderness life, like the hero's restoration, provided a major theme in most wilderness novels. Through the French Canadian or perhaps through his own unaided pluck, urban man redeemed himself on the Long Trail. His natural heroine affirmed the virtues he found in the simple life and sharply pointed up the shallowness of society women. The villain gave wilderness novelists an opportunity to illustrate evil and its circumvention in "the spirit of that big clean fighting North which makes men out of a beginning of flesh and blood." [34]

In an age which many observers saw committed to progress, urbanization and the industrial revolution, the wilderness hero lost his taste for the world of "balls and clubs and cities." Only when the Curwood hero was choking an insulter of the Woman did he show more fury than he turned on American urban life. "It's what we call civilization—but it's mostly hell," Curwood wrote in one novel; "it's a hell of big cities, of strife, of blood-letting, of wickedness." [35] The dollar-hunting wolves of the city tore at virtue and sincerity for the sake of success; [36] the wilderness, by contrast, "meant the mountains, the vast tundras, the immeasurable spaces into which civilization had not yet come with its clang and clamor." [37] Harold Bell Wright called it "a land where a man, to live, must be a man . . . . a land of far-arched and unstained skies, where the wind sweeps free and untainted and the atmosphere is the atmosphere of those places that remain as God made them . . . ." [38]

"Wilderness" could be a state of mind, however, and as applicable to "the Harvester's" six-hundred-acre woods in Indiana as to the arctic tundra. In *The Shepherd of the Hills,* Harold Bell Wright brought peace of mind to his disillusioned Chicago minister tending sheep in the Ozark Mountains. In *When a Man's a Man,* he sent Larry Knight, effete Eastern millionaire, to wrestle with his soul as "Patches" the cowhand on the western plains. But for Curwood, "things were as God meant them to be" only in the far wilderness and the isolated trader's post. There the Curwood hero found "the joy of companionship and of life—which had so terribly eluded and escaped him in his own home of wealth and luxury." Chivalry "was born and bred of the mountains and the open and had nothing in common with the insincere brand which develops in the softer and more luxurious laps of civilization." In the wilderness environment, love of the Woman could come to the hero "as it had come to *Tristan* and *Isolde,* to *Paola* and *Francesca*—sudden and irresistible, but, unlike theirs, as pure as the air of the world which he breathed." [39] Whatever their settings, however, the wilderness novels brought to urban readers a vision of peaceful forests and quiet streams, where even the rapids ran in sunshine and snow fell on snug old cabins where fires roared and life was good.

But twentieth-century man could no longer trade his heritage for a mess of wilderness beans. He lived in an urban world, and he needed to make the best of it. The wilderness virtues offered a vital complement to urban life, but the Far North was an interlude in fiction and in life, from which even Curwood and his readers returned. The wilderness novelist, with occasional disclamation from Curwood, had little intention of exiling his hero forever into paradise.

Thus young Kirk Brander "gained all that he had come north to gain" in five years on the trail: "a consciousness that he could be of some good in the world after all." Having gained that,

"there seemed to be nothing left for him in the north." [40] As Zane
Grey's heroine told her forest lover, "giving yourself to a hunter's
wild life is selfish. It is wrong. You love this lonely life, but it is
not work. Work that does not help others is not real man's work."
So Milt Dale turned back to the workaday world, though he
homesteaded his rugged hunting camp in "Paradise Park" for
family vacations. To Hamlin Garland, the wilderness was "a
splendid place for a summer vacation, but a stern place in winter-
time, and for a lifelong residence . . . not inspiring." [41]

Wilderness could be savored for a week or a month or a year;
prolonged contact eroded intellectual sophistication and weakened its inspiration. Pure wildness, therefore, gave way from time
to time to the Romantic combination of wilderness life and
the remnant grandeur that might be associated with Canada's
"Old Regime." The First Men of the North were not Indians
and Eskimos but French and English aristocrats who brought
high culture to the outposts. Remote trading posts were lined
with books and ancient hangings, graced with silver and fine
linen, pianos and other remembrances of another world carefully preserved in the timeless forest. The narrator of Mary
Waller's best-selling *Cry in the Wilderness* starved in the city,
then turned governess in Canada at the Seigniory of Lamoral.
There the ancient manor house gleamed with polished marble,
wood paneling and oil paintings dark with age. The forest breeze,
"so strong, so free, so soft, as if it were blowing straight from the
great Northland, over unending virgin plains, through primeval
unending forests," [42] spoke of wildness, but the Seigniory itself
was owned by a progressive New Englander, who practiced scientific forestry and revelled in historical romance. Fiercely loyal to
the wilderness, Waller's heroine lived in peace and contentment,
redecorating the manor house in *Art Nouveau* and planning a
summer camp.

Just as Mary Waller surrounded her heroine with civilized conveniences, so Jack London was satisfied in real life with a single
winter in the Alaskan wilderness. No matter how often he turned

to it in his stories, he abandoned the Far North for a suburban Arcadia on the side of Sonoma Mountain near San Francisco. The 130 acre hobby farm he bought in 1905 developed, in the tradition of the literary commuters, into a major part of his life. By 1913 he owned 1,100 contiguous acres and kept thirty-five men at work on his palatial "Wolf House," a stone and redwood mansion that burned on the eve of occupancy. Earning $75,000 a year and spending $100,000, he turned from his Alaskan stories to put into *Burning Daylight* and *The Valley of the Moon* the simple Arcadian life he was unable to lead for himself.

Back from the Yukon, London's hero, "Burning Daylight," launched himself in the financial wilderness of San Francisco with an $11,000,000 grubstake. "The grim Yukon life had failed to make Daylight hard. It required civilization to produce this result," London wrote as he bitterly reversed the theme of *Call of the Wild.* Reverting to savagery in San Francisco's financial circles, London's hero lost the mental largeness and physical tone bred of the wilderness. Heavy-handed and heavy-paunched, he set out one day to climb suburban Sonoma Mountain. "All the sordidness, meanness and viciousness that filled the dirty pool of city existence" fell away as he talked to nature lovers in the Sonoma Valley. "I'm sick of living in the city and playing business," he announced, as he turned his back on thirty million dollars for "the sunshine, and the country and the green grass." In his "little ranch house in one of the prettiest bits of country God ever made," he lived a new life of simple fare and simple pleasures, calculating in squabs instead of stocks and bonds. When a landslide uncovered a vein of gold worth fifty thousand dollars a ton, he rushed to bury it again to preserve his Arcadia undefiled by worldly wealth, though London remarked that "it was easier for one who has gorged at the flesh-pots to content himself with the meagerness of a crust, than for one who has known only the crust." [43]

In *Burning Daylight* London explored the evils of wealth. In *The Valley of the Moon* he dealt with the evils of poverty. Billy Roberts, teamster, and Saxon Brown, ironing-woman, courted and married in the Oakland slums, where social conventions beat down any effort of the poor to better themselves. Inspired by a cinema idyll of rural life, hero and heroine set out on a vagabond search for land and work in the California back country. They found freedom from the stereotyped roles of laundry girl and union teamster almost immediately and soon settled instead on a little abandoned ranch in the Sonoma Valley, where Saxon turned to truck gardening and Billy to horse-trading and both grew in wisdom and in stature.

Though London spent his time at "Glen Ellen," other novelists counted themselves among the fortunate who could pursue wilderness adventure in life as in fiction. They refused to live there, but Curwood and Stewart Edward White camped repeatedly on the trails they followed in fiction. Charles G. D. Roberts, born and raised in New Brunswick, delineated his landscapes with the crispness of a winter frost, and Dillon Wallace vividly turned his own adventures into twenty wilderness novels for boys. Similarly, Harold Bell Wright and Gene Stratton Porter inserted themselves wholeheartedly into their own sentimental novels.

Gene Stratton Porter attracted a vast audience with "a freshness of feeling and a transparent sincerity" in her Limberlost novels.[44] Born and raised in the country herself, she married a successful druggist and came to live in a fourteen room log cabin near Rome City, Indiana. An ardent nature-photographer, she arranged with her publishers to alternate a volume of natural history with each nature novel. *Freckles* languished for three years before the nature movement gained sufficient popularity to justify the sketches on its margins. *The Girl of the Limberlost* promoted honor and virtue in the forest as did *The Harvester*, which Mrs. Porter had dedicated to Henry David Thoreau and drawn from memories of her father.

The wilderness, Harold Bell Wright wrote in defense of his works, "will give you great treasure that you may give again to others who have not your good strength to escape from the things that men make or do in the restless world over there."

Nature writing was a "noble craft" that publicized "the good things God has written on this page of His great book." [45] Wright went to the out-of-doors for his health in the 1890's, and preached for a time in the Ozarks. Later he bought a horse ranch in California's Imperial Valley, where he set *The Winning of Barbara Worth,* as well as a ranch in Arizona and a 160-acre estate near Tucson. He wrote himself into his books and lived with the aid of royalties and movie rights, something approximating the life he preached. But he, like other nature novelists, ran into stiff opposition from critics who demanded less attractive views of life.

Welcoming the gift of vision and the opportunity to improve it, Curwood, White, Mrs. Porter and Wright brought wild nature to urban Americans with missionary zeal. They wrote without strain and without humor of things they knew full well, convinced that they fulfilled a vital role in urban society. If their heroes and heroines were sentimental and idealized, it was not a device of the popular novel but a proof of wilderness virtue. When critics questioned Mrs. Porter's sincerity, she stormed back against those who prejudged life "by the atmosphere of the average city newspaper and magazine office." In the Limberlost country, life at its best seemed "*just as true and legitimate*" as life at its worst. "What do I care for the newspaper or magazine critic yammering that there is not such a thing as a moral man, and that my pictures of life are sentimental and idealized," she wrote in 1911. "They are! and I glory in them!" she added. "They are straight, living pictures from the lives of men and women of morals, honour, and loving kindness . . . copied from life where it touches religion, chastity, love, home, and hope of heaven ultimately." [46]

Analyzing the literary criticism of his day, Grant Overton noted that "an inveterate tradition of the minority brands the majority as sentimental." [47] Literary critics praising "realism" and "naturalism" looked on "sentimentality" as the portrayal of nice people. To them wilderness fiction was not the record of heroic virtue but "cheap dope" as W. H. Boynton called it, for city dwellers.[48] Woe to him who painted icons in an iconoclastic era; Charles Baldwin said Harold Bell Wright specialized in "leaving stones unturned," enshrining "the shibboleths and superstitions of our fathers, making old creeds and antique fables sacred in the eyes of all." Wright was "not a member of society but an individualist growing rich through the sale of tenth rate novels . . . a bigot standing directly in the path of progress."[49] *When a Man's a Man* called on Eastern intellectuals to sample outdoor life where "a man's soul must be as the unstained skies, the unburdened wind, and the untainted atmosphere." Baldwin denounced the book as "dangerous propaganda," broadcast by an "irresponsible" who undermined the superiority of culture. Like other wilderness novelists, Wright did not share the preoccupation with congenital faults that haunted many urban critics. The remedy for failure was as simple as a vacation in the woods or a good sensible book. Baldwin found Wright "empty and shallow and inconsequential when he isn't vicious."[50]

But Wright's books remained on view in humble parlors where *Main Street* had been discarded and *Sister Carrie* had never entered. Grant Overton decided that most people had no intellectual criteria by which to judge a book. Their standards were drawn instead from "principles of living not far removed from their own." Literary critics who put aside intellectual purity for popular psychology would see at once that "the usual person unsentimentally proceeds through life with the assistance of attainable ideals"—ideals which popular fiction did much to perpetuate.[51] Wright's excesses of sentimentality, another critic noted wryly, were "rendered sacred by the standard of thought and conduct accepted by millions of Americans." In his books, the average reader found himself "not merely reflected, but magnified and exalted, in all his socially shaped moral being . . . ."[52] Curwood's books, like most of the wilderness novels, were standardized products, with stereotyped characters and conventional settings, but their roots went deep into "those universal emotions which never fail in their appeal," a *New York Times* reviewer concluded. Moreover, he added, "Mr. Curwood sees to it that his

yarns, swept by pine-laden breezes as they are, have a whole-
someness about them that would offset many more defects than
can ever be truly ascribed to him." [53]

Portraying not the eccentric but the type, popular novels offered a variety of roles which readers could temporarily assume,
testing them always against their own experience. Readers of
popular fiction actively if unconsciously explored new lives for
themselves, accepting or rejecting the manner and dress of fictional characters as a means of projecting their own personalities,
and emulating as best they could the conventional behavior of
heroic stereotypes. In the city, where contact between classes was
limited chiefly to service functions, popular novels offered a
versatile introduction to customs and patterns of living otherwise
inaccessible. Wilderness fiction brought nature to city dwellers
purified of black flies and mosquitoes, frigid cold and steaming
summer heat. Those who appraised its value spoke of a simple
and timeless way of life. Readers learned more than the behavior
patterns and conventional symbols of the outdoorsman—the
mackinaw jacket and khaki breeches, the knee-high boots and
briar pipe. They learned also a view of nature and the city and
of man's role in life that was essentially Arcadian. And if the
myth seemed always clearer in literature than in life, it was no
less real for its fictional presentation.

13

The Church in the Wildwood

Just as provision is made for the study of God's Word, so ought we to make at least a little provision for the study of God's works.

Earle Amos Brooks, *A Handbook of the Outdoors*
(New York: George Doran, 1925), p. 42.

When geologist Nathaniel Shaler suggested that his work could not go forward without "spiritual reconciliation with nature," churchmen, educators and journalists agreed. Capitalizing on America's discovery of the out-of-doors, they began to argue about the significance of God's Works as well as His Word. To one or another interpreter, trees, flowers, brooks and birds' nests seemed all "the smiles of God." Nature signified "the visible garment of God," the "art of God," the "thoughts of God," or to Lyman Abbott of the *Outlook*, "the playground of the soul." [1]

Hugh MacMillan lamented in the 1890's that Christianity was "almost wholly an indoor religion." He held "the uncertainty of our weather and the general inclemency of our climate" partly responsible, but the weather seemed no reason "to confine our ideas of God . . . to sermons and cathedrals." If Americans would bring to nature "the same devout frame of mind" they brought to church, God would surely reveal Himself "and make the lonely wood, or hill, or sea-shore to us holy ground." Natural objects, MacMillan assured his readers, must then be symbols of the highest Truth. William Channing Gannet tried his hand at sermons on the seasons in the 1880's. When he came to Winter, he saw a powerful image in tiny snowflakes: like them, we were "a moment's vision, then we melt and vanish," yet he declared himself "willing to trust for life and love while . . . the Power and Beauty which molds the snow-flake is around me and in me." But churchmen soon discovered that nature which served so well for Gospel parables was a treacherous source for transcendental wisdom. Hugh MacMillan revealed in his *Cyclopaedia of Nature Teachings* that so simple a thing as "dew" carried many equally transcendent meanings. Dew was "transitory piety," the very archetype of "instability." On the other hand, MacMillan announced, Christians could be counted "as a dew from the Lord." As dew evaporated, so Christians could also be delivered from early surroundings.[2]

However uncertain as substitutes for His Word, God's Works provoked a healthy flow of sentiment. Sunday worshipers found themselves singing

> "Field and forest, vale and mountain,
> Flowery meadow, flashing sea,
> Chanting bird and flowing fountain,
> Call us to rejoice in Thee"

in Henry Van Dyke's "Joyful, Joyful, We Adore Thee." Little children and many of their parents learned that, whatever the state of Biblical scholarship, this was still their "Father's world" where they would "hear Him pass in the rustling grass," speaking to them everywhere. Fresh from the "alabaster city" in Chicago, Katherine Lee Bates wrote "America the Beautiful." After a visit to Pikes Peak in 1893 she combined thoughts on God, nature and America so suitably that her lines were sung to more than seventy tunes in the next half century.

Gene Stratton Porter and other novelists like James Oliver Curwood and Harold Bell Wright further popularized the "nature creed." Wright called for preachers "with a wilderness training like John the Baptist, who will show us the way of the Lord, rather than a thousand theological, hot-house posies, who will show us only the opinions of the authorities."[3] No popular novelist probed "the Religion of the Woods" as consistently as the Reverend Charles W. Gordon. After two years at Banff and a tour as missioner in the Far North, Gordon settled down to publish twenty-two novels of outdoor life under the pen name "Ralph Connor." His first novel, *Black Rock: a Tale of the Selkirks,* was one of the best-sellers of the era. He continued in *The Sky Pilot* and other volumes to create a cycle of wilderness heroes struggling for "strong, clean, God-conquered" manhood. His urban missionaries predictably learned to judge old creeds by the standards of the North and to dress their Bible tales in the vernacular of the foothills. Like Gordon, Sir Gilbert Parker sent his own university theologian to hard-muscled service in the Athabasca Country; James Oliver Curwood's missioners cared for the sick and buried the dead in ten thousand miles of wilderness. They left theology to those in the city, secure in the belief that their charges learned more of natural virtue from outdoor life than they could ever teach them. On occasion Curwood's missioner confided, "it may be that I've learned one thing better than most of you who live down in civilization. And that's how to find yourself . . . ." [4]

Religious educators were most interested in helping others to find themselves. They discovered an "almost tantalizing fascination" among young people for outdoor life, and they determined to put it to use. "So wholesome is the effect of long walks in the open woods and leisurely rambles through the fields that . . . outdoor activities ought to be required . . . in every Church program" wrote Amos Brooks, Instructor in Field Laboratory Sciences at Boston University's School of Religious Education and Social Service. According to Amos Brooks, "the religious worker" must be trained "to make effective, in the building of Christian character, all the interesting experiences of a hike or a camping trip." [5] Sunday school teachers tried as best they could, but churchmen found no real way to control children's exposure to the out-of-doors until the Boy Scouting movement began in 1910. Psychologist Norman Richardson noted that well over a fourth of all scoutmasters were ministers in 1912, and that Methodist,

Presbyterian, Congregationalist and Baptist churches sponsored two-thirds of the existing 6,868 scout troops.

The patriarch of nature writers, John Burroughs, did indeed assure his readers that "every walk in the woods is a religious rite." "If we do not go to church as much as did our fathers," he wrote in 1912, "we go to the woods much more, and . . . we now use the word nature very much as our fathers used the word God." [6] New York City's fisherman-preacher Henry Van Dyke counseled a whole generation of nature lovers in volumes of essays like *Fisherman's Luck* and *Camp Fires and Guide Posts*. His best-selling *Out-of-Doors in the Holy Land* typified the new belief; but the Reverend O. Warren Smith, "Outdoors W. Smith," as he called himself, offered the most fitting benediction. "Bless, you," he told his readers, "a week of pack-sack sauntering in the wilderness near home will teach you more than a hundred and one sermons." [7] One Baptist journalist called summer camping "a life as simple and unostentatious, as benevolent and unselfish, as that of our Lord," a life far removed from "fashion and display and dissipation." Writing from Pacific Theological Seminary, mountain climber William Badé noted "that thousands of tired and overworked people now annually go into the Sierra Nevada with the unpretentious equipment with which religious art is accustomed to endow Joseph and Mary on their journey to Egypt." Liberty Hyde Bailey turned the whole conservation movement into a religious crusade: if nature was holy, then "the greedy division of the resources and privileges of the earth was a form of sinfulness." Every American had "a divine obligation" to preserve what he could of the world around him. [8]

By 1924, when Bruce Barton's *The Man Nobody Knows* made best-seller lists, the "Religion of the Fields" was well established; to a writer in *Good Housekeeping*, it was "pastoral Christianity, like that preached in Judea or Galilee." The New Testament offered "a fishin' religion" to one writer and "a country religion" to another. To the Reverend E. P. Powell, outdoor columnist for *Independent* magazine, simplicity and naturalness in suburbia were "the handmaids of piety." Journalist James Buckham found school-room nature-study "a pure, sweet, religious thing"; biologist Clifton Hodge of Clark University claimed it laid "the surest possible foundation for religious character." [9] No one spoke of pastoral themes with greater enthusiasm than Bishop William Quayle—"the Skylark of Methodism." Bruce Barton called Christ "the founder of modern business" and proclaimed Him an archetypal outdoorsman in the same breath, but Quayle went even further. It was, he announced, "the out-of-doorsness" of Jesus that made Christianity relevant for modern Americans. Jesus was categorically "the most out-of-doors man that ever lived." Moreover, "what he said and did was out-of-doors talk and out-of-doors doing." [10]

To Archibald Rutledge, it seemed in the 1930's that "the natural world, spiritually discerned," might bring "peace in the heart" to troubled Americans. An old watchman spoke for Rutledge of the virtues of solitude where " 'Ceptin' the deer and things, ain't nobody but me and God.' " Only in the woods, it seemed to Rutledge, did "resentment for the general system of life" fade into insignificance.[11] Men like Hugh MacMillan, Henry Van Dyke and Bishop Quayle were all convinced that average Americans could best find Christian values in the out-of-doors. Their analogies might be trite and their efforts to capitalize on the secular nature movement transparent. Nevertheless, they continued to offer nature sermons with a cheerful faith in their necessity, assured that they had found in "nature," as one writer noted, a source of inspiration "unclouded by intellectual error." [12]

14

Nature and the Camera

More and more, as it becomes necessary to preserve the
game, let us hope that the camera will largely supplant the
rifle . . . . The shot is, after all, only a small part of the free
life of the wilderness. The chief attractions lie in the physical
hardihood for which the life calls, the sense of limitless freedom which it brings, and the remoteness and wild charm and
beauty of primitive nature. All of this we get exactly as much
in hunting with the camera as in hunting with the rifle . . . .

Theodore Roosevelt, introduction to A. G. Wallihan,
Camera Shots at Big Game (New York:
Doubleday, Page, 1901), p. 5.

Nature lovers appreciated landscape in some more easily managed form than cumbersome reality. In large measure, art and
literature freed them from the vagaries of time and place and
temperature. But, however much they might admire an artist's
taste, they could not completely escape the feeling that what
they saw and read was not "real." Still, men found it hard to contemplate only what was best in real landscape. In 1898, geologist
Nathaniel Shaler noted that pushing against the winds in open
country or peering from a mountain top virtually precluded
"spiritual contact" with nature. Shaler found it difficult to focus
on single themes when he was surrounded by beauty. In "The
Landscape as a Means of Culture," he laid out for readers of *The
Atlantic Monthly* a scheme to limit the field of vision by scientific
principles, and so reduce landscape to a static impression which
he could view without distraction. First of all, he wrote, "a certain
reconnoitering of the ground is required before one determines
just how one shall face the vista." Since he found eye motion
distracting, Shaler suggested a "frame device." He reasoned that
the proper viewing radius for the human eye was no more than

fifteen degrees, and he stationed himself in precise relation to rocks or tree trunks, doorways or window frames to insure that he could best see into "the heart of things." [1]

Eighteenth-century Romantics could stroll through their land-scaped gardens with a "plano-convex mirror," an engaging device for turning reality into two-dimensional art by erasing fore-ground distinctions. Nineteenth-century nature lovers discovered photography, and with it the proper blending of reality and art to preserve the Arcadian vision. Civil War photographers Mat-thew Brady, Alexander Gardner and George S. Cook turned to landscape scenes when their primitive equipment failed to cap-ture dramatic action. William Henry Jackson's realistic photo-graphs of the Yellowstone country convinced Congress to set the area aside in 1872 as America's first scenic reservation. His work also paved the way for landscape photographers in the 1880's who brought the wilderness into stereoscopic viewers across the country. With inexpensive cameras and all-purpose films, George Eastman set out to put "Kodak" snapshots in every family album at the end of the century. New methods in printing made the glossy photograph a common sight in books and magazines; periodicals like *The World's Work* began to specialize in "photo-stories."

From stereoscopic slides and magazine illustrations, the aver-age American learned to appreciate the magnificence of America's mountain ranges, lakes and forests. Unlike artists' landscapes, stereoscopic views offered "real" nature in three dimensions. But professional photographers' scenic views were far more than snap-shots. They learned to compose precisely as landscape artists did, eliminating with their view finders any undesirable intrusions and isolating only the best of scenery. In the twentieth century, care-fully selected reproductions in the popular National Park "Port-folios" blended naturalness and artificiality in compositions which seemed all the more real for their studied carelessness. Such artis-tic presentations of American scenery prepared tourists for their first views of Yosemite Valley or Yellowstone's geysers and fur-nished readers with possible settings for wilderness novels.

Landscape photography particularly benefited railroad advertising. Sprawling enlargements, reminding prospective travellers of distant attractions, were spread like murals across the walls of ticket offices in smoky Eastern cities. Scenic vignettes dotted the advertising sections of national magazines as one railroad after another set out to prove that its route tapped the nation's most inspiring countryside. In 1913, ten different lines vied with each other in one issue of the *Literary Digest*. The New York Central claimed Hudson River scenery as its own; the New England Lines glorified Maine's Mount Desert Island. The Northern Pacific flaunted Yellowstone Park; the White Pass and Yukon offered visitors all of Alaska. The Delaware and Hudson advertised Saratoga and Lake George; and the Chicago, Milwaukee and St. Paul claimed a monopoly on the Midwest's "Vacation Land." "Come early to Canada this year," the Canadian Pacific urged readers, who saw the full-page picture of Lake Louise in the *Ladies' Home Journal*.

Such gratuitous visions of landscape scenery did much to bring nature at its best into the city, but they lacked the animation and the human interest of wildlife photography. To American sportsmen harassed by sentimentalists, the camera offered a perfect compromise between the masculine joys of field sports and the moral values of wildlife. Hunting seemed about to undergo its final refinement.

The first of the pioneer wildlife photographers to win a national audience was a Pittsburgh lawyer, George Shiras, III. A naturalist in the tradition of Gilbert White of Selbourne, Shiras did most of his work at his Whitefish Lake camp near Marquette, Michigan, to which he made annual excursions for sixty-five summers. One of the first to experiment with primitive fire-flashlight pictures in the 1890's, Shiras was requested by the government to exhibit a series of night photographs at the 1900 World Exposition in Paris. The pictures of whitetail deer which he took from his canoe won the highest award in both the Forestry and Photography divisions. The same series took the grand prize at the Louisiana Purchase Exposition in St. Louis in 1904. Men like

Arthur Dugmore made a career of wildlife photography. Unlike many others who depended on free-lance sales, Dugmore worked under contract for nature-book publishers, photographing subjects that varied from nestling birds to charging rhinos. Dugmore was a yachtsman, an explorer and an artist as well as the author of sixteen nature books which he illustrated with his own work. These ranged from African adventures to popular handbooks like *Nature and the Camera*, published in 1902.[2]

Wild birds offered the greatest challenge to modern photograph hunters. As naturalist Herbert K. Job noted, in his work with American shorebirds, their nervousness and small size required an exceedingly careful and close approach. Yet a photograph of them seemed worth the effort to Job, because they expressed all the romance and mystery of the Far North from which they came—the primitive wilderness beyond men's imaginings. "They and their lone surroundings are the unsullied handiwork of God," Job wrote of the creatures he framed in his camera's lens. "No trace is here of man's vandalism . . . the wildness of the scene might have been matched at creation's dawn."[3]

Man's own physical presence posed a barrier to his communion with "creation's dawn." The wild creatures which met his eye were usually nervous and looked unnatural. Only rarely could he surprise them unaware. Serious hobbyists learned to fasten simple triggers to their cameras so that birds and animals could take their own portraits. Day and night, such cameras stood watch over birds' nests and woodland trails—patient proxies for impatient men. Thus nature lovers found a way to enjoy, second hand, realities of nature which they might otherwise never have seen.

Still-photography captured only a single moment, however artistic the composition and however accurate the camera. When the wilderness flickered across the movie screen, however, nature really seemed to come to life. As early as 1899, Thomas Edison recorded the Great Falls of the Yellowstone and cranked away at a cinema drama called *Poker at Dawson City*. American Mutoscope and Biograph followed Edison in 1903 with films of *Glacier*

Point and *Trappers Crossing Bald Mountain.* S. Lubin produced
A Romance of the Fur Country in 1908 and *Glimpses of Yellow-stone Park* in 1909.

Some of the early movies spoofed the Arcadian tradition. Such
was *Back to the Simple Life* in 1914. It made much of the comic
misadventures of those who "pictured the most charmingly Arcadian scenes . . . amid the peaceful clucking of chickens and
the lowing of kine," and went about trading "a comfortable little
apartment in the outskirts of the city" for a hobby farm in the
country. In 1918, Vitagraph's *Back to Eden* sent Miss Constance
and her niece to a little place in the country, there to be wooed
by their wealthy landlord and his son. In *Back to the Woods,*
Mabel Norman fled the fortune hunters of the city, disguised as
a lumbercamp schoolmarm. There in the forest she met her hero,
who appeared to have "lived all his life in the great outdoors . . .
free from the taint of the city," though he was revealed at last to
be a sophisticated newspaperman.[4]

The impact of the "people's theater" on American life was as
astonishing as it was immediate. As early as 1914, seventy theaters
in Indianapolis were serving 350,000 customers a week. A few
years later, 45,000 crowded into Toledo's fifty-eight movie houses
every day. In 1922, the Federal Trade Committee estimated nationwide daily attendance at twenty million, almost a sixth of the
population. Catering to public taste, motion picture companies
produced a wide variety of celluloid melodramas, and the pros
and cons of censorship were the talk of the day.

But "big outdoor productions," like the fledgling "westerns,"
were far removed from city bedrooms. "Away up in the Canadian
Rockies, amid the mighty forces of Nature, a man must be a man
even to survive," press releases proudly announced for James
Oliver Curwood's *The Valley of Silent Men* in 1922. If wilderness novels and magazine illustrations brought a limited and
vicarious enjoyment of outdoor life to urban Americans, the movies
brought them unbounded thrills. For a few pennies they could
turn from the streets to a world of far-off adventure. Wilderness
melodramas unfolded in scenic splendor, while Wallace Beery,

NATURE AND THE CAMERA

Lon Chaney and Tom Mix played the villains against Lewis
Stone, Lew Cody, Thomas Meighan, Louise Lovely, Nell Ship-
man as "Rin tin tin" and the faithful dogs looked on.[5]

Early press releases for these outdoor pictures appealed to the
public interest in both scenery and action. In 1915, James Oliver
Curwood's agents advertised *In the Days of Famine* as "A Supreme Test of Manhood That Shows What Real Character Is. It
Surpasses Belief and Overwhelms Our Sense of the Beautiful." In
addition to his wilderness novels, Curwood wrote scripts for one
hundred and two movies. Peter B. Kyne had a hand in another
forty-three, and Gene Stratton Porter formed her own company
to film her Limberlost novels. All offered what the trade flyer for
World Pictures' *Forest Rivals* in 1919 called "fast action, a strong
love interest, thrilling incidents," and, of course, "beautiful
scenery." *Forest Rivals,* the flyer continued, told "a wonderful
story of life in the north woods, revealed with marvelous dramatic
effect! A scenic setting that will make your audience gasp!" Not
to be outdone, Paramount Artcraft sent out posters for Peter B.
Kyne's *Valley of the Giants* featuring a desperate struggle in the
forest with the caption:

> It was War! They had gone too far. The friends of his youth—
> his redwoods—towering on the slopes he loved, to those vandal
> "pioneers" were only "lumber!" And when they felled the hoary
> giant that guarded his mother's grave—then it was man against
> man, camp against camp—to the death!
> A picture of rugged hills and of rugged hearts. Filled with
> the tang of boundless forests. Rich with the blood of untamed
> men. Come!

The motion picture industry firmly molded its material to the
Arcadian image. To insure public recognition, the movie version
of Curwood's *Wapi the Walrus* was entitled *Back to God's Country* in 1919. Directed by David Hartman, much of the production
was filmed, according to advance notices, "at a temperature of 52
degrees below zero." In one press release, Curwood claimed for it
"the distinction of having been made further north than any other

picture in the history of the screen . . . on the far shore of Lesser
Slave Lake, north of the 56th parallel." Lobby announcements
aimed at those who "love God's great out-of-doors, the land of
frozen forests and everlasting snows where the gaunt wolf stalks
its prey, where men loom large and life is big . . . ."

Motion picture companies nurtured the public's appetite for
"powerful acting, scenic splendor and tense situations," as releases described Curwood's *Jan of the Big Snows* in 1922. Dis-
tributors provided layouts for lobby cards, press releases, and pre-
written newspaper reviews. "Bearing in mind the phenomenal success of *Back to God's Country* there should be little need to urge
the importance of publicity on *Nomads of the North*," theater
owners were told in 1921. Curwood had put into it the "thrill,
heart-punch and spectacular sensation which have made him
famous as a word-painter of life in the Far North." With Lewis S.
Stone as Corporal O'Connor and Lon Chaney as Raoul Challoner,
the picture was to "be exploited from angles which will bring it
home to every section of your community." The Famous Players
Lasky Corporation ballyhooed *The Alaskan* in 1924. "At last!" they
told their exhibitors, "the most consistent male star of to-day . . .
in James Oliver Curwood's magnificent story of the far north . . . .
Thomas Meighan in an outdoor picture redolent of the pines and
the open spaces." The review prepared for local distribution described Curwood's powerful romance unfolding amid "green valleys crowded with forests of pine, mountain ranges whose peaks
are eternally white with snow, colossal glaciers and swift-rushing
rivers" in the "picturesque and scenically beautiful background"
of Alaska—"America's last frontier."

In 1926, Somerset Maugham's *The Land of Promise* appeared
as *The Canadian* to fit the wilderness formula. Starring Thomas
Meighan and filmed in the foothills of Alberta, *The Canadian*
dealt with wheat farming in the northwest, but publicity suggestions tied it to Canada Dry Ginger Ale, to sporting goods promo-
tions, and to poster-men who walked the streets in Stetson hats
and woods clothing. The American Cinema Association suggested
that *God's Great Wilderness*, a story of Paul and Mary Good-

heart's love in the logging camps, should be announced with an on-stage "Wilderness Demonstration" by local Boy Scouts. The placard accompanying the demonstration would read, "Nature's stage is the setting for *God's Great Wilderness,* an action picture with strong appeal. This photoplay was made in Yellowstone Park —Don't fail to see it." Curwood's *The Flaming Forest,* which Metro-Goldwyn-Mayer released in 1926, brought to the screen "a desperate battle between settlers and Indians and a burning forest, set ablaze to trap the three hundred Mounted Police who appear in the picture." The outdoor scenes, the press release continued, "were filmed in Canada and Montana and are scenically beautiful."

Peering through a stereoscope in some Victorian parlor, or staring at the flickering screen while cameras closed in on Roger McKay in his lone canoe, Americans saw a photographic version of nature tailored to the emotional needs of an urban world. Even railroad posters gave them a vision of rushing rivers and roaring waterfalls, of towering mountains and sprawling glaciers, of northern lakes and forests, which complemented city streets and crowded buildings. The camera enabled nature lovers to shut out the undesirable and, through the principles of art, to refine the world into permanently beautiful form. As early as 1903, Frank Chapman of the American Museum of Natural History noted that many sportsmen were finding "a photograph of a wild animal in its haunts . . . more highly prized than the animal itself." [6] National Park publicist Enos Mills declared in 1932 that "the kodak is helping to save the wilderness. It is one of the most influential factors in promoting a more rational and refined view of the flowers, the birds, and the trees . . . it throws the robe of beauty artistically over everything." [7] As the "Model T" made touring a national pastime, vacationers wandered from one national park to another, pulling off the road and taking snapshots at carefully planned "scenic" overlooks where nature seemed to equal everything they had been led to expect.

15

The Search for Scenery

The National Parks are set apart primarily in order to preserve to the people for all time the opportunity of a peculiar
kind of enjoyment and recreation, not measurable in economic
terms and to be obtained only from the remarkable scenery
which they contain—scenery of those primeval types which are
in most parts of the world rapidly vanishing for all eternity
before the increased thoroughness of the economic use of land.

Frederick Law Olmsted, Jr.,
as quoted in Victor Shelford, ed., *Naturalist's Guide to the
Americas* (Baltimore: Wilkins and Wilkins, 1926), p. 8.

"Love of beauty is practically a universal passion," wrote the
publicity director of the National Park Service in 1919. "It is that
which lures millions into the fields, valleys, woods, and mountains
on every holiday, which crowds our ocean lanes and railroads." [1]
These "millions" searching for scenery on weekends and summer
vacations pushed federal and state governments into more and
more active preservation of natural beauty. The sublime in nature
was, after all, God's gift to the American people, an antidote to
the artificial and the ugly in civilized life and a heritage for
future generations.

As early as 1864, Abraham Lincoln had given Yosemite Valley
and the Mariposa Redwoods to California as a scenic reservation
"for public use, resort and recreation . . . inalienable for all
times." Congress designated the Yellowstone country "a public
park or pleasuring-ground for the benefit and enjoyment of the
people," four years before General George Custer rode to his
death a few miles to the east.[2] Only a handful of tourists with
leisure and funds for lengthy pilgrimages visited Yellowstone or
Yosemite in the nineteenth century.

By 1900, however, John Muir noted optimistically that "the

scenery habit, even in its most artificial forms, mixed with spectacles, silliness and kodaks," was part of the American way of life.[3] Sixty-nine thousand travellers managed to find their way into the eleven National Parks in 1908. In 1910, the number grew to 198,606 and to 334,799 in 1915, when the Panama-Pacific Exposition spurred tourist travel. Automobiles brought a tidal wave of visitors sometimes answering the call of the wild less than the call of the road. In 1921, more than a million, and by 1928, some three million people toured national parks and monuments that ranged from tiny Sully's Hill in North Dakota to sprawling Yellowstone, Yosemite and Glacier. However polite, the squadron of cavalry and the machine-gun platoon staffing Yellowstone Park could hardly meet the needs of all of the tourists. In 1916, the National Park Service came into being as a branch of the Interior Department charged with adjusting unspoiled nature to the expectations of urban travellers and with interpreting natural scenery to visitors who found themselves a little ill at ease in the wilderness.

The most ardent tourists were not impressed by wildness itself. They looked instead for the unique, the spectacular or the sublime, drawing their standards from stereoscopic views, picture postcards, railroad advertising, magazine illustrations, Romantic literature and landscape art. Scenic beauty was an art form, and its inspiration a preconditioned experience. It was almost as meaningful in the monumental canvases of Albert Bierstadt and Thomas Moran or in three-dimensional stereoscopic views as it was in reality; but so long as tourists could travel to National Parks in reasonable comfort, they were willing to see for themselves. There they found undisciplined nature as they had always imagined it—towering redwoods, mountain peaks and waterfalls, paint pots and petrified forests, geysers and boiling springs, all spectacular and all unmarred by man. Much of Western scenery was far more shaggy than the pastoral landscapes of the Hudson Valley and the Berkshire Hills, however, and not always pleasing to Eastern tastes. John Muir, the white-bearded John the Baptist of the High Sierras, might argue that "none of Nature's landscapes are ugly so long as they are wild." John Burroughs, his

Eastern counterpart, found the Badlands of Utah "as new and red as butcher's meat," and called much of the West "the dumping ground of creation." [4]

The man on the street looked to the Federal Government to preserve the National Parks as symbols of wild nature, even at the expense of the man on the land, who found himself a trespasser on the public domain. Even nature lovers who had never been West thought of National Parks as reservoirs of stability in a volatile world, resting places where rocks and trees and running brooks were just as they had always been.

Government turned policeman in the twentieth century in the name of a "people" who seemed very far away to the man on the land. Men who saw a wealth of natural resources in idle park land steadily contested the right of urban Americans to wilderness scenery. Waterfalls were power sites, valleys potential irrigation reservoirs, and mountain meadows pastures for sheep and cattle. Opportunists measured redwood trees in board feet and dynamited ancient Sequoias, too massive even for modern saws, into stakes for California vineyards. Against such interests, nature lovers had little recourse but to place their faith in government regulation of the wilderness. The nation's scenic reservations could hardly remain "unharmed and free to all the people," J. Horace McFarland warned the American Civic Association in 1911, "if the hand of the Federal Government were withdrawn from them." [5] But the question "once a park, always a park?" echoed more than once in Congressional hearings. [6]

Washington, caught between conflicting responsibilities to settlers and city dwellers, sometimes withdrew its protection. One such case, a tiny valley called "Hetch-Hetchy" deep inside Yosemite Park became a *cause célèbre* when the city of San Francisco applied to use it as a water reservoir in 1901. In the furor that followed, nature lovers and a sympathetic press made the valley an indelible part of the nature movement. The sanctity of scenery and spiritual values was at stake, roared one enthusiast, when San Francisco "stood against the nation" for Yosemite. [7] Only the hardiest of wilderness travelers ever reached

Hetch-Hetchy. Mayor James D. Phelan saw it as an ideal water reservoir site, unlike a dozen others, free for the asking. When Secretary of the Interior Hitchcock refused his request, he turned again to Secretary James Garfield in 1908. Phelan and Warren Olney, one-time Oakland mayor, argued that the reservoir would replace one kind of scenery with another by exchanging "a beautiful but somewhat unusable 'meadow'" for "a lake of rare beauty." But the Government's responsibility to San Francisco was far more important, Phelan wrote in 1909, than "the relative beauties of a meadow or a lake." [8]

John Muir insisted that wilderness would soon be scarcer than water and that future generations would need it more. Aided by special-interest groups already supplying water and power to the San Francisco area, Muir and his supporters attempted to mobilize the national press. They argued that San Francisco was using the Hetch-Hetchy application to browbeat its present suppliers, and that the city would rather take park land for nothing than develop any of thirteen other possible sites. But most important they insisted that the government's responsibility to the nation was greater than to the people of San Francisco. The urban migration of the twentieth century might well have created a water shortage in San Francisco, but it also increased federal responsibility to keep the public domain in trust for those who visited the valley. Led by *Outlook, Independent,* and *The World's Work,* Eastern periodicals insisted that National Parks served the whole nation in a higher capacity as scenery than as reservoir sites. J. Horace McFarland, president of the American Civic Association, sent out a barrage of correspondence warning that to allow San Francisco to triumph would set a dangerous precedent.[9]

Failing to move Secretary Garfield, park supporters turned to the Department of Agriculture and its Forest Service. But Theodore Roosevelt's "conservation conscience," Chief Forester Gifford Pinchot, turned a deaf ear to preservationist pleas. A practical man with little time for scenery or symbolism, Pinchot measured Hetch-Hetchy's value according to its use. "To put it baldly," he wrote to Frederick Noble of the Spokane *Review,* "the intermit-

tent esthetic enjoyment of one per cent is being balanced against
the daily comfort and welfare of 99 per cent. For that reason,
from the very beginning I have been in favor of the Tuolumne
water supply for the city of San Francisco." He saw the "Hetch-
Hetchy fight" as a struggle by honest government against private
monopoly. To those who agreed with him, Pinchot was not playing politics or selling out the parks to further his own conservation program, but steadfastly refusing "to play into the hands of
the interests who were capitalizing [upon] the whole nature
loving sentiment of the country." [10]

The House Public Lands Committee dodged the question of
San Francisco's present need in 1909, declaring that there must
be "not merely enough, but an ample supply of water for the
western metropolis," for "fifty years hence this nation will have
200,000,000 population, with a growing proportion of them on
the Pacific slope." Two of Yosemite's eleven hundred square miles
seemed a small price to pay for progress. Congressmen were
moved by thoughts of tenement children crying for water, but
they were hardly anxious to hurry the issue. For four years, off
and on, they listened politely to what some called "the protests
of the Nature fakers," then granted San Francisco her request in
1913. Suspecting chicanery, nature lovers bowed to claims of
urgent need a little bitterly. The reservoir was impounded in
1923, and work began at last on the forty-seven mile aqueduct in
1931.

Nature lovers lost Hetch-Hetchy, but they alerted the public to
the need for a distinct agency to safeguard the National Parks.
Gifford Pinchot's position made it clear that policies appropriate
to National Forests were inappropriate to National Parks. Landscape architect Frederick Law Olmsted, Jr., supplied the basic
distinction:

> The National *Forests* are set apart for economic ends, and
> their use for recreation is a by-product properly to be secured
> only in so far as it does not interfere with the economic effi-
> ciency of the forest management. The National *Parks* are set
> apart primarily in order to preserve to the people for all time

the opportunity of a peculiar kind of enjoyment and recreation
not measurable in economic terms and to be obtained only from
the remarkable scenery which they contain . . . .[11]

As early as 1910, J. Horace McFarland threw the weight of his
American Civic Association behind a bill creating a "Park Service"
in the Interior Department. Pinchot, embroiled in a feud with
Secretary Richard A. Ballinger, opposed the bill. Pinchot believed
the parks belonged to the Forest Service, not to the Interior Department. Insisting "they are all crooks over there," he continued
to ignore McFarland's evidence of good intent, until McFarland
concluded irascibly, "I have not any confidence in your own
harmony with the underlying economic and sociological purposes
of parks." [12] It seemed to McFarland that by 1914 Pinchot had
"ceased to be a useful force for real conservation." "If we are to
get anywhere with the national park service," he wrote to Allen
Chamberlain, "we have got to do it over Pinchot's opposition, and
through him, over the opposition, direct or indirect, of the Forest
Service itself." [13] Mrs. John Dickinson Sherman, chairman of the
powerful Conservation Committee of the General Federation of
Women's Clubs, came to McFarland's aid in 1916. In the belief
that scenery was "one of our noblest resources," [14] the Chicago
socialite who summered on a "stone and timber claim" at Long's
Peak, Colorado, marshalled newspaper editorials and mailed
seven hundred personal letters supporting the Park Service idea.[15]
Urged on by McFarland and Mrs. Sherman, Congress approved a
National Park Service in August of 1916. Stephen T. Mather, a
wealthy young borax merchant "with obsessions to do good," [16]
brought altruism and business enterprise to the new Service as its
first Director.

Mather furthered the wartime "See America First" campaign to
turn the National Parks into "the people's playgrounds." He and
his staff soon emerged as the nation's foremost scenery salesmen.
Traditionally, railroad advertising provided most National Park
publicity; in 1915, the Union Pacific and the Santa Fe Railroad
spent nearly half a million dollars on exhibits at the San Francisco

160 BACK TO NATURE

Exposition, with the Union Pacific's replica of Yellowstone's Old Faithful Inn enhanced by an artificial geyser that erupted every hour. But the next year, Mather supplemented $43,000 donated by seventeen western railroads with $5,000 of his own money to prepare 275,000 free copies of *The National Parks Portfolio*, an elegant collection of landscape photographs aimed at sophisticated nature lovers in Women's Clubs, colleges and universities. In 1917, the Service distributed 128,000 information circulars, 117,000 "Glimpses of Our National Parks," 83,000 automobile guide maps, 3,431 slides and 348,000 feet of motion picture film, in addition to a sale edition of the *Portfolio* now scheduled to appear annually. Meanwhile, the United States Railroad Administration established a special bureau to funnel information from the Park Service and the railroads to the public. In 1919, this bureau distributed some two and a half million pieces of literature and saw to it that Eastern ticket offices displayed enticing pictures of park scenery.

The war in Europe turned tourists to the West in increasing numbers. As humorist Irving Cobb put it in his version of a tourist guidebook, most of them went "to see the country and rough it—rough it on overland trains better equipped and more luxurious than any to be found in the East; rough it at ten-dollar-a-day hotels; rough it by touring car over the most magnificent automobile roads to be found on this continent." [17]

Cobb paid little attention to automobiles in 1915, but within a few years automobile touring permanently altered National Park travel, changing the wilderness from a gallery reserved for a discriminating few to a playground where all might absorb what they could. W. A. Clarke and his wife first steamed over the rough roads from Oakland to Yosemite in 1902. "At Curry Camp," Clarke wrote, "we ran our machine into the midst of a circle of Eastern tourists seated around a large campfire. To say that the apparition of an automobile . . . called forth generous applause and hearty congratulations but feebly expresses it." [18] Mount Rainier was officially opened to automobiles and motorcycles in 1908, as was Crater Lake in 1911 and Glacier in 1912. At Mount

Rainier, drivers who paid the five-dollar fee could take the road to Paradise Valley between eight in the morning and six-thirty in the evening, honking at every bend and driving no faster than six miles an hour, unless the roads were otherwise posted. On meeting horsemen, they were to pull to the outside lane and stop until signalled to drive on. The same regulations applied at Crater Lake, except that roads were open for no more than three hours in the early morning and three in late afternoon.

To British Ambassador James Bryce, the automobiles slithering over mountain roads were serpents in paradise, carrying to the parks a new class of tourists, destroying "the sentimental charm of the landscape" and threatening to envelop even Yosemite in a pall of dust. "If you were to realize what the result of the automobile will be in that wonderful, that incomparable valley," he told the American Civic Association in 1912, "you will keep it out." [19] But Yosemite and Sequoia Parks were opened in 1913 and Mesa Verde in 1914. In 1914 the only road designated for automobiles in Yellowstone Park was too rough for any car to travel. But the following year, a triumphant Ford, "so loaded with tenting and cooking utensils that the occupants scarcely could be seen," chugged into the center of the park. It was the first of nearly a thousand to be registered that season. "Those who laughed and those who groaned at the sight of it, and there were both, were no seers," wrote Robert Sterling Yard, "for that minute Yellowstone entered upon her destiny." [20] Automobiles registered in the National Parks in 1917 numbered 55,296; in 1926, more than four hundred thousand.[21] "It was inevitable that the automobile would revolutionize the park tour," Stephen Mather noted in 1919, "just as it changed travel conditions everywhere and turned into memories cherished methods of seeing and doing things." [22] The parks were not only for lovers of solitude, but also for "people too old, too young, too unsound, or too sedentary to rough it." [23]

Secretary of the Interior Franklin K. Lane officially declared in 1918 that parks "must be maintained in absolutely unimpaired form for the use of future generations as well as those of our own time." They were "set apart for the use, observation, health, and pleasure of the people," he continued, and only "the national interest" should control public decisions and private enterprise. There would be no lumbering, cabin leasing or other economic development, and the parks were to be "kept accessible by any means practicable." In addition, Lane directed Mather to extend "the splendid cooperation developed during the last three years among chambers of commerce, tourist bureaus, and automobile-highway associations for the purpose of spreading information about our national parks and facilitating their use and enjoyment." [24] But George Lorimer, editor of *The Saturday Evening Post*, warned the following year that "selling scenery" was a risky business. It would prove extremely difficult, he argued, "to popularize our national parks without destroying the very thing we are trying to save; to sell them to the public without claptrap commercialism." [25]

Mather's publicity brought a new group of tourists to the parks. Many thousands of them were simply "devotees of the recently born craze for touring." For them "the parks were merely the latest travel sensation." The great surge of visitors demonstrated only that "tourist crowds awheel will swing off their courses, whenever new roads of high quality offer opportunity, to see anything new and well advertised." [26] National parks were "roadside points of interest," holding the auto tourist for a few hours or a few days; "selling scenery" had become a matter of making park features attractive to a transient, largely inexperienced audience.

In the days before roadside cabin camps, few tourists enjoyed the comfort of overnight hotels; all but 1,500 of the 51,506 who registered at Yellowstone in 1922 found themselves "roughing it." These impromptu campers, with "tent and camp equipment piled high on the running boards or carried in neat trailers fastened on behind," were to Mather "the most wholesome aspect of our national park popularity." [27] But most who camped from necessity had little skill in woodcraft. Mather soon discovered they needed guidance even beyond carefully managed camping facilities and emphatic warnings against feeding the bears. The Park Service,

THE SEARCH FOR SCENERY
                                                         163

once concerned with protecting scenery from commercial exploitation, now turned to protecting it from visitors. Superintendents in Yosemite found themselves steadily battling health
and sanitation problems while as many as four thousand tourists
a day camped, cooked and bathed in a three-quarter square mile
area. Yosemite Creek and the Merced River, which flowed across
the valley floor with all the appearance of wild streams, were
sadly polluted by 1913. Mount Rainier had once appealed to John
Muir as a place "for rest, inspiration, and prayers," but by 1919,
Rainier's superintendent was not so much concerned with inspiration as he was with installing a six-inch pipeline to carry "the
sewage of Paradise Inn to the Paradise River." [28]

   In many respects tourist crowds could be controlled as subtly
in a great national park as in a suburban garden. To Robert
Sterling Yard, motorists could be "concentrated because they re-
fuse to be anything else." [29] They lived by the road, and they most
enjoyed the wilderness as it was framed in their windshields. To
offer scenic beauty without destroying the wilderness it was only
necessary to build a limited but carefully designed road network
between major park attractions. In 1918, with Charles Punchard
as its head, the "Landscape-Architecture Division" of the Park
Service set out to reconcile the auto and the wilderness. Highways were no longer access routes; like the pathways of the
Romantic garden, they were routed so that in passing tourists
could enjoy beauties which were left unspoiled. Punchard was responsible for far more than entrance gates and service buildings.
Combining engineering and art, his division controlled the image
that thousands of auto tourists carried away from the parks. His
staff designed, among other things, the "scenic turnouts," those
masterful compromises between convenience and contemplation
that offered postcard views of glaciers, mountain peaks and
canyons and opportune rest for overheated engines. Like
Punchard, John C. Merriam believed that parks should be developed through the same techniques used by landscape artists.
Merriam, who led the National Parks Association's "Advisory
Board on the Educational and Inspirational Uses of the National

Parks," even toured European art museums to work out the plans
for trails and turnouts at Crater Lake.

Well-planned roads and scenic turnouts, however carefully
conceived, offered ordinary travelers only "scenery, magnificent,
incomparable, meaningless." Many visitors were "content to wonder, not to know," yet, Robert Yard concluded, "with scenery, to
know is to begin fully to enjoy." [30] Through a variety of pamphlets, bulletins, campfire talks and other educational devices,
the Park Service translated nature into the language of ordinary
Americans. Scientific descriptions took on a spiritual connotation
in the "trailside Shrines" that blossomed out at strategic points
and parking lots. For the 1924 season, Yosemite Park offered a
summary of its attractions in a specially designed museum made
possible by a $70,500 Rockefeller grant. In 1927, a smaller grant
financed a similar museum at Grand Canyon.

But the real responsibility for making nature intelligible fell to
Park Rangers and "Nature Guides." "In our great National Parks
we have an unrivalled outdoor school that is always open; in it
is a library, a museum, a zoological garden, and a type of the
wilderness frontier," wrote Enos Mills, the flamboyant instigator
of "Nature Guiding" in Rocky Mountain National Park. The
modern automobile tourist, unlike his nineteenth-century counterpart, was not an explorer. "In visiting our great parks and wild
places," Mills concluded, "he not only wants, but needs a
guide." [31] Yet those who managed tourists differed markedly
from the "wild and woolly gun-carrying guides" of the older
West. No matter how he might disguise himself, the nature guide
talked the language and anticipated the needs of the city. He
"must play many parts, athletic instructor, pack animal, photographer, counsellor, physician, and clown," Mills wrote half humorously. "He must explain miles of geography, talk botany, quote
poetry, and above all, give intelligent answers to unintelligent
questions." [32] Mills might spoof the nature guide's sophistication,
but the Park Service took it seriously. According to the *Yosemite
Ranger Naturalist's Manual*, the good guide:

must have ready for immediate use ecology, ethnology, history, legend and tradition and a score of natural sciences. If, in addition he be endowed with a sense of the aesthetic and artistic, if he possesses a background of experience and an acquaintance with human ideals, aspirations and transactions, if he be able to draw aid and example from the world's best literature . . . and, above all, if he be favored with an unbounded enthusiasm for Nature . . . he cannot fail to interest, yea even inspire, his listeners, and to impart in unceasing measure a portion of his own bountiful self and his abundant life.[33]

City tourists could hardly penetrate the wilderness on an afternoon hike, but like so many Arcadian pleasures, "the essence of Nature Guiding" was, Mills wrote, "to travel gracefully rather than arrive." [34]

Travelling gracefully meant a great deal to many park visitors. To them the parks were a series of well-designed highways, graced by viewpoints and picnic grounds that led eventually to comfortable accommodations. Sprawling log hotels like Many Glacier and Old Faithful Inn were far more than monuments to rustic architecture. In their day they offered the precise blend of luxury and nature that tourists thought appropriate to Western life. Time-table travelers appreciated nature best as static scenery, always available whenever they could schedule it. Old Faithful geyser erupted at predictable intervals. Birds and animals usually seen only by expert woodsmen grew tame at feeding stations and garbage pits maintained by the Park Service. "The frontier no longer exists, and the days of the wilderness are gone forever," Enos Mills concluded in 1917,[35] but with the aid of the Park Service the tourist could create in his mind a new wilderness, embellished with his own version of the frontier world.

In the 1920's, then, public parks were more and more the urban American's last refuge from "the tyranny of the no-trespassing sign." [36] Citizens of New York and Chicago, Pittsburgh and Boston, moved by little more than sentiment over Hetch-Hetchy, came to "have a direct personal interest in recreational grounds where they can feel free to camp and enjoy themselves in their own way . . . ." [37] Such visitors fell into three groups. The first liked nature, but not wilderness. Their "idea of wild life in the Rockies," as *Post* editor George Lorimer put it, was "a set of tennis or eighteen holes of golf"; they expected "a Dame Nature with a permanent wave and the new figure." [38] A second and larger group enjoyed the parks, but they were of the sort, Robert Yard declared, that "can travel, or think they can travel, only in vehicles, and can find satisfactory accommodations only in good hotels." [39] Nature alone was not enough; they must have entertainment. They were the tourists for whom "the wind in the pines must be supplemented by a jazz band and for whom vaudeville under the stars is the last word in communing with Nature." A third and smaller group left the hotel concerts and the beaten pathways and travelled "man-fashion, on foot or on horseback, living a simple, clean, close-to-the-ground life, and leaving undone those things that have been their routine pleasures at home." [40]

Whatever the merits of these latter-day woodsmen, the Park Service devoted most of its effort to meeting the needs of the first two groups. Still, enthusiast Harlean James found romance in the parks despite their tent cities and tourist hotels. So long as there remained some balance between use and preservation, automobiles were no real threat to nature lovers. It was true "that the full aesthetic and emotional effect of delicate scenic pictures" was lost on those who hurried through the parks by car, unless they stopped "to make use of the many 'look-outs' provided by a thoughtful government." But automobiles made it possible at last "for everyone to reach the high places on the face of the earth," to leave the stifling city behind and perhaps to find "in the soul-satisfying beauties of our national parks and other sacred regions" some relief from the real or imagined strains of urban life. Even with fellow tourists crowding into the wilderness, it seemed to James that the search for scenery was still worthwhile; it was always possible that "only a few hundred yards from the highway, one may find lonesome-looking places and may sense in some degree the excitement of standing alone to gaze on far distant views." [41]

16

The Search for Solitude

It is the wild that we are after . . . . to the modern man in the Adirondacks, the roar of the rapids, the gaunt dead trees around the lake, the wet carry, the big rotten trunks that impede his steps, even the punkies that defy his smudge, are sources of joy and refreshment unspeakable. He sees in them the unconsciousness, the spontaneity, the coarse health of the great mother from whom we all are sprung, to whom we all return, but whose existence we have forgotten in the cities.

Henry Beers, "The Modern Feeling for Nature," in *Points at Issue* (New York: MacMillan, 1904), p. 148.

Superintendent Stephen Mather thought of Western parks as "national museums of our American wilderness." His publicity staff urged throngs of sightseers to tour these "primeval galleries of American scenery." [1] There they could feel themselves "a part of the real wilderness," the *Nature-Study Review* informed America's school teachers, on trails which were "as broad and wide as city sidewalks and far safer for travel." [2] National parks undoubtedly offered incomparable scenery, but nature lovers soon began to wonder whether they could ever again provide solitude to match their scenery. To those who wanted to get away from it all, "the horn-blowing, pistol-firing, peanut-eating tourist" seemed everywhere. [3] True, John Muir rejoiced in 1901 that "thousands of tired, nerve-shaken, over-civilized people [found] that going to the mountains is going home; that wildness is a necessity." He was sure that visitors to the Western parks would "mar them hardly more than the butterflies that hover over them," [4] but other observers were less tolerant. Stewart Edward White was well along on a five-month pack trip when he wound his way into Yosemite in 1904, past puffing tourists who with toy climbing axes and artificial Edelweiss were "playing wilderness where no wilderness exists." He could hardly agree with Muir that Yosemite was "a paradise that makes even the loss of Eden seem insignificant." Instead he found it "marred by the swarms of tourists," who enjoyed "a nice, easy, healthful, jolly kind of time up there in the mountains," but missed the tonic of solitude.[5]

On a visit to Grand Canyon, Ernest Thompson Seton and his wife found the painted wooden bricks, the paper marble, the artificial flowers and the civilized comforts of their hotel—even the captive scenery framed in its windows—a disappointment; there was "nothing honest but the fly-papers and the spittoon." [6] Even John Muir warned that "nothing can be done well at a speed of forty miles a day . . . the multitude of mixed, novel impressions rapidly piled on one another make only a dreamy, bewildering, swirling blur, most of which is unrememberable." He cautioned that real understanding of nature came only to those who left the crowd for a time, who camped in wild meadows and travelled the back country trails, who climbed the mountains to "get their good tidings." [7]

Urban Americans experimented with temporary wilderness living in the Adirondacks, the "Canoe Country" of Maine and Minnesota, and the mountains of the West. They made the cabin in the woods a new symbol of weekend freedom, building their rustic retreats on mountainsides, in isolated corners on suburban estates, and even hidden in den rooms behind the facades of wealth. Their hornet's nests and Navajo blankets, diamond-paned windows, mission furniture, oriental rugs and Morris chairs served to complement the simple life. Though the frame cottages and tar paper shanties on Lake Minniemashie may well have been the rule, an early distinction between "cabin" and "cottage" underlined both the expense and the status associated with log construction. Real log cabins represented more than artful simplicity; they expressed an attitude toward life itself. Experienced architects successfully integrated wiring, plumbing and powder rooms with what one enthusiast called "the picturesqueness of pioneer days." [8] Most patterned the elaborate log retreats of the rich after

German and Swiss chalets rather than pioneer cabins—those quaint reminders of the past suited wilderness movies but not the new wilderness life.

Americans yearning to recover the healthy glow that physicians attributed to balsam boughs and open air turned to "roughing it" with a vengeance in the twentieth century. Inexperienced travelers trusted themselves to professional guides, who wrangled horses and portaged canoes, pitched tents and flapjacks with equal ease, and generally smoothed away the troubles of the trail for days or even weeks. Some followed literary guidebooks: Elon Jessup's *Roughing It Smoothly,* or the woodcraft manuals of Horace Kephart, Warren Miller, and others who evoked the inspiration of the out-of-doors with practical discussions of diamond hitches, packsacks, footgear and sourdough.[9] Such writers told direction by moss or stars, swore by Indian moccasins or rubber boots, warned against rattlesnakes and poison oak and dashed off a line or two on instinct psychology and the ungovernable need for outdoor life. Many wrote of method but few of meaning; it was easier to take for granted that wildness *was* a necessity than to analyze its place in industrial society.

Stewart Edward White managed to spell out campcraft and its meaning in a popular trilogy—*The Forest, The Mountains* and *The Cabin*—which he completed in 1911. A reviewer in the New York *Times* happily called *The Cabin* something more than a "nature-book," a term that suggested "almost as much discredit as to say of a bird that it is an English sparrow." It was, instead, a "forest book," which he found "beautiful or whimsical by turns with . . . home-brewed philosophy."[10] White made elaborate play of building a summer camp in the Sierras, seventy miles from the railroad, but he reminded his readers that even temporary solitude required stamina and resourcefulness rarely called for in the city. As the "Cabin" took shape, it became for White the measure of himself. Building it, he learned the restraint of careful craftsmanship, the value of axe and adze, and the caution brewed of time and solitude. In the year that he and his wife spent in the woods he claimed to have acquired a sense of competence in small things that urban intellectuals rarely knew.[11]

If White found physical rewards in the wilderness, Stanton Davis Kirkham, another Sierra camper, discovered in 1910 that "the most precious gift of the hills" was "the mountain thoughts they inspire." [12] Paradise was "a trout stream and a snow-capped mountain"; Kirkham asked simply that "it be rude and savage that I may see the hand of God." An outdoor philosopher little known even among nature lovers, he ranged in a half-dozen volumes from botanical description to poignant sentiment. Like White, he was always ready to criticize a sedentary generation. "Few dare go to the woods alone," he wrote in 1912. Those who did "must first organize a club and hold a meeting, and then with bird book, opera-glass, and overshoes they may venture in quest of the sparrow." [13]

The ability of writers like White and Muir and Kirkham to share their experiences made it possible for them to combine pleasure and business without the limitations of ordinary travelers. Whether for philosophy or adventure, more and more writers "took to the woods" and returned to publish the pleasures of solitude. Some had special business in the wilderness, as did Dillon Wallace, the intrepid if inefficient Labrador explorer, and Hudson Stuck, self-styled Episcopal "Archdeacon of the Yukon," who listed the conquest of Mount McKinley among his accomplishments. Hamlin Garland trekked over 760 miles on the lonely "Telegraph Trail" to observe the Gold Rush in 1898. Charles Sheldon of the Boone and Crockett Club followed the Yukon miners to study color variation in mountain sheep and published his report as a eulogy on the masculine joys of wilderness hunting. Others went for the sake of escape or merely for publicity. In the summer of 1913, paunchy, middle-aged Joseph Knowles, a wildlife painter from Vermont, stripped to his breechclout for a photographer and a panel of judges and strode into the woods of Northern Maine. He lived by his wits for two months, scrawling artistic messages on birch-bark and organizing his thoughts for a volume he called *Alone in the Wilderness*.[14]

In 1920, Rockwell Kent, a far better artist, recorded a winter spent in Alaska with his young son. Illustrated with strangely feminine supermen posing against a mountain backdrop, Kent's journal was a classic "of quiet adventure in the wilderness." In a fetching combination of breeziness and whimsy, he made it clear that only the sophisticated could indulge in the luxury of simplicity. "Seen close to," Kent wrote, "those who made their living in the woods [seemed] damnably stupid and coarse." He and his son preferred to spend their time "in uneventful solitude"; Kent told his readers, "if we have not . . . fled from its loneliness, it is because of the wealth of our own souls that filled the void with imagery, warmed it, and gave it speech and understanding." [15]

White and Kirkham and Kent, and even Joseph Knowles, described a solitary world. National Parks, however spectacular their scenery, seemed artificial by contrast; Liberty Bailey noted sadly in 1923 that men had "not yet learned how, in any large way, to live in the presence of free nature without defiling it." [16] A Romantic like *Century* editor Robert Underwood Johnson might still find himself "continually in a state between awe and rapture" in Yosemite, but when John C. Merriam looked down on Yosemite Valley a quarter of a century after Stewart Edward White, he saw little more than "long stretches of wide road, innumerable buildings, hotels, automobiles, and parking places." To Merriam, a member of the Interior Department's "Advisory Board on National Park Policy," it was no longer a shrine but "a resort . . . promoted by business for profit." [17] Even the grizzly bears fed under electric lights at government expense. They were stars of "a play staged in Yosemite, taken over and arranged by the National Park Service." [18] In 1930, Merriam preferred "to go to any one of a thousand other places to enjoy nature," and a surprising number of vocal Americans agreed with him.

Few could find their way to Hudson's Bay or the Yukon, or the far places so popular in wilderness fiction. Some turned instead to Western dude ranches where, as Mary Roberts Rinehart put it, they could satisfy the "hunger of the civilized to get away from civilization and yet avoid the hardships few of us can easily endure." A curious grafting of Eastern ideals on Western culture, dude ranching offered the artistic side of rustic life, as rancher Struthers Burt expressed it, with "home-made bedsteads but forty-pound mattresses." With sympathetic guides and a restricted clientele, it preserved "the impression of wildness and isolation" that parks could not.[19] Summer boarding farms were nothing new to Easterners. Even in the 1890's, "the red chairs set out, and the hammock swung aloft" advertised the summer boarding house as accurately as carved wooden signs did the wayside inns of earlier times.[20] According to the Census Bureau in 1930, the majority of the nation's sixty-two hundred boarding farms were still in New England and the Middle Atlantic States, but three hundred and sixty-six Western ranchers reported the major portion of their income from boarders, lodgers and campers.

The dude rancher was a new type in the West—a progressive businessman who chose his land for its view and opposed the grazing, mining, logging and hunting for profit that spelled progress to his neighbors. Transplanted Easterners often anticipated far better than Westerners the hopes and fears of their guests; they knew from experience something of the urge that propelled city dwellers into the edge of the wilderness. Struthers Burt had himself been an English instructor at Princeton. An avid outdoorsman, he combined success and solitude as a dude rancher in Wyoming's "Jackson Hole" country. Beautiful scenery, wild game and the lure of the wild were his business assets, he explained in a series of articles for *The Saturday Evening Post*.

Mystery writer Mary Roberts Rinehart discovered "the call of the mountains" on a three-hundred-mile horseback tour through the Rockies to Glacier Park in 1915. Forty-two people rode with Howard Eaton on this wandering pilgrimage. Eaton, a native of Pittsburgh with a lifetime of Western experience, was credited with discovering "the dude-business" when Eastern friends overran his South Dakota horse ranch. From a base at Wolf, Wyoming, he led his horseback caravans as far as British Columbia, advertising the wilderness on winter tours of Eastern

Athletic Clubs and bringing into his parties not only Mrs. Rinehart but such notables as Rex Beach and Charles Russell as well.
For them, as for Mrs. Rinehart, the "Long Trail" was a "six-inch
path of glory" that "poor followers of the pavements" never
knew.[21]

But the Long Trail grew shorter year by year as automobile
roadways pushed along the footpaths of the past. Long before the
ubiquitous "Model A," touring cars spelled the end to wilderness
lovers as prairie schooners had to the Indians. Tourist associations
and auto clubs, local promoters and even nature enthusiasts urged
that primitive areas be opened up with roads and hotels and all
the advantages of national parks. Critics of Theodore Roosevelt's
conservation programs had long argued that national forests were
"locked up" and inaccessible, but Gifford Pinchot's vision of "producing forests" had so far come to pass in the 1920's that conservation by controlled harvest threatened the last remaining
virgin lands in the national forest system. Deeply concerned that
wilderness might well become extinct in the twentieth century,
men like Aldo Leopold and Robert Marshall set to work within
the Forest Service to establish permanent reservations.

Leopold had graduated from the Yale Forestry School in 1908.
A year later he explored the half-dozen remaining roadless areas
in the Southwest, looking for some way to preserve them from
destruction. Just as "canoeing in the wake of a motor launch or
down a lane of summer cottages" was not a canoe trip, so Leopold
was sure that taking a pack train down a graded highway was
"merely exercise, with about the same flavor as lifting dumb-
bells." [22] He advocated "Wilderness Areas" as monuments to ordinary and everyday nature. They were to be "wild regions big
enough to absorb the average man's two-week vacation without
getting him tangled up in his own backtrack . . . free from motor
roads, summer cottages, launches, or other manifestations of gaso-
line." In 1924, the Forest Service established the Gila Wilderness
in New Mexico as the first of a number of such areas within the
national forests.

The first major study of recreation on Federal lands concluded in 1928:

> City planning can make possible adequate playgrounds and parks to meet local needs, and counties and states can provide large parks and forests for transient enjoyment and relaxation out of doors, but man cannot replace the wilderness and the remaining wilderness of America, modified as it inevitably has been, is now found only in Federal ownership.[23]

The Federal Government, the same report continued, must protect "those forms of outdoor life and recreation which it alone can give and which are associated only with the wilderness." Other voices amplified the principle that government must serve the minority that searched for solitude as well as the majority of automobile tourists. Professional biologists asked for wilderness areas as ecological laboratories where the natural balance between plant and animal life could continue undisturbed, and where threatened species might still find refuge. Even to ecologists the social potential of natural areas outweighed their economic importance. "The wilderness, like the forests, was once a great hindrance to our civilization," Charles C. Adams wrote for the *Naturalist's Guide to the Americas*. Now, he argued, it must be maintained at great expense because society could not do without it.[24] Liberty Bailey asked that Americans slow the development of power sites in wilderness regions for the sake of future generations "in the days when electricity and other present aids" to power would no longer be needed.[25]

In 1930, Robert Marshall took the case to *The Scientific Monthly*. He revised Leopold's definition of "wilderness" to include only "a region which contains no permanent inhabitants, possesses no possibility of conveyance by any mechanical means, and is sufficiently spacious that a person crossing it must have the experience of sleeping out."[26] Marshall was more than concerned that "asphalt spotted with chewing gum" had replaced twin-flower and woods sorrel as the native American "ground-cover." He warned his readers that, without government intervention, it would be "only a few years until the last escape from society will be barricaded." When it was gone, the Long Trail would cease to be; now it offered the adventure of new ground, the exercise of new muscles and new skills, and the greatest test of mental and physical readiness available to a peaceful people. In 1935, Marshall joined with Leopold, Bernard Frank, Robert Sterling Yard and regional planner Benton MacKaye to organize the "Wilderness Society," dedicating themselves to preserving the distinction between scenery and solitude.

Retreat to the wilderness was a middle-class response to urban pressures. The autobiographical hero in Melville Ferguson's *Motor Camping on Western Trails* confessed:

> He had been looking at brick walls, the asphalt pavements, the hard, narrow canyons of cut stone, for forty-eight years. He hated alarm-clocks, the cellar heater, and the face of the conductor who twice daily punched his ticket on the suburban train. He longed for the open spaces, the scent of the moist forest, the roar of the mountain torrent, the acrid tang of burning wood. He knew that he must go.
> He went for a year . . . .[27]

Similarly, Sigurd Olson, then a professional guide in the Hudson Bay country, found himself catering to vacationing executives. "I have seen them come from the cities down below, worried and sick at heart, and have watched them change under the stimulus of wilderness living," he wrote with all the fervor of a Curwood novel, "into happy carefree, joyous men, to whom the successful taking of a trout or the running of a rapids meant far more than the rise and fall of stocks and bonds." [28]

Wild nature was a nuisance to the man on the land unless he profited by it. But those who dealt in symbols and myths found the wilderness a major force in shaping American character. "It has given bodily vigor, self-taught resourcefulness, and moral stamina to every generation of Americans," Forest Service Chief William B. Greeley wrote in 1925. "The restoring and preserving influences of the open spaces" seemed vital "as cities multiply and everyday living strikes a faster pace." [29] To men like Greeley, Marshall and Leopold, "the opportunity to disappear into the tall uncut," as Leopold put it, ought to be for city dwellers "one of the fixed facts of nature." [30]

But the taste for the primitive was a sophisticated appetite. Overindulged it led to spiritual indigestion; as one realist noted in the *Yale Review*, "any protracted, genuine association with nature means a reversion to a state of brutal savagery." [31] In spite of the educational work of the Wilderness Society, the average American knew pure solitude and virgin wilderness most intimately in volumes of wilderness adventure written by those who took his place on the Long Trail. Arm-chair adventures into primeval solitude were far less arduous than those of reality, and in so far as men like White and Kent succeeded in its portrayal, so far did the appreciation of wilderness solitude penetrate American thought. Both the tourists who gaped at Yellowstone and Yosemite and those who searched for solitude responded to the publicity that modern prophets gave to wild nature. The camping trip, as Henry Busch described it in *The Encyclopaedia of the Social Sciences*, became "a folkway of an urban society." Only "city people," he continued, adopted "the temporary but periodic retreat to the out of doors as a form of recreation and a phase of the accepted ways of living." [32]

17

The New Frontier

Some day we shall construct great pictures out-of-doors. We shall assemble the houses, control the architecture, arrange the trees and the forest, direct the roads and fences, display the slopes of the hills, lay out the farms, remove every feature that offends a sensitive eye; and persons will leave the galleries, with their limitations and imitations, to go to the country to see some of the greatest works of art that man can make . . . .

Liberty Bailey, *The Outlook to Nature*
(New York: MacMillan, 1905), p. 86.

Men like Robert Marshall found the problems of modern living so great that wilderness seemed "a psychic necessity." Marshall was certain that "only the possibility of convalescing in the wilderness" could ease "the terrible neural tension of modern existence."[1] Medical metaphors were nothing new in Marshall's time, but many wilderness lovers seemed almost obsessed. After all, as one of Zane Grey's heroines pointed out, they were no Indians; however much they loved the wilderness, they owed their lives to the world's work.[2] T. K. Whipple urbanely noted that "the old inevitable fallacy of the remote" pushed such men to abandon even temporarily their urban heritage. However comforting the common belief "that the last refinement of sophistication is a taste for simplicity," Whipple still insisted that such a rationalization abandoned responsibility for urban problems.[3] Nevertheless, however much Whipple might bewail the nature lover's flight from reality, the American city occasionally seemed sick even to sympathetic observers.

The decade of the 1920's saw the rise of "The New Exploration" as Benton MacKaye was to call it—an examination not of geographic resources, but of the city and the conditions that made up city life. Surveyor's transit and chain gave way to the scientific tools of psychologists, sociologists and city planners. The first reports of the new explorers gave surprising credence to nature lovers' complaints, however silly and sentimental they seemed to others. "The city of our dreams," wrote Clarence Stein, "is lost in another city which could occur to a sane mind only in a nightmare." [4] Citing evidence for New York, Stein traced successive breakdowns of the city's physical functions. Growing water and sewage problems reflected the mushrooming of residential areas around the perimeter of the old city. By 1928, 475 outlets emptied 1,100,000,000 gallons of sewage per day into the Hudson, the East, and the Harlem Rivers. The Passaic Valley sewer contributed another billion gallons at Robbins Reef. As one cynic remarked in 1913, beaches were areas of land washed by water, except in New York, where they were washed by garbage. Swimmers found themselves restricted to two per cent of the city's 190 mile waterfront, and oil pollution made even that area less than pleasant.

Traffic controls were frequently as primitive as sewage disposal. With the development of the skyscraper, two to six new "cities" rose from the streets of the old; massive traffic jams became a daily hazard of urban life. "Every day the congestion increases," Stein concluded, "in spite of traffic policemen, curb setbacks, one-way streets, electric traffic signals." Subways were equally crowded by 1925.[5]

Noise seemed the natural accompaniment to urban expansion. Sound proofing was in its infancy in building construction and in the transportation industry. City office workers contracted neuroses similar to shell shock as iron tires, klaxon horns, chain drives, traffic whistles, trolley bells and the thunder of elevated trains joined the air hammers and rivet guns of new construction.[6] E. E. Free, science editor for The Forum, found in a study of noise in New York City, which was repeated across the country, that commercial districts created a sound threshold equivalent to from one-third to one-half deafness in city workers. With the objectivity of a science fiction horror story, Free's analysis suggested that the irritation of audible sounds might well be less than the psychological assault of sounds which could only be registered by instruments.[7] New York City's Noise Abatement Commission went on to conclude that "a tiger from Siberia or Bengal could roar or snarl indefinitely" on many streets "without attracting the auditory attention of passersby."[8] Recognizing that jangled nerves were inevitable, the Commission suggested mild controls ranging from stifling random tugboat whistles to muffling exhaust pipes on federal mail trucks. They induced the Interborough Rapid Transit Company to pad nine hundred subway turnstiles when a bank of five in Grand Central Station was rated noisier than an elevated train.

The physical transition from rural to urban life gave rise to fears of the city that sociologists further defined. Rural sociologist Charles Galpin saw city life as "immured in brick and stone, gaining its outlook, as it were, through periscopes."[9] Early urban sociologists seemed equally concerned. In 1909, Charles Cooley gave an emotion-laden vocabulary to a generation of investigators with his theories of "primary" and "secondary" relationships. He characterized primary relationships as the "intimate face-to-face association and cooperation" characteristic of rural life.[10] Cooley's followers found secondary contact typical of life in cities where men became symbols for the services they performed. The study of etiquette replaced the study of human nature, said Chicago's Robert E. Park, whenever "the individual's status is determined to a considerable degree by conventional signs—by fashion and 'front'—and the art of life is largely reduced to skating on thin surfaces and a scrupulous study of style and manners."[11]

Led by Robert Park, the University of Chicago's sociology department became a leading center for urban research. Park saw the city as "a clinic" in which human nature could be examined under stress. The "Chicago school" favored objective and heavily documented studies, but when its investigators asked such questions as "Are Modern Industry and City Life Unfavorable to the Family,"[12] with results that could only horrify most readers, it was clear that urban sociologists were deeply disturbed by their own culture.

Students of urban society responded enthusiastically to Jacob Riis' *How the Other Half Lives*. Among other things, Harvey Zorbaugh commented, "Riis did more than anyone else to make 'slumming' a popular sport." [13] By the nineteen-twenties, urban sociology was itself becoming a kind of intellectual slumming. Such studies as *The Hobo, The Social Evil in Chicago, Five Hundred Criminal Careers, Prostitution in the United States, The Unadjusted Girl*, and *The City Where Crime Is Play* indicated an almost pathological interest in human failure. In 1929, Chicago's dignified "Sociological Series" included *Suicide, Family Disorganization, Sex Freedom and Social Control, Domestic Discord, Map of Chicago's Gangland, The Ghetto* and *The Strike*. Robert Park concluded that "our great cities, as those who have studied them have learned, are full of junk, much of it human." [14]

In view of the case against the city, such scholars were hard put to account for the continued surge of population into the towns. Niles Carpenter found the "lure of the city" too great for the American people, who were being conditioned to seek the "enthralment of the urban way of life." Urbanism had reached "a point never before attained in human history." Americans, Carpenter felt, would continue to move to the cities knowing that economic opportunity was closed to them by the sheer numbers of their fellow migrants; he predicted a time when the average American might well become "so completely conditioned to urban life that he simply could not conceive of living outside a city." Only Roman history offered useful parallels to modern urbanization, yet this was a most disturbing comparison, Carpenter noted, "for the end of the Roman urban society was wilderness and manorial feudalism." [15] Boston University's Ernest Groves also found urban life a "self-chosen enslavement." He reported that "the psychological causes of urban drift are socially most sinister." The individual's adjustment to city life was sociology's tormenting problem. "The mere pressing together of population, the congestion of the city, gives the impression of bigness," Groves declared, and "unless he identifies himself with this manpower, the crowd becomes an alien force and he flees from it with morbid fear." [16]

The flight from the crowd took various directions—to city parks, suburbs, country places, or to the wilderness. One of the most idealistic escapes involved the short-lived "garden city" concept. Though A. T. Stewart platted Garden City, Long Island, in 1869, Ebenezer Howard, a romantic Englishman who saw in the countryside around London "the very embodiment of Divine Love for man," did most to popularize the idea in the 1890's. In *Garden Cities of Tomorrow*, he imagined a series of carefully controlled communities which would combine selected industries with boulevards, parks and workers' cottages.[17] Howard outlined his goals much more clearly than his methods. As a result, early garden cities rarely succeeded. Perhaps the most spectacular disappointment to social reformers was the 104-acre Forest Hills Gardens on Long Island. Shortly after the turn of the century the Russell Sage Foundation Homes Company hired landscape architect Frederick Law Olmsted, Jr., to lay out the community. Artistic public buildings absorbed so much capital that the community was soon unable to offer homes to workingmen at all. Twenty years later it was "one of the most beautiful, most artistic, most expensive and most exclusive residential parks in the world." [18]

If "garden cities" failed in their purpose, conventional suburbs multiplied with astonishing rapidity. As early as 1906, the *World Today* could truthfully announce, "suburbia is still crude, too often a hodge-podge of jerry-built atrocities, but it is the city of the future." [19] In the construction boom after World War I, as Booth Tarkington complained:

> A new house would appear upon a country road; the country road would transform itself into an asphalt street with a brick drug store at the corner of a meadow . . . . What was in

spring a quiet lane through fields and woods was in autumn a constantly lengthening street with trolley-cars gonging and new house-owners hurriedly putting up wooden garages in their freshly sodded "side yards." [20]

By 1925, New York had one hundred and twenty-nine incorporated satellites, Chicago fifty-seven and Boston fifty-five. These "bedroom towns," as sociologist Nels Anderson called them, dominated the landscape around all major cities; sociologists found in them the standardization, divided loyalties and disinterest that would plague them a generation later. To one angry housewife, suburban living sapped the individuality and sophistication that brought it forth. "If you have the rubber soul and cast-iron nerve necessary for social climbing," she wrote, "you will get all the bridge parties, country club life, teas, telephone gossip, and invitations your soul craves, if you 'play the game' suburban fashion, and aren't overly particular." Narrow houses and tiny suburban yards failed to supply the nature promised in the Arcadian dream. Happiness lay further from the city, somewhere in the "real" country. "By country," she wrote, "I do not mean a farm or many acres or huge castles built in imitation of English country houses." Arcadia was instead "a simple home built along a country road, near hills or water, from a quarter of a mile to two or three miles from the railway station, and within one and one-half hours' commuting distance from the city." [21]

Such "real" country rapidly retreated before junkyards, satellite industries and real estate developments. In 1925, *Century* magazine's search for "the wildness" of New York, Boston, and Philadelphia yielded only a meager harvest of sidewalk ants, dandelions, butterflies and nighthawks.[22] All too often the feeling of vast distance and the original conditions of life were available to city dwellers only in ecological groupings at the natural history museum. Clever and exaggerated habitat settings, where painted backgrounds, waxen plants, and carefully postured animals offered "a glimpse of wild life as it is, or more often, as it has been, before man took complete possession of the land." [23] Nighthawks

and painted forests could hardly recompense nature lovers for an
Arcadia that seemed attainable in actuality through intelligent
urban planning.

City planners had been meeting since 1909 in national conferences on the problems of simple "congestion," but now they
turned to exploring the possibilities of the "metropolitan district." [24] In 1925, Lewis Mumford edited a special issue of *The
Survey Graphic* which argued that regional planning was "the
New Conservation," aimed at utilizing natural resources exclusively to benefit city dwellers. Mumford's contributors were
members of the Regional Planning Association of America, men
who had failed to remold the city to suit their fancy and had
turned instead to planning a metropolitan environment "not as a
temporary refuge but as a permanent seat of life and culture,
urban in its advantages, permanently rural in its situation." [25]

The Russell Sage Foundation sponsored a "Regional Survey of
New York and Its Environs" in 1924 to develop a master plan
for New York City. Mapping out a 5,500 square mile "region"
which included four hundred twenty municipalities and one-
twelfth of the country's population, the survey suggested guide-
lines for efficient suburban expansion, traced logical traffic patterns, laid out badly needed parklands for public recreation, and
in ten fat volumes surveyed the past and future prospects of the
nation's largest city. "Mastering a Metropolis" on paper simply
required directing its growth along the course prescribed by social scientists and city planners. Even in New York wild nature
could be preserved with careful forethought. In spite of the inevitable doubling of population, "the New Yorker of 1965" would
still be able to "answer the call of the wild and feel the thrill of
great open spaces . . . if we plan wisely now." [26]

There was an element of urgency in the Regional Planning
movement—a feeling that cities at flood tide could overrun the
countryside. Benton MacKaye, in his *New Exploration, a Philosophy of Regional Planning*, borrowed his metaphors from engineering as he pleaded for legislative control of the metropolitan
flood. Parkways and parks and public reserves were the tools he

planned to use in halting the encroachment of city on country. They would be forbidden areas legislated to channel the flow of population into practical "catch-basins"; they would be levees protecting the "indigenous environment." [27]

The new exploration moved rapidly from the old realm of what was to the realm of what could be, from mapping to planning. The explorer gave way to social scientists, economists and engineers. If parks and open spaces were dikes against the flow of urbanization, highways, to these planners, were its channels. Older cities had followed rail and trolley lines; new developments would hinge on road construction. MacKaye and other planners designed their roadways not only to move traffic but to insure that such traffic would whisk past bits of undisturbed nature that still remained.

But MacKaye, along with his friend Walter Prichard Eaton, conceived his main defense as nothing less than a "wilderness foot-path" running the whole length of the East Coast. Such a monument to outdoor life, as Eaton put it, would provide something of "the wilderness beauties, the wilderness health, the wilderness virtues, which we have so largely lost." [28] The version of such a trail that MacKaye announced in the journal of the American Institute of Architects in 1921 as "An Appalachian Trail: a Project in Regional Planning," provided for a series of public parks and open ways to cluster around the trail as a constant reminder to coastal residents that the whole world was not a city.

The nation's social planners of the 1920's left little doubt that the Arcadian mythology influenced them. Engineers hoped to remake both city and country according to its dictates. An affection for nature had become a part of the accepted way of American living. President Calvin Coolidge told delegates from 128 organizations, whom he summoned to the National Conference on Outdoor Recreation in 1924, that the right to outdoor life was as important as the right to work. Woodcraft skills should be "cultivated and cherished," he added, "like a knowledge of the humanities and the sciences." [29] Herbert Hoover explained to the

Conference convened in 1926 that "the spiritual uplift, the good will, cheerfulness, and optimism that accompanies every expedition to the outdoors is the peculiar spirit that our people need in troublous times of suspicion and doubt." Believing as he did that "man and boy, the American is a fisherman," Hoover urged that unpolluted streams be preserved as wild rivers, that restorable streams be surveyed, and that only irrecoverable waters be given to industry.[30]

In high circles and in low, as Geoffrey Scott put it, "Naturalism became the aesthetic method, and the love of Nature the most genuine emotion of our age."[31] Even so astute a critic as Henry S. Canby found the "note of woods longing" a key to American thought. Bradford Torrey, John Burroughs and Stewart Edward White were not great writers, but their popularity demonstrated to Canby that "with most Americans you reach intimacy most quickly by talking about the woods."[32] Even though they dealt with a witches' brew of bats and snakes and toads, with beetles as well as bluebirds, American nature writers made "vivid and warm and sympathetic our background of nature" and touched in some not too subtle way the great American subconscious. "Say your worst of it," Canby concluded, "still the fact remains that more Americans go back to nature for one reason or another, annually, than any civilized men before them. And more Americans, I fancy, are studying nature in clubs and public schools— or, in summer camps and the Boy Scouts . . . than even statistics could make believable."

For all their publicity and all of Canby's euphoria, however, nature lovers seemed to take themselves a bit too seriously. Whatever cause they had for bewailing the city, they were happy to earn their living there, and the country life they pictured in their essays seemed to a cosmopolitan critic like Heywood Broun, "a little too much like one of these big musical comedies—there is more beauty in it than fun."[33] John Preston noted in *The Saturday Review* that nature essayists gave to "a warbler, a hepatica, a hermit thrush, an islanded pine left from the great woods . . . a quality which is less philosophic but more immediately human"

than the concerns of much greater writers. Still, suburban shelves
were too often stocked with "canned fruit, canned vegetables,
canned music, and canned emotions." After all, he wrote, "Camp-
bell's Soup tastes the same in the wilderness as it does in some
monstrous and neurotic apartment house." He went on to conclude
with some concern:

> The wilderness is still at suburban backdoors, still deep if no
> longer wide. But the mind has changed. We are all for analyz-
> ing now, all for groping in the minds of others. The contem-
> plative mood has passed. It is the chemist with his test tube
> or the physicist with his ray who is the modern symbol of lit-
> erature. We are too much interested in our neighbors' com-
> plexes, or our own inhibitions, to be concerned with expansion
> of soul.[34]

In spite of Preston's concern, and in spite of the insistent
clamoring of social reformers, the city continued to thrive. "The
notion that the world is plunging headlong into the fatal abyss
of urbanism is a part of the creed of many for whom the country
symbolizes all that is good in life," sociologists Noel Gist and
L. A. Halbert noted in their study of "Urban Society." "While it
is true that the growth of cities has been accompanied by many
forms of maladjustment and social injustice," they added, "there
seems to be no scientific evidence that urbanism is a pathological
manifestation of a sick society . . . ."[35]

Nature worship continued in fashion in the 1920's, but the urgency with which turn-of-the-century intellectuals resisted the
city had begun to evaporate. In 1900, all of the systems by which
men classified experience had elevated nature. "Crowd psychology" and "instinct psychology" had turned intellectuals away from
the city. "Behaviorism" and "environmentalism" had praised moral
values in country life. As cities grew larger and dire catastrophes
failed to materialize, sociologists like Gist and Halbert found new
ways to rationalize the fact of city existence. "The Red God's
Call" might echo faintly in sporting magazines, but instinct psychology, with its implicit denial of urbanization, was fast becom-

ing obsolete. Recapitulation psychology, with its oppressive condemnation of urban childhood, was also giving way to more benign approaches to education. Even G. Stanley Hall was willing to admit that outdoor life was no longer a condition for human survival.

Gist and Halbert recognized urban life as a positive force. "Secondary relationships," the nemeses of early psychologists, suddenly ceased to be destructive. Impersonality no longer led to disintegration of rural mores but to increased freedom for individuals to choose the roles they wished to play. "Since the major portion of social contacts in the city are of the touch-and-go type, external appearance assumes a pronounced social value," they concluded; "because of the exaggerated emphasis on external form, many urban persons live behind a mask which conceals the real self." City dwellers learned to express their personalities by closely adhering to conventions and customs symbolic of their attitudes toward life. As Gist and Halbert concluded:

> This masquerading, posing, playing a role, gives the outward impression of hypocrisy, and to the rural person, who deliberately avoids artificiality and who cannot understand the basis of urban relationships, the metropolite is hypocritical, untrustworthy, a "slicker." Yet withal it is a natural phenomenon, a form of social adjustment that has grown out of the exigencies of urban life.

"Social ritual," as they saw it, became "at the same time a measure of exclusiveness for the social group and a mark of prestige for the individual who accepts it as part of his pattern of behavior."

Thus nature lovers found themselves behaving according to stereotyped conventions, not because their salvation depended upon it, but because certain patterns of behavior naturally accompanied the role of country squire or suburban commuter. The nature movement lingered on in corduroy hunting coats and briar pipes, in suburban barbecues and "city homes on country lanes," but the desperate vitality that electrified it in 1900 ebbed away. Nature essays appealed to magazine editors more and more for vacation editions in May and June. Yet, no matter how much overt expression might dwindle, the myth remained as a significant part of American culture. Geoffrey Scott designated as the "Biological Fallacy" the idea that institutions and ideologies must have a birth, a growth, a decline and an end. The Arcadian view of nature did not begin with Andrew Jackson Downing or Frederick Law Olmsted. Neither did it decline with the Depression. It is as popular at midcentury, if not as well articulated, as it was when Dallas Sharp, John Burroughs, James Oliver Curwood, and Gene Stratton Porter were the writers of the hour.

As John Erskine put it in 1926, "he knows little about us who overlooks our buying up of deserted farms and converting them into a refuge from something or other." [36] If Erskine and others found it difficult to describe their feeling with great precision, they were quite convinced that it was not an extension of "agrarian" values in the twentieth century. Sportsmen condemning pot-hunters, commuters shunning "natives," landscape architects planning suburban estates, summer camp directors and city tourists, all believed that rural Americans failed to appreciate the urban response to nature. Nostalgia for some remembered agricultural past played as little part in Erskine's philosophy as it did in Theodore Roosevelt's enjoyment of "Sagamore Hill" on Long Island. If the Arcadian myth was not simply a reversion to Thomas Jefferson's agrarianism, neither was it a revival of nineteenth-century "Transcendentalism." Here again, landscape architects felt they must improve on nature with axe and hoe; they must find aesthetic, not philosophical meaning in nature. Wilderness novelists and landscape photographers composed their scenes with the techniques of English Romantic artists. Churchmen agreed that nature was a Great Book, but it yielded them only good Christian parables. Suburbanites saw no inconsistency in coming face to face with nature only in John Burroughs's essays or Ernest Thompson Seton's nature-study readers. Finally, a mythology so full of urbane illusions offered poor support for any naive primitivism. The Arcadian tradition spread most widely through the mass media, but it was hardly unsophisticated. Presidents and preachers, journalists, university professors and business executives spoke for simple outdoor values that seemed attainable only through a system of unlimited complexity.

At whatever level it appeared, from nature-study classroom to the White House, the Arcadian myth embodied an urban response to nature that seemed most appropriate for an urban age. No matter how indifferently it actually transformed city life, most Americans came to link it with status and sophistication. Many adopted the role with no understanding of its intricate philosophy. Yet in so far as they believed that country life and city culture offered more in conjunction than as opposites, they seemed to welcome the contact with "Nature."

Notes

[This study has grown out of extended reading in the materials of "popular culture" which encompassed something over a thousand books and articles. For additional documentation see "Call of the Wild, the Arcadian Myth in Urban America, 1900–1930," Ph.D. dissertation, University of Minnesota, 1966.]

CHAPTER 1

1. Robert Marshall, "The Problem of the Wilderness," *Scientific Monthly*, xxx (February, 1930), p. 143.
2. Robert Dunn, "The Town Man in Camp," *Collier's Outdoor America*, xlvi (October 15, 1910), p. 29.
3. Liberty Hyde Bailey, "What This Magazine Stands For," *Country Life in America*, i (November, 1901), p. 24. For a perceptive discussion of the agrarian myth see "The Agrarian Myth and Commercial Realities," in Richard Hofstadter, *The Age of Reform* (New York, 1955).
4. In stable countries like England or Germany, Romantics could achieve, in the landscaped gardens of the gentry at least, the associations they sought—particularly when their emotions were keyed by literary allusions. In such gardens, ruined towers of painted canvas and crumbling plaster suggested man's impermanence, and strands of ivy hid his necessary intrusions, as, by act of will or hired labor, Romantics attempted to make nature conform to poetry and landscape art. Critic Geoffrey Scott suggested that Romantic literary fashion ruled the other arts in "the most extreme example of the triumph of association over direct experiences which the history of culture contains"; see *The Architecture of Humanism: a Study in the History of Taste* (London: Constable, 1914), p. 63.
5. Lewis Mumford, *The Golden Day* (New York: Boni & Liveright, 1926), p. 80.
6. Andrew Jackson Downing, "Hints to Rural Improvers," *Horticul-*

ture (July, 1848), reprinted in Downing, *Rural Essays* (New York: Leavitt, Allen, 1857), p. 111.

7. Donald G. Mitchell, *My Farm of Edgewood* (New York: Scribner's, 1894, 1st ed. 1863), pp. 258, 256.

8. *Ibid.*, p. 4; Mitchell, *Out-of-Town Places: With Hints for Their Improvements* (New York: Scribner's, 1907, 1st ed. 1867), p. 285; cf. Robert B. Roosevelt, *Five Acres Too Much* (New York: Harper, 1869), p. xvi.

9. Mitchell, *My Farm of Edgewood*, p. 83.

10. J. P. Mowbray, pseud., *A Journey to Nature* (New York: Doubleday, Page, 1901), p. 55.

11. "The Native Sons . . . ," *House and Garden*, XLVII (April, 1925), p. 62; for an early sociological study of rural-urban differences see Count R. N. Coudenhove-Kalergi, "The New Nobility," *Century*, CIX (November, 1924), pp. 3–7.

12. William H. H. Murray, *Adventures in the Wilderness: or Camp-Life in the Adirondacks* (Boston: Lee & Sheperd, 1869), p. 19.

13. Charles Dudley Warner, *In the Wilderness* (Boston: Houghton, Mifflin, Riverside Literature Series, 1905, 1st ed. 1878), p. 75.

14. Herbert produced a number of romances and historical accounts, but he is known almost entirely by the works he published as "Frank Forester."

15. Roosevelt, *Florida and Game Water Birds* (New York: Orange Judd, 1884), p. 399.

16. Lewis, *American Sportsman* (Philadelphia: Lippincott, 3rd ed. 1879, 1st ed. 1856), p. 40.

17. Lewis, *American Sportsman*, p. 86; Robert Roosevelt, *Florida and Game Water Birds*, p. 147.

18. Hornaday, *Our Vanishing Wildlife* (New York: New York Zoological Society, 1913), p. 63.

19. Murray, *Adventures in the Wilderness*, p. 38.

20. William Boardman, *The Lovers of the Woods* (New York: McClure & Phillips, 1901), p. 21.

21. Edward S. Martin, "Country Clubs and Hunt Clubs in America," in *Athletic Sports* (New York: Scribner's, Out of Door Library, 1897), p. 292.

22. *Ibid.*, p. 295.

23. Gustav Kobbe, "The Country Club and Its Influence on American Social Life," *Outlook*, LXVIII (June 1, 1901), p. 266.

24. *Ibid.*, p. 256. To Caspar Whitney it seemed "impossible to overestimate the blessing of the country club in adding comforts to country living"; see Whitney, "Evolution of the Country Club," *Harper's New Monthly Magazine*, XC (December, 1894), p. 18. By 1928, New York City's metropolitan region included one hundred fifty-nine clubs offering some twenty thousand landscaped acres to nearly fifty-two thousand members; see Lee F. Hanmer,

Public Recreation, Regional Plan of New York and Its Environs, v (New York: RPNYE, 1928), p. 240.

25. Claude P. Fordyce, *Touring Afoot,* Outing Handbook No. 52 (New York: Outing Publishing Company, 1916), p. 9; Bliss Carman, *The Making of Personality* (Boston: L. C. Page, 1908), p. 315.

26. Emerson Hough, "Deathless Heathen," *Reader,* vii (April, 1906), p. 532.

27. Theodore Roosevelt to "Needham," July 19, 1905, in Theodore Roosevelt Papers, box 150, Library of Congress.

28. Theodore Roosevelt, *A Book-Lover's Holidays in the Open* (New York: Scribner's, 1926, 1st ed. 1916), pp. vii, viii.

29. James G. Needham, "Outdoor Equipment," *Nature-Study Review,* x (March, 1914), p. 94.

30. Austin Carey, "Forestry Policy of Typical States—New York," *Annals of the American Academy,* xxxv (March, 1910), p. 251.

31. Gifford Pinchot, "Forest Destruction," *Annual Report of the Board of Regents of the Smithsonian Institute for 1901,* pp. 404, 401.

32. Frank A. Waugh, "Conservation Ad Absurdum," *Scientific Monthly,* xvii (November, 1923), pp. 501, 498.

33. Emerson Hough, "The Slaughter of the Trees," *Everybody's Magazine,* xviii (May, 1908), p. 579.

34. The "pillow-tent" was only one of several devices described in "Sleeping Outdoors in the House," *Ladies' Home Journal,* xxv (September, 1908), p. 27.

35. Primary commuter lines like the Long Island Railroad, with its "Sunrise Homeland" campaign, provided some of the most persuasive literature in the Arcadian tradition. Henry H. Richardson's Romanesque stations set in grounds designed by Frederick Law Olmsted, Sr., provided prototypes for many suburban stations emerging as "the real civic centers of the suburbanite."

36. William F. Dix, "The Automobile as a Vacation Agent," *Independent,* lvi (June 2, 1904), p. 1256; Eugene A. Clancy, "The Car and the Country Home," *Harper's Weekly,* lv (May 6, 1911), p. 30.

37. John Erskine, "A House in the Country," *Century,* cxii (July, 1926), p. 374.

38. See "The Making of a Country Home," *Country Life in America,* i (April, 1902), p. 201; Edward Powell, *The Country Home* (New York: McClure, Phillips, 1904), p. 14. Landscape philosopher John C. Van Dyke held that beauty lay only in "wildness," but he recognized the abandoned farm as the commuter's alternative. "Very commonplace is the ten-acre pasture," he wrote, "with its small knolls, its tufts of tall grass, its smooth-cropped inter-spaces, its wild-flowers, and its ivy-wound fence of stone; yet in this patched irregularity there is a whole world of loveliness"; *Nature for Its Own Sake, First Studies in Natural Appearances* (New York: Scribner's, 1898), p. 282.

39. Truman DeWeese, *The Bend in the Road and How a Man of the City Found It* (New York: Harper, 1913), p. 14.
40. Clancy, "The Car and the Country House," p. 30.
41. Liberty Bailey, *The Country-Life Movement in the United States* (New York: MacMillan, 1911), p. 17.
42. "Successful Houses," *House Beautiful*, v (May, 1899), p. 267.
43. J. C. Nichols, "Real Estate Subdivisions," American Civic Association Bulletin, Series II, No. 5 (November, 1912), p. 6.
44. "Belle-Terre," *Country Life in America*, IV (September, 1903), pp. 351–352. Many residential colonies were similar to the "Heathcote Association" near Scarsdale. Heathcote organized in 1901 with nine "colonists" and hired an engineer to lay out three- to fifteen-acre building sites on 130 acres of abandoned farm land. All agreed in 1904 that the social advantages of such a colony made it better in all respects than "a crowded suburban community." See Philip Colt, "The Making of a Suburban Colony," *Country Life in America*, VI (August, 1904), p. 350; cf. Colt, "A Cooperative Country Colony," *ibid.* (July, 1904), p. 250; "An Inexpensive Vacation Club in the Country," *ibid.* (May, 1904), p. 84; Miles Roberts, "The 'Abandoned Farm' Club," *ibid.*, x (June, 1906), p. 176.
45. Henry H. Moore, "Country Club and the Abandoned Farm," *Outlook*, CXI (September 22, 1915), p. 203.
46. Dallas Lore Sharp, *The Lay of the Land* (Boston: Houghton, Mifflin, 1908), p. 118.

CHAPTER 2

1. Olmsted, Vaux and Company, *Preliminary Report upon the Proposed Suburban Village at Riverside, Near Chicago* (New York: Sutton, Browne, 1868), pp. 5, 7.
2. H. A. Caparn, "Parallelogram Park—Suburban Life by the Square Mile," *Craftsman*, x (September, 1906), pp. 767–774.
3. "Rapid Transit and Home Life," *Harper's Bazaar*, XXXIII (December, 1900), p. 2003.
4. Grace Goodwin, "The Commuter's Wife," *Good Housekeeping*, XLIX (October, 1909), pp. 362, 363.
5. Review of J. P. Mowbray [pseud. for Andrew Carpenter Wheeler], "A Journey to Nature," as quoted by Doubleday, Page in *Country Life in America*, II (August, 1902), p. xc. The charmingly superficial essays which called out this praise first appeared in the New York *Evening Post*. They purported to be notes of a stock-broker sent to the hills by his physician to begin a monastic communion with nature in a rustic hovel a hundred miles from New York. There he tried on the simple life with a blue flannel shirt and a pair of baseball shoes, whistling an operatic air while his hired neighbor stood by to help with chores.

6. Dallas Lore Sharp, *The Face of the Fields* (Boston: Houghton, Mifflin, 1911), p. 228.

7. Sharp, *The Hills of Hingham* (Boston: Houghton, Mifflin, 1916), p. 19.

8. Sharp, *The Seer of Slabsides* (Boston: Houghton, Mifflin, 1921), p. 56.

9. Sharp, "The Nature Writer," *Outlook*, xciv (April 30, 1910), p. 955.

10. Sharp, *Lay of the Land*, pp. 121, 70, 72.

11. Sharp, *Face of the Fields*, pp. 85, 86.

12. Louise C. Willcox, "Outdoor Books," *North American Review*, clxxxiii (July, 1906), p. 119. See also Mabel Osgood Wright, "Life Outdoors and Its Effect upon Literature," *Critic*, xlii (April, 1903), p. 310.

13. Sharp, *Seer of Slabsides*, p. 33.

14. John Burroughs, *Far and Near* (Boston: Houghton, Mifflin, 1904), p. 132.

15. Clara Barrus, *Our Friend John Burroughs* (Boston: Houghton, Mifflin, 1914), pp. 199, 201.

16. Mabel Osgood Wright, *The Garden of a Commuter's Wife* (New York: MacMillan, 1903), p. 181.

17. Sharp, *Seer of Slabsides*, pp. 48, 50.

18. Samuel Schmucker, *The Study of Nature* (Philadelphia: Lippincott, 1928, 1st ed. 1908), p. 50.

19. Quoted in Barrus, *Our Friend John Burroughs*, p. 129.

20. Burroughs, *Birds and Poets*, Writings of John Burroughs, iii (Boston: Houghton, Mifflin, 1904), p. 58.

21. Roosevelt to Burroughs, May 4, 1906, in the Theodore Roosevelt Papers, box 153; Burroughs to Dallas Lore Sharp, Nov. 18, 1920, in the Sharp Papers, Boston University.

22. Frost to Eaton, July 15, 1915, in the Eaton Papers, University of Virginia.

23. Sullivan to Eaton, March 3, 1917, in the Eaton Papers.

24. Frances K. Hutchinson, *Our Country Home: How We Transformed a Wisconsin Woodland* (Chicago: McClurg, 1908, 1st ed. 1907).

25. *Our Country Home*, pp. 2, 7, 18, 42, 84.

26. Hutchinson, *Our Country Life* (Chicago: McClurg, 1912), p. 33.

27. Dorothy Canfield Fisher, "Why Don't I Live Somewhere Else," *American Magazine*, ci (May, 1926), p. 37; Grant Overton, *Authors of the Day* (New York: George Doran, 1922), p. 114.

28. *World's Work*, iv (October, 1902), pp. 2603–2611.

29. Mrs. Theodore Thomas, *Our Mountain Garden* (New York: MacMillan, 1904), pp. 32, 85, 24.

30. "Fine Country Estates," *House Beautiful*, x (November, 1901), 333.

31. Maurice Thompson, *My Winter Garden* (New York: Century, 1900), p. 103.

32. E. P. Powell, "Down the Valley," *Independent*, lxv (September 24, 1908), p. 689.

33. E. P. Powell, *The Country Home* (New York: McClure, Phillips, 1904), frontispiece.
34. Caspar Whitney, "What We Stand For," Outdoor America Section, *Collier's Weekly*, XLII (March 13, 1909), p. 15.
35. *Country Life in America*, v (November, 1903), pp. 31–34.
36. Leonidas Hubbard, Jr., "Country Homes on Long Island; Where Weary Men Find Rest," *Outing*, XXXVII (January, 1902), 342.
37. "Back to Nature," *Outlook*, LXXIV (June 6, 1903), 305.
38. "What This Magazine Stands For," *Country Life in America*, I (November, 1901), 24.
39. Theodore Roosevelt's address as quoted in *Homes of Doubleday, Doran and Company, Inc.* (Garden City, 1930), n.p.
40. *The Country Life Press* (Garden City: Doubleday, Page, 1913), pp. 54, 18; Louise Green, "A Nature Creed in the Concrete," *Nature-Study Review*, VII (October, 1911), p. 187.
41. Edwin E. Slosson, "Back to Nature? Never! Forward to the Machine," *Independent*, CI (January 3, 1920), p. 38; Lyman Abbott, "Letters to Unknown Friends," *Outlook*, CI (June 22, 1912), pp. 382–383.
42. Walter Dyer, "This Farm of Mine, I Want to be a Countryman," *Century*, CXIV (October, 1927), p. 739.
43. Edith L. and H. B. Fullerton, "Discovering a Country Home: How We Abandoned a City Flat, Tried a Rented House in the Suburbs, and Found Happiness in the Real Country," *Country Life in America*, IV (June, 1903), p. 739.
44. Sharp, *Lay of the Land*, p. 125.
45. "Going Into the Country," as reprinted in *Living Age*, CCXCIV (July 14, 1917), pp. 113, 114, 115.

CHAPTER 3

1. Philip Hicks, *The Development of the Natural History Essay in American Literature*, Ph.D. thesis, University of Pennsylvania (Philadelphia, 1924), p. 40.
2. Edith Patch, *Bird Stories* (Chicago: E. M. Hale, original copyright, Atlantic Monthly Press, 1921), pp. 1, 17.
3. As late as 1917, when T. Gilbert Pearson of the Audubon Society put together his monumental *Birds of America*, many species still carried a string of local or regional nicknames.
4. Theodore Roosevelt's son wrote of a bayman who identified his ring-necked plover as "one of them 'sand peeps.' Our father and mother took care," he added, "that we did not grow up blind in this way," as quoted in H. A. Haring, ed., *The Slabsides Book of John Burroughs* (Boston: Houghton, Mifflin, 1931), p. 139.
5. Frank M. Chapman, *Fifty Years of American Ornithology* (New York: American Ornithologists' Union, 1933), p. 203.
6. Mabel O. Wright and Elliot Coues, *Citizen Bird: Scenes from Bird*

Life in Plain English for Beginners (New York: MacMillan, 1897).

7. Neltje Blanchan Doubleday, *Bird Neighbors* (New York: Doubleday, McClure, 1897); Jenny H. Stickney, *Bird World, a Bird Book for Children* (Boston: Ginn & Co., 1898); Sara V. Prueser, *Our Dooryard Friends* (Chicago: the Platform, 1915); Gilbert Trafton, *Bird Friends* (Boston: Houghton, Mifflin, 1916); S. Louise Patteson, *How To Have Bird Neighbors* (Boston: D. C. Heath, 1917).

8. J. W. Muller, *First Aid to Naturers* (New York: Platt, Peck, 1913), p. 83.

9. Sharp, *Where Rolls the Oregon* (Boston: Houghton, Mifflin, 1914), p. 196.

10. See, for example, Charles Abbott, *Bird-land Echoes* (Philadelphia: Lippincott, 1896), p. 22.

11. *Bird Stories*, pp. 16, 3. Even John Burroughs called the chickadee "a truly Emersonian bird . . . . Hardy, active, social . . . with a note the most cheering and reassuring to be heard in our January woods," in *Birds and Poets*, Writings of John Burroughs, III (Boston: Houghton, Mifflin, 1904), p. 39.

12. *Bird Stories*, pp. 18, 40.

13. Walter B. Barrows, *The English Sparrow in North America . . .* (Washington: Government Printing Office, 1889), p. 34. Cf. Samuel Schmucker, *The Meaning of Evolution* (New York: MacMillan, 1913), pp. 62–86.

14. Ernest Thompson Seton, *Lives of the Hunted* (New York: Scribner's, 1901), p. 109.

15. Henry Van Dyke, *Fisherman's Luck* (New York: Scribner's, 1899), p. 57.

16. Barrows, *English Sparrow*, pp. 107, 121.

17. *Ibid.*, p. 150.

18. *Ibid.*, p. 39.

19. Included in three feather sales on the London Market in 1911 were 41,000 hummingbird skins and the plumes of some 129,000 egrets according to William Hornaday, *Our Vanishing Wildlife* (New York: New York Zoological Society, 1913), p. 121.

20. The Wild Flower Preservation Society, for example, was founded in 1902. In 1930, it claimed 10,000 adult and 100,000 junior members.

21. "How One Man Secured a Law in Thirty-two States," *World's Work*, XII (October, 1906), p. 8138. Without widespread support, however, such laws were unevenly effective. In North Carolina, for example, the Society had the powers of a State Game Commission, but in such states as Virginia, which passed the model law in 1903, funds to enforce it were unavailable.

22. Stanton Davis Kirkham, *Outdoor Philosophy, the Meditations of a Naturalist* (New York: Putnam's, 1912), p. 77.

CHAPTER 4

1. John Burroughs, *Wake-Robin* (Boston: Houghton, Mifflin, 1904, 1st ed. 1871), 1895 preface, p. xiv.
2. Burroughs, *Ways of Nature* (Boston: Houghton, Mifflin, 1905), p. 15; *Leaf and Tendril* (Boston: Houghton, Mifflin, 1908), p. 103.
3. Sharp, "Out-of-doors from Labrador to Africa," *Critic*, xlviii (February, 1906), p. 121.
4. Ernest Thompson Seton, *Trail of an Artist-Naturalist* (New York: Scribner's, 1940), pp. 352, 99.
5. Seton, *Lives of the Hunted* (New York: Scribner's, 1901), p. 9.
6. Roberts, *Kindred of the Wild* (Boston: L. C. Page, 1902), pp. 24, 29.
7. Seton, *Lives of the Hunted*, p. 9; Roberts, *Kindred of the Wild*, p. 24.
8. Wright, "Nature as a Field for Fiction," *The New York Times Book Review* (December 19, 1905), p. 872.
9. Burroughs, "Real and Sham Natural History," *Atlantic Monthly*, xci (March, 1903), pp. 298–301.
10. Burroughs, *Ways of Nature*, p. 101.
11. Burroughs, *Leaf and Tendril*, p. 101.
12. For a balanced discussion of personalities involved see Mark Sullivan, *Our Times*, iii (New York: Scribner's, 1930), pp. 146–162.
13. William J. Long, *School of the Woods* (Boston: Ginn, 1902), p. 21.
14. William J. Long, "The Modern School of Nature-Study and Its Critics," *North American Review*, clxxvi (May, 1903), p. 691.
15. *Wood Folk at School*, Wood Folk Series, Book iv (Boston: Ginn, 1902), p. vi.
16. Roosevelt to John Burroughs, June 11, 1903, in Roosevelt Papers, box 145; Roosevelt to Burroughs, June 8, 1907, box 156; Roosevelt to Burroughs, June 2, 1907, box 156. From 1903 to 1911, Roosevelt's private correspondence shows repeated irritation with Long.
17. Ellen Hayes, "The Writings of William J. Long," *Science*, n.s. xix (April 15, 1904), p. 626.
18. Long, "Modern School of Nature-Study," p. 688.
19. William J. Long, "Animal Surgery," *Outlook*, lxxv (September 12, 1903), pp. 126, 125.
20. Long, "Modern School of Nature-Study," p. 692.
21. Long, "Animal Surgery," p. 126.
22. See, for example, William M. Wheeler, "Woodcock Surgery," *Science*, n.s. xix (February 26, 1904), p. 349.
23. *Ways of Nature*, p. 147.
24. Frank Chapman, "The Case of William J. Long," *Science*, n.s. xix (March 4, 1904), p. 387.
25. William J. Long, "Science, Nature, and Criticism," *Science*, n.s. xix (May 13, 1904), p. 762.

26. Roosevelt, "Nature Fakers," *Everybody's Magazine*, xvii (September, 1907), p. 428.
27. William J. Long, *Northern Trails* (Boston: Ginn, 1905), p. 16; Roosevelt to C. Hart Merriam, June 8, 1907, in the Roosevelt Papers, box 156.
28. Roosevelt, "Nature Fakers," 430. Long replied to Roosevelt immediately. "Your high position gives weight even to your foolish words," he warned on May 22, 1907, "and for the sake of truth, and of the thousands who read and love my books, I am obliged to answer you publically." On May 29, he mailed proof sheets of the open letter he was offering to major newspapers across the country. In it he portrayed Roosevelt as a bloodthirsty killer, himself as a Natty Bumppo. "For him to produce eyewitnesses of his feats is easy," he wrote, "for he goes into the woods with dogs, horses, guides, followers, men servants, reporters and a camera man. For myself, it is more difficult, for I go alone into the woods, follow the animals silently, never kill unless in need of food, and spend many weeks each year in the solitude of the wilderness"; see Roosevelt Papers, box 120.
29. Long, *Northern Trails*, p. 217.
30. *Ibid.*, p. 214.
31. Long, "Science, Nature, and Criticism," p. 763.
32. Hornaday to Roosevelt, May 19, 1907, in the Roosevelt Papers, box 120.
33. Charles Daniels, "Discord in the Forest," Boston *Evening Transcript* (March 7, 1903), p. 23.
34. Wright, "Life Outdoors and Its Effect Upon Literature," *Critic*, xlii (April, 1903), p. 311.
35. Sharp, "Out-of-doors from Labrador to Africa," p. 122.
36. "Criticism of Connecticut Naturalists," *Connecticut Magazine*, vii (No. 1, 1903), p. 147.
37. Burroughs, "Real and Sham Natural History," p. 306.
38. Typescript copy addressed to Theodore Roosevelt, June 11, 1907, in the Roosevelt Papers, box 120.

CHAPTER 5

1. Andrew Jackson Downing, *A Treatise on the Theory and Practice of Landscape Gardening* (New York: Orange Judd, 8th ed. 1859), p. 67.
2. See Frederick Law Olmsted, Jr., "Landscape Design," in *Significance of the Fine Arts* (Boston: Marshall Jones, 1923), p. 328; cf. Downing, *Theory and Practice of Landscape Gardening*, p. 74.
3. Olmsted, "Landscape Design," p. 329.
4. Henry Vincent Hubbard and Theodora Kimball, *An Introduction to the Study of Landscape Design* (New York: MacMillan, 1938, 1st ed. 1917), p. 58.

5. Frederick Law Olmsted, Jr. and Theodora Kimball, *Frederick Law Olmsted, Landscape Architect, 1822–1903* (New York: Putnam's, 1922), p. 70; Charles W. Eliot, Sr., *Charles Eliot, Landscape Architect, a Lover of Nature and of His Kind Who Trained Himself for a New Profession* . . . (Boston: Houghton Mifflin, 1902), p. 219. Even as late as 1915, Samuel Parsons laced together with modern examples the Romantic theories of Thomas Whately, Sir Humphrey Repton and the German designer, Puckler-Muskau, in *The Art of Landscape Architecture* (New York: Putnam's, 1915), p. vii.

6. Sir Uvedale Price, *An Essay on the Picturesque as Compared with the Sublime and the Beautiful: And on the Use of Studying Pictures, for the Purpose of Improving Real Landscape* (London: J. Robson, 1794, 1798), vol. I, pp. 11, 10, xv.

7. Reverend William Gilpin, *Remarks on Forest Scenery, and Other Woodland Views (Relative Chiefly to Picturesque Beauty)* . . . (London: R. Blamire, 1791), vol. I, i; Price, *Essay on the Picturesque*, p. 29.

8. Gilpin, *Remarks on Forest Scenery*, p. 9.

9. Mrs. Schuyler Van Rensselaer, *Art Out-of-Doors: Hints on Good Taste in Gardening* (New York: Scribner's, 1893), p. 358.

10. As quoted in Olmsted, *Frederick Law Olmsted*, p. 68.

11. Frank A. Waugh, *The Natural Style in Landscape Gardening* (Boston: R. G. Badger, 1917), pp. 55, 59.

12. Hubbard, *Introduction to the Study of Landscape Design*, pp. 78, 56, 16.

13. Eliot, *Charles Eliot, Landscape Architect*, p. 50.

14. Eliot to the editor of *Garden and Forest*, February 13, 1889, as quoted in Eliot, *Charles Eliot*, p. 262.

15. Herbert Kellaway, *How to Lay Out Suburban Home Grounds* (New York: J. Wiley, 1907), p. 70.

16. *Ibid.*, p. 52.

17. Linnie Marsh Wolfe, *Son of the Wilderness: The Life of John Muir* (New York: Knopf, 1945), p. 278.

18. Quoted in Parsons, *Art of Landscape Architecture*, p. 159.

19. Mrs. Schuyler Van Rensselaer, "A Suburban Country Place," *Century*, LIV (May, 1897), pp. 3, 12, 14.

20. Wilhelm Miller, "The Sargent Home Near Boston," *Country Life in America*, III (March, 1903), p. 201.

21. J. Wilkinson Elliott, "Flowers by the Ten Thousand," *Country Life in America*, VI (September, 1904), p. 405.

22. Frances K. Hutchinson, *Our Country Life* (Chicago: McClurg, 1912), p. 22.

23. James J. Allen, "An Experience with the Soil: Wild Gardening in Little—the Trials of a Suburbanite and the Rewards," *Country Life in America*, I (February, 1902), p. 131.

24. *Art Out-of-Doors*, p. 313.

25. Samuel Parsons, *How to Plan the Home Grounds* (New York: Doubleday, McClure, 1899), p. 45.
26. Charles Eliot, "The Need of Conserving the Beauty and Freedom of Nature in Modern Life," *National Geographic,* XXVI (July, 1914), p. 69.

CHAPTER 6

1. "State and Prospects of Horticulture," *Horticulture* (December, 1851), as quoted in Andrew Jackson Downing, *Rural Essays* (New York: Leavitt, Allen, 1857), p. 81.
2. As quoted in Henry Vincent Hubbard and Theodora Kimball, *An Introduction to the Study of Landscape Design* (New York: Mac-Millan, 1938, 1st ed. 1917), p. 1.
3. Charles Eliot, "The Need of Parks," as quoted in Charles Eliot, Sr., *Charles Eliot, Landscape Architect* . . . (Boston: Houghton Mifflin, 1902), pp. 339, 341.
4. Eliot, *Charles Eliot,* p. 655.
5. Louis Windmuller, "Disposal of the Dead in Cities," *Municipal Affairs,* VI (Fall, 1902), p. 474.
6. "An American Idea in Landscape Art," *Country Life in America,* IV (September, 1903), p. 349.
7. Ossian Simonds, *Landscape Gardening,* in L. H. Bailey Rural Science Series (New York: MacMillan, 1920), p. 299.
8. "An American Idea in Landscape Art," p. 349.
9. Bayley Smith, "An Outdoor Room on a Cemetery Lot," *Country Life in America,* XVII (March, 1910), p. 539.
10. Ossian Simonds, "The Planning and Administration of a Landscape Cemetery," *Country Life in America,* IV (September, 1903), p. 350.
11. Nathaniel Shaler, "The Landscape as a Means of Culture," *Atlantic Monthly,* LXXXII (December, 1898), p. 777.
12. Hubbard, *Introduction to the Study of Landscape Design,* p. 299.
13. *Ibid.,* p. 69. In the flowing irregularity of the pasture motif, landscape philosopher John C. Van Dyke found "a whole world of loveliness. The quaint lines, the warmth and glow of color, and above all, the broad area of sunlight, affect one emotionally. Take any man from the bustle of the city and place him there and he will instinctively breathe deeper, and though he may say little, yet be sure he is making confession in his secret soul," *Nature for Its Own Sake, First Studies in Natural Appearances* (New York: Scribner's, 1898), p. 282.
14. "A Proposed Speed-road in Central Park," *Garden and Forest,* I (March 21, 1888), p. 38.
15. In 1928, the National Recreation Association found 248,627 acres of parks in 15,702 American towns. Cities of 5,000 or more numbered ten per cent of the total, but they controlled ninety-six per

cent of the park land. See *Park Recreation in the United States*
(Washington: Government Printing Office, 1928), p. 18.

16. "American Cities and Public Open Spaces," *Charities,* xvi (July
7, 1906), p. 424.

17. "American Civic Association," American Park and Outdoor Art
Association and American League for Civic Improvement, joint
issue, *Bulletin Number 1* (n.p., n.d.).

18. J. Horace McFarland, *The Awakening of Harrisburg* (Harrisburg:
n.p., 1906), pp. 2, 8.

19. See Lee F. Hanmer, *Public Recreation,* Regional Plan of New York
and Its Environs, v (New York: RPNYE, 1928), p. 41.

20. Charles Eliot, "The Need of Conserving the Beauty and Freedom
of Nature in Modern Life," *National Geographic,* xxvi (July,
1914), p. 67.

21. Samuel Parsons, Jr., *The Art of Landscape Architecture* (New
York: Putnam's, 1915), p. 274.

22. Eliot, "Parks and Squares of United States Cities," as quoted in
Eliot, *Charles Eliot,* p. 305.

23. Joseph Lee, "Play as Landscape," *Charities,* xvi (July 7, 1906),
pp. 430, 427, 432.

24. Joseph Lee, *Constructive and Preventive Philanthropy* (New York:
MacMillan, 1902), pp. 166, 123.

25. Lee, "Play as Landscape," p. 431. U.S. Commissioner of Education
Elmer Elsworth Brown insisted in 1907 that "the most beautiful
thing of all in our public parks today is a lot of children hard at
play where there is room to play and nobody cares whether the
grass grows or not"; see "Health, Morality and the Playground,"
Playground Association of America, *Proceedings,* 1 (August, 1907),
p. 30.

26. For an institutional history of the playground movement see Clar-
ence E. Rainwater's Ph.D. dissertation in sociology, *The Play
Movement in the United States* (Chicago: University of Chicago
Press, 1922), 371 pp.

27. Luther Gulick, "Play and Democracy," Playground Association of
America, *Proceedings,* 1 (August, 1907), p. 12.

28. Henry S. Curtis, "Playground Progress and Tendencies of the
Year," Playground Association of America, *Proceedings,* 1 (August,
1907), p. 27.

29. National Recreation Association, *Rural and Small Community
Recreation* (New York: Playground and Recreation Association
of America, 1929), pp. 7, 36, *passim.*

30. Graham R. Taylor, "How They Played at Chicago," Playground
Association of America, *Proceedings,* 1 (August, 1907), p. 3; National Recreation Association, *Park Recreation Areas,* p. 49.

31. Olmsted, "Landscape Design," p. 331; cf. Weir, *Parks: A Manual
of Municipal and Country Parks* (New York: Barnes, 1923), vol.
1, p. xix.

CHAPTER 7

1. Francis Parker, "The Child," *Addresses and Proceedings of the National Education Association*, 1889, p. 480.
2. Granville Stanley Hall, "The Contents of Children's Minds on Entering School," *Pedagogical Seminary*, I (1891), pp. 146–150, 155, 156. Hall cited a Kansas City study done in 1883 which showed, though few educators seemed to recognize it, that children mastered adult preoccupations and verbal awareness during their first year of school.
3. *Ibid.*, 155.
4. Hall, "The Natural Activities of Children," *Addresses and Proceedings of the National Education Association*, 1904, p. 445.
5. Hall, *Adolescence* (New York: Appleton, 1904), I, p. 202.
6. *Ibid.*, I, p. 207. See also Luther Halsey Gulick, "Some Psychical Aspects of Muscular Exercise," *Popular Science Monthly*, LIII (October, 1898), pp. 793–805; a serious and thoroughly reasoned study by a well-known playground psychologist.
7. Hall, "Natural Activities of Children," p. 446.
8. Hall, *Adolescence*, I, p. xi; II, pp. 215, 216.
9. *Ibid.*, I, pp. xv, xiv.
10. Francis Parker, "The Child," *Addresses and Proceedings of the National Education Association*, 1889, p. 479.
11. Hall, *Adolescence*, I, pp. xi, x.
12. Hall, Introduction to Clifton F. Hodge, *Nature Study and Life* (Boston: Ginn & Co., 1902), p. xv.
13. Liberty Hyde Bailey's *The Nature Study Idea* (New York: Doubleday, Page, 1903) was not popular as a text, but it is the best coverage of the sentiment and pedagogic theory of nature-study.
14. J. G. Wood, *The Common Objects of the Country* (London: Routledge, 14th ed. 1892), p. 109.
15. Barney Standish, *Common Things with Common Eyes: An Illustrated Course of Nature Study for Schools, about Insects, Fishes, Quadrupeds, Flowers, Trees and Birds* (Minneapolis: Standish and Standish, 1897), pref., p. 15.
16. Dietrich Lange, *Handbook of Nature Study: For Teachers and Pupils in Elementary Schools* (New York: MacMillan, 1902, 1st ed. 1898), pp. 132, 135.
17. John C. Wilson, *How to Study Nature in Elementary Schools* (Syracuse: C. W. Bardeen, 1900), p. 36.
18. Charles Scott, *Nature Study and the Child* (Boston: Heath, 1900), pp. 126, 185.
19. Ira B. Meyer, "The Evolution of Aim and Method in the Teaching of Nature-Study in the Common Schools of the United States," *Elementary School Teacher*, I (December, 1910), p. 245.
20. Bailey, *Nature Study Idea*, p. 121. Anna B. Comstock, his colleague at Cornell University, argued forcefully if circuitously that

"adventures with animals may always be read with safety, as these do not, strictly speaking, belong to nature-study. They belong rather to literature and may be used most successfully to interest the child in nature," "Suggestions for Nature-Study Work," in *Cornell Nature-Study Leaflets . . .* (Albany: J. B. Lyons, 1904), p. 55. A decade later, however, Comstock referred to this period as the "cute and fluffy" stage which "rendered soggy" the whole curriculum; see "The Growth and Influence of the Nature-Study Idea," p. 11.

21. Bailey, *Nature Study Idea*, pp. 21, 87.
22. Clifton F. Hodge, *Nature Study and Life*, pp. vii, xvi.
23. W. G. Latta, "Agriculture in the Public Schools," *Nature-Study Review*, III (February, 1907), p. 45.
24. Mary C. Dickerson, "Nature-Study in City Primary Schools," *Nature-Study Review*, II (March, 1906), p. 100.
25. Francis Parker, "The Farm As the Center of Interest," *NEA Report of the Committee of Twelve on Rural Schools* (Chicago, 1897), pp. 152–161.
26. Lida McMurray, *Nature Study Lessons for Primary Grades* (New York: MacMillan, 1905), p. ix. See also Frank Owen Payne, *One Hundred Lessons in Nature Study Around My School* (New York: E. L. Kellogg, 1895), p. 3; Margaret Ahearne, "Nature-Study in the Gary Schools," *Nature-Study Review*, XI (February, 1915), pp. 59–63.

CHAPTER 8

1. Porter E. Sargent, *A Handbook of American Private Schools* (Boston: Sargent, 1918), pp. 181, 173; also pp. 159, 160, 609.
2. John M. Coulter, John G. Coulter, Alice Patterson, *Practical Nature Study and Elementary Agriculture: A Manual for the Use of Teachers and Normal Students* (New York: D. Appleton, 1909), pp. 12, 26, vii, 5.
3. Maurice Bigelow, "Training Teachers of Nature-Study: A Series of Reports from Many Normal Schools and Colleges," *Nature-Study Review*, II (April, 1906), p. 121.
4. Maurice Bigelow, "The Established Principles of Nature-Study," *ibid.*, 4.
5. J. V. Crone, "True Nature-Study: Its Fundamentals, and Its Relation to Some Other Subjects," *Nature-Study Review*, II (May, 1906), p. 184.
6. Clifton Hodge, "Nature-Study and Its Relation to Natural Science," *Nature-Study Review*, III (January, 1907), 7.
7. Samuel Schmucker, *The Study of Nature* (Philadelphia: Lippincott, 1928, 1st ed. 1908), pp. 9, 59. See also Schmucker, "Science and Nature-Study," *Nature-Study Review*, XIV (February, 1918), pp. 50, 52.

8. Anna B. Comstock, "What Nature-Study Does for the Child and for the Teacher," *Nature-Study Review*, VII (May, 1911), p. 134.
9. Dallas Lore Sharp, *The Lay of the Land* (Boston: Houghton, Mifflin, 1908), p. 214.
10. Sharp, *Ways of the Woods*, Riverside Literature Series (Boston: Houghton, Mifflin, 1912).
11. Stanley Coulter, "The Field Trip in Nature-Study," *Nature-Study Review*, II (October, 1906), p. 231.
12. Dickerson, "Nature-Study in City Primary Schools," *Nature-Study Review*, II (March, 1906), p. 102.
13. Frank Owen Payne, *One Hundred Lessons in Nature Study Around My School* (New York: Kellogg, 1895), p. 186.
14. Maurice Bigelow, "Are Children Naturally Naturalists?" *Nature-Study Review*, II (November, 1907), p. 237.
15. John Brittain, *Elementary Agriculture and Nature Study* (Toronto: Educational Book Company, 1909), p. 148.
16. Winterburn, *Methods in Teaching: Being the Stockton Methods in Elementary Schools* (New York: MacMillan, 1908), p. 173.
17. C. A. Stebbins, "Correlation in Nature-Study," *Nature-Study Review*, V (September, 1909), p. 156.
18. H. D. Hemenway, "School-Gardens at the School of Horticulture, Hartford, Connecticut," *Nature-Study Review*, I (January, 1905), p. 36.
19. Nellie Salton, "Spring Day in the Children's Greenhouse," *Nature-Study Review*, X (May, 1914), p. 185.
20. Hodge, *Nature Study and Life*, pp. 132, 10.
21. C. A. Stebbins, "Correlation in Nature-Study," 157.
22. Fannie G. Parsons, "A Day at the Children's School Farm in New York City," *Nature-Study Review*, I (November, 1905), p. 255.
23. Quoted in Maria Greene, *Among School Gardens* (New York: Charities Publications Committee, 1910), p. 4.
24. R. J. Floody, "Worcester Garden City Plan: Or, the Good Citizens' Factory," *Nature-Study Review*, VIII (April, 1912), p. 145.
25. Alice V. Joyce, "The School Garden a Laboratory for Industrial Education," *Nature-Study Review*, XI (November, 1915), p. 362.
26. Alice Patterson, "Educational Values of Children's Gardens," *Nature-Study Review*, XII (March, 1916), pp. 126, 127.
27. "The United States School Garden Army," *Nature-Study Review*, XV (March, 1919), p. 102.
28. Ira Meyer, "Evolution of Aim and Method in Nature Study . . . ," *Elementary School Teacher*, XI (December, 1910), p. 212. "The stints become monotonous, mechanical, factory work to the pupil," wrote G. Stanley Hall, "but to the teacher they acquire an excessive value, as if the world of knowledge had been canonized and certain things set apart," *Adolescence*, II, p. 509.
29. Van Evrie Kilpatrick, "Neglect of Nature-Study," *Journal of Education*, CXI (May 12, 1930), p. 528. As the National Recreation

Association concluded in 1933, "the state of nature study in the schools is still cause for much weeping and wailing. The need of it is not yet widely recognized though city dwellers stand to lose something precious in the face of growing cities and disappearance therein of so much that makes up the nature world. Nature lovers cannot be made out of the content of books; either nature must be brought to people or they must go where nature is if they are to learn much about it, and too few schools do either of these things as yet." See *The New Leisure Challenges the Schools: Shall Recreation Enrich or Impoverish Life?* (Washington: National Education Association, 1933), p. 266.

30. Hodge, "Learning Disease Prevention in School, the House Fly as a Practical Lesson," *Nature-Study Review*, IX (November, 1913), pp. 245–250; Comstock, "The Bracket Fungus, a Lesson in Civic Duty," *ibid.*, pp. 236–239.

31. Kate Douglas Wiggin and Nora A. Smith, *Kindergarten Principles and Practice* (Boston: Houghton, Mifflin, 1896), p. 23.

32. Louise K. Miller, *Children's Gardens for School and Home, a Manual for Cooperative Gardening* (New York: Appleton, 1904), p. 99.

33. Alice R. Northrop, "Flower Shows in City Schools," *Nature-Study Review*, I (May, 1905), 106. Such children were sufficiently isolated from country experience that their nature-study had little meaning. A "woolly bear" caterpillar shown to several, Northrop reported, was called a frog, a lizard, a snake, a grasshopper, and a worm, but when told that it was a caterpillar, every child answered that it would turn into a chrysalis and emerge a moth or a butterfly.

34. Quoted in Clara Barrus, *Our Friend John Burroughs* (Boston: Houghton, Mifflin, 1914), p. 82.

35. Harold Fairbanks, *Conservation Reader* (New York: World Book Co., 1920), p. iii. As Clifton Hodge put it, city children must be taught that "as society becomes organized, the common goods of nature come to form a great public property—pure air, pure water, forests and roadside trees and flowers, game and fishes, birds, and other beneficent animals," *Nature Study and Life*, p. 18.

36. Edith M. Patch and Harrison Howe, *Hunting* (New York: MacMillan, 1933), p. 6.

CHAPTER 9

1. Porter Sargent, *Handbook of the Best Private Schools* (Boston: n.p., 1915), p. 225.

2. Liberty Hyde Bailey, *The Nature Study Idea* (New York: Doubleday, Page, 1903), p. 151.

3. Holtz, *Nature-Study: A Manual for Teachers and Students* (New York: Scribner's, 1909), p. 16.

4. William Cole, "Country Week," *New England Magazine*, XIV (July, 1896), p. 531.

5. Walter S. Ufford, *Fresh Air Charity in the United States*, Ph.D. dissertation, Columbia University (New York: Bonnell, Silver & Co., 1897), pp. 10–12, 28, 83. Ufford's study gives the best coverage of the Fresh Air movement in the nineteenth century.

6. Cole concluded that "adoptions into country families would be more frequent, were the parents more willing to give up their children," see "Country Week," pp. 528, 529.

7. Cole, "Country Week," p. 530. "It is worse than mockery," A. H. Stewart noted, to argue that city children could "repeat in their play the history of the race by climbing, hunting, fishing, building fires, and constructing houses if they have not even a microscopic back yard in which to follow out these instincts." Stewart was an "environmentalist," and brought slightly more perspective than Cole to the recapitulation theory. See *American Bad Boys in the Making* (New York: Lechner, 1912), p. 146.

8. Dan Beard Outdoor School to Master Len Grinker, Denver, Colorado, April 7, 1917, copy in Beard Papers, box 227, Library of Congress.

9. Dan Beard Outdoor School to Mrs. J. C. Gibbons, Paris, Texas, April 14, 1917; Beard to Mr. George F. Ogden, Batavia, New York, April 13, 1916, copies in Beard Papers.

10. Dan Beard Outdoor School to Miss Rose B. Selig, Philadelphia, Pennsylvania, April 18, 1917, in Beard Papers.

11. Beard to Hon. H. G. Morison, Johnson City, Tennessee, February 20, 1922, in Beard Papers, box 250.

12. Frances D. Maning to Beard [1924], in Beard Papers.

13. Hedley S. Dimock, Charles E. Hendry, *Camping and Character* (New York: Association Press, 1931), pp. xiii, 4, 128, 66.

14. Carlos Ward, *Organized Camping and Progressive Education* (Nashville: Cullom & Ghertner, 1935), p. 39.

15. Quoted in H. W. Gibson, *Camp Management, a Manual on Organized Camping* (New York: Greenberg, 1923, rev. ed. 1939), p. 3.

16. Emory Stephen Bogardus, *The City Boy and His Problems, a Survey of Boy Life in Los Angeles* (Los Angeles: Rotary Club, 1926), p. 13.

17. H. W. Gibson, *Camping for Boys* (New York: Association Press, 1911), p. 7; Sigmund Spaeth, "Boy Rampant," *Collier's Outdoor America*, XLVII (August 12, 1911), p. 16.

18. Peixotto, "The Aims of a Boy's Club," p. 1346; cf. Sargent, *Handbook of Summer Camps*, p. 15.

19. Joshua Lieberman, *Creative Camping: A Coeducational Experiment in Personality Development and Social Living* . . . (New York: Association Press, 1931), pp. xi, xiii.

20. William H. Kilpatrick, *Summer Vacation Activities of the School Child* (New York: Century, 1933), pp. 38, 40.

21. Porter E. Sargent, *Handbook of Summer Camps, an Annual Survey* (Boston: P. Sargent, 12th ed., 1935), p. 22.

22. James W. F. Davies, *Out of Doors with Youth* (Chicago: U. of Chicago, 1927), p. 8. "Twenty years ago," Elizabeth Frazer wrote in 1926, "the chief aim was simply to install a group of children in tents along the wooded shore of some lake and let them absorb the atmosphere near to nature's heart. Now the movement has become highly organized and placed on a firm scientific and educational basis," "Young America Takes to the Wilds," *Saturday Evening Post*, cxcviii (May 22, 1926), p. 48.
23. Sargent, *Handbook of Summer Camps*, p. 28; Lloyd Burgess Sharp, *Education and the Summer Camp* (New York: Teachers' Coll., Columbia U., 1930), p. 2.
24. George W. Hinckley, *Roughing It with Boys: Actual Experiences of Boys at Summer and Winter Camps in the Maine Woods* (New York: Association Press, 1913), pp. 13, 12.
25. Davies, *Out of Doors with Youth*, p. 25.
26. Lieberman, *Creative Camping*, p. 42.

CHAPTER 10

1. Ernest Thompson Seton, *The Book of Woodcraft* (Garden City: Doubleday, Page, 1917, 1st ed. 1912), p. 3.
2. Sir Robert Baden-Powell, *Scoutmastership, a Handbook for Scoutmasters on the Theory of Scout Training* (New York: Putnam's, 1920), p. 6.
3. Seton, *Book of Woodcraft*, p. v.
4. Seton, *The Trail of an Artist-Naturalist* (New York: Scribner's, 1940), p. 384.
5. As quoted in William D. Murray, *The History of the Boy Scouts of America* (New York: Boy Scouts of America, 1937), p. 16.
6. Seton, *Manual of the Woodcraft Indians* (Garden City: Doubleday, Page, 1915, 14th edition), pp. xiii, 3.
7. Burroughs to Roosevelt, July 2, 1906, in Theodore Roosevelt Papers, box 107.
8. Unsigned, undated typescript history of Seton's group in Beard Papers, box 224.
9. An award suggested to Beard by John Muir in a letter of May 30, 1907, in Beard Papers, box 16.
10. Beard, *The Buckskin Book of the Boy Pioneers of America* (n.p.: Pictorial Review, 1911), p. 5.
11. Baden-Powell, *Scoutmastership*, p. 82.
12. R. S. S. Baden-Powell, "Boy Scouts," photostatic copy of the two-page flyer dated May, 1907, in Beard Papers.
13. *Scoutmastership*, pp. 64, 82, 6–13.
14. Baden-Powell, "Boy Scouts."
15. "The Boy Scout Scheme," 24-page pamphlet published by the Boy Scouts of America, July, 1914, in Beard Papers, box 224, Library of Congress.

16. Quoted in Murray, *History of the Boy Scouts*, p. 42.
17. Helen Buckler, Mary Fiedler, Martha Allen, *Wo-He-Lo, the Story of the Camp Fire Girls* (New York: Holt, Rinehart, Winston, 1961), p. 83. In 1929, nearly two hundred and twenty thousand Camp Fire Girls met in nine thousand local groups, and eighty-six thousand members spent two to four weeks in more than a hundred official camps.
18. E.g., Harrison Fisher's cover illustration for *The Ladies' Home Journal*, xxxix (August, 1912).
19. Percy K. Fitzhugh, *Westy Martin in the Rockies*, in *Out West with Westy Martin* (New York: Grosset and Dunlap, reprint of 1925 edition), p. 2.
20. Beard to Pratt, Pratt Institute, Brooklyn, January 22, 1913, in Beard Papers, box 17.
21. When Seton once introduced him as the father of Scouting, Baden-Powell insisted he was only "one of the uncles of the movement." See reprint of this speech in the New York *Tribune*, September 24, 1910.
22. Beard to Editorial Board, Boy Scouts of America, December 17, 1912, copy in Beard Papers, box 17.
23. Murray, *History of the Boy Scouts*, pp. 429, 138, 238.
24. John Alexander, "Boy Scouts," illustrated pamphlet [c. 1911], no pagination. This lavish booklet was the first major publicity for the Scouts. It was sponsored by the "Minute Tapioca Company" in an edition of 500,000 copies.
25. Norman E. Richardson and Ormond Loomis, *Boy Scout Movement Applied by the Church* (New York: Scribner's, 1915), p. 14.
26. Carlos Ward, *Organized Camping and Progressive Education* (Nashville: Cullom & Ghertner, 1935), p. 42. Porter Sargent complained that national control of the Scout movement was militaristic, almost fascist in its power. The "patrol" unit, originally designed to give educational purpose to the "gang instinct," seemed to have lost its place under "an increasing tendency to standardize activities and suppress initiative"; see *A Handbook of Summer Camps, an Annual Survey* (Boston: Porter Sargent, 12th ed. 1935), p. 104.
27. *Thirteenth Annual Report of the Boy Scouts of America*, 68th Congress, 1st Session (Washington: Government Printing Office, 1924, serial no. 8265), pp. 16, 22.
28. *Ibid.*, p. 16.

CHAPTER 11

1. There were twelve "Curlytops" volumes in 1918 and seventeen "Buddy" stories in 1929, all dealing with the out-of-doors for younger readers, published by Cupples and Leon in New York.

2. William Graydon, *Canoe Boys and Campfires: Or Adventures on Winding Waters* (New York: World Syndicate, 1907), p. 14.
3. Ruel Perley Smith, *The Rival Campers Afloat* (Boston: Page, 1906), p. 30.
4. Quincy Allen, *The Outdoor Chums at Cabin Point* (New York: Grosset and Dunlap, 1916), p. 4.
5. Graydon, *Canoe Boys and Campfires*, p. 11.
6. Walter Eaton, *Boy Scouts in Glacier Park* (Boston: W. A. Wilde, 1918), p. 234; Margaret Vandercook, *The Camp Fire Girls amid the Snows* (Philadelphia: John Winston, 1913), p. 14.
7. Howard Garis, *Dick Hamilton's Touring Car: Or a Young Millionaire's Race for a Fortune* (Cleveland: Goldsmith, 1913); Smith, *Rival Campers Afloat*.
8. Quincy Allen, *The Outdoor Chums: Or the First Tour of the Rod, Gun and Camera Club* (New York: Grosset and Dunlap, 1911).
9. Harvey Ralphson, *Boy Scouts on the Columbia River* (Chicago: M. A. Donohue, n.d.), pp. 11, 134.
10. Janet Aldridge, *The Meadow-Brook Girls under Canvas, or Fun and Frolic in the Summer Camp* (Philadelphia: Henry Altemus, 1913).
11. Katherine Stokes, *The Motor Maids at Sunrise Camp* (New York: Hurst, 1914), p. 10.
12. Thornton Burgess, *The Boy Scouts in a Trapper's Camp* (Philadelphia: Penn Publishing Co., 1915). In *Heroes of the Wilds* (New York: T. Crowell, 1923), Chelsea Fraser offered his readers not local pioneers, but forest rangers, surveyors, explorers, big-game hunters, wild-life photographers and similar urban "outposters of toiling humanity."
13. Margaret Love Sanderson, *The Camp Fire Girls at Pine Tree Camp* (Chicago: Reilly and Britton, 1914), pp. 19, 33. Jane Stewart, Stella Francis, Hildegard Frey and Edith Lavell all published similar series with six to ten titles each.
14. Sanderson, *Camp Fire Girls at Pine Tree Camp*, pp. 55, 146.
15. Thornton Burgess, *The Boy Scouts of Woodcraft Camp* (Philadelphia: Penn Publishing Company, 1912), pp. 5, 36. Burgess made a life-long career as a writer of children's nature stories. In addition to his "Boy Scout" series, he published "Mother West Wind" tales, and he began in 1912 to syndicate "Bedtime Stories" in American and Canadian newspapers. By 1934, he had written over seven thousand bedtime anecdotes including "Peter Rabbit," "Reddy Fox," "Green Meadows," and "Green Forest."
16. Burgess, *Boy Scouts in a Trapper's Camp*, introduction, 358.
17. Advertisement for *The Campfires of the Wolf Patrol* in Alan Douglas, *Woodcraft: Or How a Patrol Leader Made Good* (New York: New York Book Company, 1913).
18. Gordon Stuart, *The Boy Scouts of the Air at Eagle Camp* (Chi-

cago: Reilly and Britton, 1912); Harvey Ralphson, *Boy Scouts on the Columbia River*, p. 184.

19. Gordon Stuart, *The Boy Scouts of the Air in Indian Land* (Chicago: Reilly and Britton, 1912).

20. Roy Rockwood, *Through the Air to the North Pole* (New York: Cupples and Leon, 1906).

21. George Bird Grinnell, *Jack the Young Ranchman: Or a Boy's Adventures in the Rockies* (New York: Fred A. Stokes, 1899), p. 4.

22. Dillon Wallace, *Bobby of the Labrador* (Chicago: McClurg, 1916), p. 202.

23. Wallace, *The Fur Trail Adventurers* (Chicago: McClurg, 1915); *The Arctic Stowaways* (Chicago: McClurg, 1917), p. 6; *The Wilderness Castaways* (Chicago: McClurg, 1913), p. 6; *With Dog and Canoe: A Story of the Big North Woods* (New York, Chicago: Revell, 1928), p. 20.

24. Wallace, *The Arctic Stowaways*, p. 85.

25. Burgess, *Boy Scouts in a Trapper's Camp*, p. 101.

26. Dillon Wallace, *Troop One of the Labrador* (New York, 1920), p. 35.

27. Wallace, *Wilderness Castaways*, pp. 309, 315.

28. Morris T. Longstreth, *Ade of the Marcy Mounted* (New York: Century, 1926), p. 194.

CHAPTER 12

1. Edward Weeks, "The Best Sellers Since 1875," *Publisher's Weekly*, cxxv (April 21, 1934), pp. 1503–1506. Issuing chiefly reprints of established works, Grosset and Dunlap employed the most elaborate distribution system in the country. They sent out 1,226,066 copies of Porter's *Freckles*, their "biggest seller ever issued." *A Girl of the Limberlost* was second with 1,106,165 copies. Their total sales for Porter novels reached 6,071,269 by 1936. See George T. Dunlap, *The Fleeting Years: A Memoir* (New York, n.p., 1937), p. 191.

2. "The Books of 1901," *Publisher's Weekly*, LXI (January 25, 1902), p. 83.

3. As quoted in Grant Overton, *Authors of the Day* (New York: George Doran, 1922), p. 157.

4. As quoted by Porter's publishers in *The Country Life Press* (Garden City: Doubleday, Page, 1919), p. 145.

5. Popular story-tellers like Zane Grey and Rex Beach occasionally wrote about wilderness, but formula novelists like James B. Hendryx, Harold Bindloss, Stanley Shaw, Robert Pinkerton, James Dorrance, Herman Whitaker, Peter McFarlane, George Marsh, Robert Stead and James Oliver Curwood made it their special province. Some, like Bindloss, Whitaker and Stead, wrote ponderous stories

of the Canadian Prairies. Others, like Louis Hemon, turned to the romantic pastoral of Quebec, where the Old World met the wilderness. Still others dealt with the "Long Trail" in the far north. All were prolific; Bindloss alone produced eighty-two novels of the Canadian and African back country.

6. Stewart Edward White, *The Blazed Trail* (New York: McClure, Phillips, 1902), p. 3. Cf. White, *The Riverman* (Garden City: Doubleday, Page, 1924, 1st ed. 1908); *The Rules of the Game* (New York: Doubleday, Page, 1910).

7. Holman Day, *King Spruce, a Novel* (New York: Harper, 1908), p. 3.

8. Irving Bacheller, *Silas Strong,* Pine Tree Edition (New York: Harper, 1906), fwd., 2.

9. White, *The Rules of the Game,* p. 22.

10. Ray Long, "James Oliver Curwood and His Far North," *Bookman,* LII (February, 1921), 493.

11. Jack London, *The Son of the Wolf: Tales of the Far North* (Boston: Houghton, Mifflin, 1900), p. 105.

12. See Gilbert Parker, *Pierre and His People,* Imperial Edition (New York: Scribner's, 1916, 1st ed. 1894), vol. I, p. 184; Parker, *A Romany of the Snows,* Imperial Edition (New York: Scribner's, 1916, 1st ed. titled *An Adventurer of the North,* 1896), p. 179; Jack London, *A Daughter of the Snows* (Philadelphia: Lippincott, 1902), p. 25; cf. the wilderness travel experiences in Hudson Stuck's *Ten Thousand Miles with a Dog Sled* (New York: Scribner's, 1914); or Dillon Wallace, *The Long Labrador Trail* (New York: Outing, 1907).

13. London, *The Call of the Wild* (New York: MacMillan, 1919, 1st ed. 1903), pp. 39, 182.

14. London, *White Fang* (New York: Regent Press, 1905), p. 3.

15. Douglas Durkin, *The Lobstick Trail* (Chicago: McClurg, 1922), p. 110; Day, *King Spruce,* p. 273; Hamlin Garland, "Hitting the Trail," *McClure's,* XII (February, 1899), pp. 298–304; Garland, *Trail of the Goldseekers* (New York: MacMillan, 1899).

16. James Oliver Curwood, *Flower of the North* (New York: Harper, 1912), p. 42.

17. James Oliver Curwood, *God's Country—and the Woman* (New York: Doubleday, Page, 1915), p. 37.

18. Durkin, *Lobstick Trail,* p. 3.

19. Curwood, *Flower of the North,* p. 129.

20. Wright, *Shepherd of the Hills* (Chicago: Book Supply Co., 1907), p. 121; see also Durkin, *Lobstick Trail,* p. 138.

21. Curwood, *God's Country—and the Woman,* p. 16; *The Valley of Silent Men* (New York: Cosmopolitan Book Corp., 1920), p. 62; *The Courage of Marge O'Doone* (New York: Grosset and Dunlap, 1918), p. 50.

22. Curwood, *Flower of the North,* p. 31; cf. Holman Day, *Joan of Arc of the North Woods* (New York: Harper, 1922), p. 219.
23. London, *A Daughter of the Snows,* p. 90.
24. James B. Hendryx, *North* (New York: A. L. Burt, 1923), p. 74.
25. See Wright, *Shepherd of the Hills,* p. 350; Hamlin Garland, *The Forester's Daughter: A Romance of the Bear-Tooth Range* (New York: Harper, 1914), p. 71.
26. Curwood's *The Alaskan* (New York: Grosset and Dunlap, 1923) was, like William McLeod Raine's *Yukon Trail* (New York: Grosset and Dunlap, 1917), an outright appeal for worthwhile development of new territory.
27. Curwood, *The Country Beyond* (New York: Cosmopolitan Book Corp., 1922), p. 14.
28. London, *A Daughter of the Snows,* p. 199.
29. James J. Tynan, *The Shooting of Dan McGrew* (New York: Grosset and Dunlap, 1924), p. 28.
30. Samuel Alexander White, *Law of the North: A Story of Love and Battle in Rupert's Land* (New York: Grosset and Dunlap, 1913), p. 72.
31. Curwood, *Honor of the Big Snows* (Indianapolis: Bobbs-Merrill, 1911), p. 19.
32. Curwood, *God's Country—and the Woman,* p. 159.
33. Curwood, *Honor of the Big Snows,* p. 300.
34. James Oliver Curwood, "Peter God," in *Back to God's Country* (New York: Grosset and Dunlap, 1920), p. 241.
35. *Honor of the Big Snows,* 285.
36. Curwood, *God's Country—and the Woman,* p. 252; *Flower of the North,* p. 29; see also Gene Stratton Porter, *The Harvester* (New York: Grosset and Dunlap, 1911), p. 5; Wright, *The Winning of Barbara Worth* (Chicago: Book Supply Company, 1911), p. 364; Harriet T. Comstock, *Joyce of the North Woods* (New York: Grosset and Dunlap, 1911), p. 379; Day, *Joan of Arc of the North Woods,* pp. 92, 118; Tynan, *Shooting of Dan McGrew,* p. 139; Kyne, *The Understanding Heart,* p. 99.
37. Curwood, *The Alaskan,* p. 12; Tynan, *Shooting of Dan McGrew,* p. 170.
38. Wright, *When a Man's a Man,* p. 11; Raine, *Yukon Trail,* p. 87.
39. Curwood, *Honor of the Big Snows,* p. 17; *Courage of Marge O'Doone,* p. 47; *The Alaskan,* p. 25; *God's Country—and the Woman,* p. 52.
40. Durkin, *Lobstick Trail,* p. 7; cf. Parker, "The Stake and the Plumb Line," in *Northern Lights,* p. 145.
41. Garland, *The Forester's Daughter,* p. 264.
42. Waller, *A Cry in the Wilderness* (Boston: Little, Brown, 1912), p. 64. Cf. J. A. Mitchell, *The Pines of Lory* (New York: Life Publishing Co., 1901).

43. Jack London, *Burning Daylight* (New York: MacMillan, 1910), pp. 162, 188, 323, 327, 340.
44. Overton, *Author's of the Day*, p. 160.
45. Wright, *The Shepherd of the Hills*, p. 350.
46. Quoted in Jeannette Porter Meehan, *Gene Stratton-Porter, Lady of the Limberlost* (Garden City: Doubleday, Page, 1928), p. 157.
47. Overton, *Authors of the Day*, p. 86.
48. W. H. Boynton, "Book Reviews," *Independent*, CIX (September 16, 1924), 137.
49. Charles C. Baldwin, *The Men Who Make Our Novels* (New York: Dodd, Mead, rev. ed. 1924, 1st ed. 1919), pp. 610, 603.
50. *Ibid.*, p. 609. See *When a Man's a Man*, p. 11.
51. *Ibid.*, p. 88.
52. W. A. Bradley, "H. B. Wright's 'The Winning of Barbara Worth,' " *Bookman*, XXXIV (September, 1911), 98.
53. *The New York Times Book Review*, July 27, 1924, p. 18.

CHAPTER 13

1. Nathaniel S. Shaler, "Faith in Nature," *International Quarterly*, VI (December, 1902), p. 281; cf. Charles W. Eliot, "The Religious Ideal in Education," *Outlook*, XCIX (October 21, 1911), p. 413; and Hamilton W. Mabie, *Essays on Nature and Culture* (New York, 1906), p. 284. See also J. Ellis, *The Charm of Nature: An Anthology for All Lovers of Nature* (New York, n.d.), title page; Archibald Rutledge, *Peace in the Heart* (Garden City, 1930), p. 1; Earle Amos Brooks, *A Handbook of the Outdoors* (New York, 1925), p. vii; "Outdoors," *Independent*, LV (April 16, 1903), p. 925; "Back to Nature," *Outlook*, LXXIV (June 6, 1903), p. 305.
2. Hugh MacMillan, *A Cyclopaedia of Nature Teachings* (New York, 1892), introduction, xi; William Channing Gannett, *A Year of Miracle, a Poem in Four Seasons* (Boston, 1881), p. 35; MacMillan, *op. cit.*, p. 30.
3. Harold Bell Wright, *That Printer of Udell's* (New York, 1911), p. 212.
4. Ralph Connor, *Black Rock: A Tale of the Selkirks* (Toronto, 1898); *The Sky Pilot: A Tale of the Foothills* (New York, 1899); Gilbert Parker, "A Man, a Famine, and a Heathen Boy," in *Northern Lights* (New York, 1909); James Oliver Curwood, *The Courage of Marge O'Doone* (New York, 1918), p. 15; cf. Curwood, *A Gentleman of Courage* (New York, 1924), p. 20; Gene Stratton Porter, *The Harvester* (New York, 1911), p. 312.
5. Brooks, *op. cit.*, pp. 42, vii; cf. Cora S. Cobb, *God's Wonder World: A Manual for Religious Instruction in Junior Grades* (Boston, 1918); Charles W. Finley and Otis Caldwell, "A Sunday Boys' Outdoor Club," *Nature-Study Review*, VI (May, 1910), pp. 130–134.

6. John Burroughs, "The Gospel of Nature," *Century*, LXXXIV (June, 1912), 196; Burroughs, "Faith of a Naturalist," *North American Review*, CCX (November, 1919), 681; cf. Stanton D. Kirkham, *Outdoor Philosophy, the Meditations of a Naturalist* (New York, London, 1912), p. 6.

7. O. Warren Smith, "By Your Lone," *Independent*, LXXXVI (June 5, 1916), 375.

8. William C. Gray, *Musing by Camp-Fire and Wayside* (New York, 1902), pp. 298, 299; William F. Badé, "Summering in the Sierra Nevada," *Independent*, LXX (June 22, 1911), p. 1363; Liberty Hyde Bailey, *The Holy Earth* (New York, 1943), pp. 11, 12.

9. Mary M. Atkeson, "The Religion of the Fields," *Good Housekeeping*, LXXIX (July, 1924), p. 190; Annie T. Slosson, *Fishin' Jimmy* (New York, 1889), p. 11; E. P. Powell, "Country Home for the Professional Man," *Independent*, LV (May 14, 1903), p. 1134; James Buckham, *Where Town and Country Meet* (Cincinnati, 1903), p. 76; Clifton Hodge, *Nature Study and Life* (Boston, London, 1902), p. 30. Bruce Barton's first chapter deals with Christ the "executive," his second with "The Outdoor Man"; see *The Man Nobody Knows, a Discovery of the Real Jesus* (New York, 1924).

10. William A. Quayle, *Out-of-Doors With Jesus* (New York, Cincinnati, 1924), pp. 9, 10.

11. Rutledge, *Peace in the Heart*, pp. 197, 296.

12. Vaughan Cornish, *The Poetic Impression of Natural Scenery* (London, 1931), pref.

CHAPTER 14

1. Nathaniel Shaler, "The Landscape as a Means of Culture," *Atlantic Monthly*, LXXXII (December, 1898), pp. 779, 778, 780.

2. Lowell Thomas, *Rolling Stone, the Life and Adventures of Arthur Radclyffe Dugmore* (Garden City: Doubleday, Page, 1931); see Dugmore, *Nature and the Camera* (New York: Doubleday, Page, 1902); *Bird Homes* (New York: Doubleday, Page, 1900); *Wild Life and the Camera* (Philadelphia: J. B. Lippincott, 1912), etc.

3. Herbert K. Job, *Wild Wings: Adventures of a Camera-Hunter* (Boston: Houghton, Mifflin, 1905), pp. 239, viii.

4. Unless otherwise indicated, movie sources are copyright declarations housed in the Library of Congress. These declarations range from typescript descriptions of setting and plot to stills and strips of film. Most frequently they are copies of the printed announcements sent to individual exhibitors. These include suggested advertisements, publicity items, and scenes from the photoplay. Films originally deposited with the copyrights have been removed.

5. Irving Cummings with "Rin tin tin" played the "Mountie" Pierre de Barre, in Curwood's 1922 photoplay, *The Man from Hell's*

216 NOTES TO PAGES 153–159

River. Wallace Beery played Gaspard the villain and Eva Novak played the feminine lead.
6. Frank Chapman, "Hunting With a Camera," *World's Work,* VI (June, 1903), 3554.
7. Enos A. Mills, *Your National Parks* (Boston: Houghton, Mifflin, 1932), p. 205.

CHAPTER 15

1. Robert Sterling Yard, *The Book of the National Parks* (New York: Scribner's, 1919), p. 5.
2. Quoted in Jenks Cameron, *The National Parks Service, its History, Activities and Organization,* Institute for Government Research Monograph 11 (New York: Appleton, 1922), pp. 98, 93.
3. John Muir, *Our National Parks* (Boston: Houghton, Mifflin, 1901), p. 2.
4. Muir, *Our National Parks,* p. 4; John Burroughs, *Far and Near* (Boston: Houghton, Mifflin, 1904), pp. 6, 7.
5. Quoted in Harlean James, *Romance of the National Parks* (New York: MacMillan, 1939), p. 72.
6. See Mary Roberts Rinehart, "Sleeping Giant," *Ladies' Home Journal,* XXXVIII (May, 1921), p. 83.
7. French Strother, "San Francisco Against the Nation for the Yosemite," *World's Work,* XVII (April, 1909), pp. 11411–11416.
8. "Granting Use of Hetch-Hetchy to City of San Francisco," *House Report #2805,* 60th Congress, 2nd Session, February, 1909, ser. no. 5384, p. 8; James D. Phelan, "Why Congress Should Pass the Hetch-Hetchy Bill," *Outlook,* XCI (February 13, 1909), 340–341.
9. The J. Horace McFarland Papers, housed in the William Penn Memorial Museum and Archives Building, Harrisburg, Pennsylvania, contain several boxes of untapped materials relating to the Hetch-Hetchy controversy.
10. Amos Pinchot, "The Hetch-Hetchy Fight," typescript in Pinchot Papers, box 1856, Library of Congress.
11. Undated enclosure in letter of James S. Pray, President, American Society of Landscape Architects, to J. Horace McFarland, February 15, 1915, in McFarland Papers, box 5.
12. See McFarland to Pinchot, February 18, 1911; McFarland to Pinchot, March 24, 1911, in McFarland Papers.
13. McFarland to Chamberlain, April 2, 1914, in McFarland Papers.
14. Mary K. Sherman, "Concerning National Park Service Bill," typescript copy in Mira L. Dock Papers, box 4, Library of Congress.
15. Sherman to Dock, April 16, 1916, in Dock Papers, box 5.
16. Robert Shankland, *Steve Mather of the National Parks* (New York: Knopf, 1951), p. 39. Shankland's biography is a key source for the early history of the Park Service.

17. Irving S. Cobb, *Roughing It DeLuxe* (New York: Doran, 1914), p. 17.
18. W. A. Clarke, "Automobiling in Yosemite Valley," *Overland Monthly*, n.s. XL (August, 1902), p. 109.
19. Right Honourable James Bryce, "National Parks—the Need of the Future," *Outlook*, CII (December 14, 1912), 813.
20. Yard, *The Book of the National Parks*, p. 209.
21. *Reports of the Department of the Interior, 1917*, vol. I, p. 79; *Reports of the Department of the Interior, 1926* (Washington: Government Printing Office, 1926), p. 16.
22. *Reports of the Department of the Interior, 1919*, p. 961.
23. Quoted in Shankland, *Steve Mather of the National Parks*, p. 158.
24. Lane to Stephen Mather, May 13, 1918, as quoted in *Reports of the Department of the Interior, 1918*, Vol. I, pp. 110–112.
25. George H. Lorimer, "Selling Scenery," *Saturday Evening Post*, CXCII (October 11, 1919), 28. As early as 1914, J. Horace McFarland wrote to his friend James Pray, "I had an interview with Mr. Lorimer . . . and got him to agree to make the National Parks a main cause in that influential periodical . . . ," see McFarland to Pray, April 17, 1914, in McFarland Papers.
26. *Recreational Resources of Federal Lands* (Washington: National Conference on Outdoor Recreation, 1928), pp. 54, 58.
27. *Reports of the Department of the Interior, 1922*, p. 89; *Reports of the Department of the Interior, 1921*, p. 113.
28. John Muir, *Our National Parks*, p. 30; *Reports of the Department of the Interior, 1919*, p. 1123.
29. As quoted in *Recreational Resources of Federal Lands*, p. 59.
30. Yard, *The Book of the National Parks*, pp. 4, 3.
31. Enos Mills, *Your National Parks* (Boston: Houghton, Mifflin, 1917), p. 366; Mills, *The Rocky Mountain National Park* (Boston: Houghton, Mifflin, 1932), p. 145.
32. Mills, *Rocky Mountain National Park*, p. 145; *Your National Parks* (1917), p. 152.
33. As quoted in *Nature Notes from Glacier National Park*, monthly mimeographed publication of the Park naturalist dated July, 1929, p. 21.
34. Enos A. Mills, "A Day With a Nature Guide," *Outlook*, CXXII (June 11, 1919), 244.
35. Mills, *Your National Parks* (1917), x.
36. Frederick E. Brimmer, *Autocamping* (Cincinnati: Stewart, Kidd, 1923), p. 19.
37. *Recreational Resources of Federal Lands*, p. 75.
38. Lorimer, "Selling Scenery," 28.
39. Yard, *The Book of the National Parks*, p. 265.
40. Lorimer, "Selling Scenery," 28.
41. James, *Romance of the National Parks*, p. 100.

CHAPTER 16

1. *Reports of the Department of the Interior, 1925* (Washington: Government Printing Office, 1925), p. 22.
2. "Editorial," *Nature-Study Review*, XVII (March, 1921), 142.
3. Frank Bolles, *At the North of Bearcamp Water: Chronicles of a Stroller in New England from July to December* (Boston: Houghton, Mifflin, 1899, 1st ed. 1893), p. 92.
4. John Muir, *Our National Parks* (Boston: Houghton, Mifflin, 1901), p. 1.
5. Stewart Edward White, *The Mountains* (New York: McClure, Phillips, 1904), pp. 205, 206, 209; Muir, *Our National Parks*, p. 101.
6. Grace Seton-Thompson, *Nimrod's Wife* (New York: Doubleday, Page, 1907), p. 60.
7. Muir, *Our National Parks*, p. 56.
8. A. R. Dee, "The Story of a $2,100 House," *Country Life in America*, III (April, 1903), pp. 227–231; Charles V. Boyd, "The Old-Fashioned Log Cabin Is the New-Fashioned Summer Camp, with All of the Comforts of Modern Life and All of the Picturesqueness of Pioneer Days," *Woman's Home Companion*, XLIII (May, 1916), p. 46; Chilson Aldrich, *The Real Log Cabin* (New York: MacMillan, 1934, 1st ed. 1928), pp. 26–28; Frederick Brimmer, *Log Cabins, Lodges and Clubhouses* (New York: Appleton, 1925).
9. See Elon Jessup, *Roughing It Smoothly* (New York: Putnam's, 1923); Warren Miller, *Camping Out* (New York: George Doran, 1918); Horace Kephart's *The Book of Camping and Woodcraft* (New York: Outing Publishing Co., 1906) went through seven editions between 1906 and 1921.
10. "The Cabin of a Novelist," *The New York Times Book Review*, April 30, 1911, p. 263.
11. Stewart Edward White, *The Cabin* (New York: Doubleday, Page, 1911), pp. 37, 134, 135.
12. Stanton Davis Kirkham, *Resources* (New York: Putnam's, 1910), p. 118.
13. Kirkham, *Outdoor Philosophy, the Meditations of a Naturalist* (New York: Putnam's, 1912), pp. 12, 187; Kirkham, *In the Open* (San Francisco: Paul Elder, 1908), p. 187.
14. Joseph Knowles, *Alone in the Wilderness* (Boston: Small, Maynard, 1913).
15. Rockwell Kent, *Wilderness, a Journal of Quiet Adventure in Alaska* (New York: Modern Library Edition, 1930, 1st ed. 1920), pp. v, 135, vii, 217.
16. Liberty Bailey, *The Seven Stars* (New York: MacMillan, 1923), p. 98.
17. John C. Merriam, undated typescript, "Memorandum of Visit to Yosemite in August, 1930," in John C. Merriam Papers, box 215, Library of Congress.

18. Outdoorsmen like Theodore Roosevelt chortled at the ironies in the contrast between "the grizzly bear of the early Rocky Mountain hunters and explorers," as he once wrote to John Burroughs, and the fact that park employees must now "remove tin cans from the bear's paws in the bear's interest"; see Roosevelt to Burroughs, dated August 15, 1904, in Theodore Roosevelt Papers, box 148.
19. Mary Roberts Rinehart, "Sleeping Giant," *Ladies' Home Journal,* XXXVIII (May, 1921), p. 21; Struthers Burt, *The Diary of a Dude Wrangler* (New York: Scribner's, 1924), pp. 50, 52.
20. Edward Hungerford, "Our Summer Migration: A Social Study," *Century,* XLII (August, 1891), p. 569.
21. Rinehart, *Tenting To-Night: A Chronicle of Sport and Adventure in Glacier Park and the Cascade Mountains* (Boston: Houghton, Mifflin, 1918), p. 2.
22. Aldo Leopold, "The Last Stand of the Wilderness," *American Forests and Forest Life,* XXXI (October, 1925), p. 601.
23. *Recreational Resources of Federal Lands* (Washington: National Conference on Outdoor Recreation, 1928), p. 139.
24. Charles C. Adams, "The Administration of Wild Life in State and National Parks," *Naturalist's Guide to the Americas* (Baltimore: Wilkins and Wilkins, 1926), p. 45. Edited by Victor Shelford, this collection was sponsored by the "Committee on the Preservation of Natural Conditions" of the Ecological Society of America as a program for the nation's remaining wilderness areas.
25. Liberty Bailey, *The Seven Stars,* p. 107.
26. Robert Marshall, "The Problem of the Wilderness," *Scientific Monthly,* XXX (February, 1930), 141. Cf. landscape architect Frank A. Waugh's "Wilderness to Keep," *Review of Reviews,* LXXXI (February, 1930), pp. 146-152.
27. Melville Ferguson, *Motor Camping on Western Trails* (New York: Century, 1925), p. 4.
28. Sigurd Olson, "Why Wilderness," *American Forests,* XLIV (September, 1938), 395.
29. William B. Greeley, "Recreation in the National Forests," in John F. Kane, ed., *Picturesque America* (New York: Resorts and Playgrounds of America, 1925, rev. ed. 1935), p. 33.
30. Quoted in *Recreational Resources of Federal Lands,* p. 88.
31. T. K. Whipple, "Aucassin in the Sierras," *Yale Review,* n.s. XVI (July, 1927), 714.
32. Henry M. Busch, "Camping," *Encyclopaedia of the Social Sciences* (New York: MacMillan, 1937), II, 168.

CHAPTER 17

1. Robert Marshall, "The Problem of the Wilderness," *Scientific Monthly,* XXX (February, 1930), 143, 144.
2. Zane Grey, *The Man of the Forest* (New York: Harper, 1920), p. 202.

3. T. K. Whipple, "Aucassin in the Sierras," *Yale Review*, n.s. XVI (July, 1927), 718, 717.

4. Clarence Stein, "Dinosaur Cities," *Survey Graphic*, LIV (May 1, 1925), 134.

5. Stein, "Dinosaur Cities," 136.

6. "The cacophony of a dozen loud-speakers, and of hundreds of rattling fenders and squeaking brakes, continuing with scarcely any interruption for hours at a time," sociologist Niles Carpenter wrote in 1931, "builds up a mass of noise that is as intensely nerve-wracking as it is peculiarly urban"; see *The Sociology of City Life* (New York, London, Toronto: Longman's Green, 1931), p. 238.

7. See Edward E. Free, "How Noisy Is New York," *Forum*, LXXV (February, 1926), pp. xxi–xxiv; Free, "Noise," *ibid.*, LXXIX (March, 1928), pp. 382–389; "We Must Outlaw Noise," *Review of Reviews*, LXXXI (January, 1930), pp. 81–82.

8. New York City Department of Health, *City Noise* (New York: Noise Abatement Commission, 1930), p. 42.

9. Charles Galpin, *Rural Life* (New York: Century, 1918), p. 11.

10. Charles E. Cooley, *Social Organization: A Study of the Larger Mind* (New York: Scribner's, 1909), p. 23.

11. Chicago's Robert E. Park advanced this idea as early as 1915. See Park, Ernest W. Burgess, Roderick D. McKenzie, *The City* (Chicago: University of Chicago Press, 1925), p. 40.

12. See Charles R. Henderson, "Are Modern Industry and City Life Unfavorable to the Family," *American Journal of Sociology*, XIV (March, 1909), pp. 668–680.

13. Harvey Zorbaugh, *Gold Coast and Slum* (Chicago: University of Chicago, 1929), p. 255.

14. Park, Burgess, McKenzie, *The City*, p. 109.

15. Carpenter, *Sociology of City Life*, pp. 218, 468.

16. Ernest Groves, "The Urban Complex," *Sociological Review*, XII (Fall, 1920), pp. 74, 76.

17. Ebenezer Howard, *Garden Cities of Tomorrow* (London: Swan Sonnenschein, 1902, 1st ed. titled *Tomorrow*, 1898), p. 13.

18. Louis Heaton Pink, *The New Day in Housing* (New York: John Day, 1928), p. 78. Sociologist Graham Taylor found in his study of "Satellite Cities," that factory workers often failed to follow their companies into the suburbs, preferring rather to commute from the cities outward. See Taylor, *Satellite Cities: A Study of Industrial Suburbs* (New York: D. Appleton, 1915), pp. 120, *passim*.

19. Frederick W. Coburn, "The Five-Hundred-Mile City," *World Today*, XI (December, 1906), 1253.

20. Booth Tarkington, *The World Does Move* (Garden City: Doubleday, Page, 1928), p. 164.

21. Christine Frederick, "Is Suburban Living a Delusion?" *Outlook*, CXLVIII (February 22, 1928), 291, 313.
22. See, for example, Lewis S. Gannett, "The Wildness of New York," *Century*, CX (July, 1925), pp. 299–304; Samuel Scoville, Jr., "The Wildness of Philadelphia," *ibid.* (November, 1925), pp. 117–124.
23. Hermon Cary Bumpus, Jr., *Hermon Cary Bumpus, Yankee Naturalist* (Minneapolis: University of Minnesota, 1948), p. 57.
24. See "City Planning Conferences in the United States," in *Proceedings*, Second National Conference on City Planning and the Problems of Congestion (Boston, 1910), p. 3.
25. Lewis Mumford, "Regions to Live In," Regional Planning Number, *The Survey Graphic*, LIV (May 1, 1925), p. 152; see also "The Fourth Migration," *ibid.*, pp. 130–133.
26. R. L. Duffus, *Mastering a Metropolis* (New York: Harper, 1930), pp. 2, 205.
27. Benton MacKaye, *The New Exploration, a Philosophy of Regional Planning* (New York: Harcourt, Brace, 1928), p. 225.
28. Walter Prichard Eaton, *Skyline Camps* . . . (Chicago: M. A. Wilde, 1922), p. 104.
29. Calvin Coolidge, "National Recreation Opportunities," *Playground*, XVIII (July, 1924), 194; also in *Proceedings*, National Conference on Outdoor Recreation (Washington: Government Printing Office, 1924), p. 12.
30. *Proceedings*, National Conference on Outdoor Recreation (Washington: Government Printing Office, 1926), p. 164; see also Herbert Hoover, "In Praise of Izaak Walton," *Atlantic Monthly*, CXXIX (June, 1927), 812.
31. Geoffrey Scott, *The Architecture of Humanism: A Study in the History of Taste* (London: Constable, 1914, 1924), p. 76.
32. Henry S. Canby, "Back to Nature," *Yale Review*, n.s. VI (July, 1917), pp. 756, 764, 762, 755.
33. Heywood Broun, "It Seems to Heywood Broun," *Nation*, CXXVI (June 13, 1928), p. 661. Even Broun admitted to owning his own country place, however.
34. John H. Preston, "Back from Nature," *Saturday Review of Literature*, III (March 12, 1927), p. 652.
35. Noel P. Gist and L. A. Halbert, *Urban Society* (New York: Thomas Crowell, 1933), pp. 48, 284, 287, 285.
36. John Erskine, "A House in the Country," *Century*, CXII (July, 1926), p. 273.

Selected Readings since 1969

Abbey, Edward. *One Life at a Time, Please.* New York: Holt, 1988.

Allen, Mary. *Animals in American Literature.* Urbana: University of Illinois Press, 1983.

Allen, Thomas. *Guardian of the Wild: The Story of the National Wildlife Federation, 1936–1986.* Bloomington: Indiana University Press, 1987.

Allin, Craig W. *The Politics of Wilderness Preservation.* Westport, Conn.: Greenwood Press, 1982.

Anglemyer, Mary, and Eleanor R. Seagraves, comps. *The Natural Environment: An Annotated Bibliography on Attitudes and Values.* Washington: Smithsonian, 1984.

Baldwin, Donald N. *The Quiet Revolution: Grass Roots of Today's Wilderness Preservation Movement.* Boulder: Pruett, 1972.

Barth, Gunther. *City People: The Rise of Modern City Culture in Nineteenth-Century America.* New York: Oxford University Press, 1980.

Belasco, Warren James. *Americans on the Road: From Autocamp to Motel, 1910–1945.* Cambridge, Mass.: MIT Press, 1979.

Bender, Thomas. *Toward an Urban Vision: Ideas and Institutions in Nineteenth-Century America.* Lexington: University Press of Kentucky, 1975.

Berry, Wendell. *Recollected Essays, 1965–1980.* Berkeley, Calif.: North Point Press, 1981.

Borne, Lawrence R. *Dude Ranching: A Complete History.* Albuquerque: University of New Mexico Press, 1983.

Bowers, William L. *The Country-Life Movement in America, 1900–1920.* Port Washington, N.Y.: Kennikat, 1974.

Bratton, Susan. "National Park Management and Values." *Environmental Ethics* 7, no. 2 (1985): 117–33.

Brooks, Paul. *The Pursuit of Wilderness.* Boston: Houghton Mifflin, 1971.

———. *Speaking for Nature: How Literary Naturalists from Henry*

Thoreau to Rachel Carson Have Shaped America. San Francisco: Sierra Club Books, 1980.

Burgess, Cheryll, "Literature and the Environment—References." Ithaca, N.Y., 1989. Manuscript.

Callicott, J. Baird. "The Land Aesthetic." *Orion Nature Quarterly* 3, no. 3 (1984): 16–23.

Cheney, Jim. "Eco-Feminism and Deep Ecology." *Environmental Ethics* 9 (Summer 1987): 115–45.

Cohen, Michael P. *The Pathless Way: John Muir and American Wilderness.* Madison: University of Wisconsin Press, 1984.

Commoner, Barry. *The Closing Circle: Nature, Man, Technology.* New York: Knopf, 1971.

Dansereau, Pierre. *Inscape and Landscape: The Human Perception of Environment.* New York: Columbia University Press, 1975.

Devall, Bill, and George Sessions. *Deep Ecology: Living as if Nature Mattered.* Salt Lake City: Gibbs M. Smith, 1985.

Dillard, Annie. *An American Childhood.* New York: Harper & Row, 1987.

Durrenberger, Robert W. *Environment and Man: A Bibliography.* Palo Alto: National Press, 1970.

Eiseley, Loren. *All the Strange Hours: The Excavation of a Life.* New York: Scribner, 1975.

Errington, Paul L. *A Question of Values.* Ames: Iowa State University Press, 1987.

———. *The Red Gods Call.* Ames: Iowa State University Press, 1973.

Evernden, Neil. *The Natural Alien: Humankind and Environment.* Toronto: University of Toronto Press, 1985.

Flader, Susan. *Thinking Like a Mountain: Aldo Leopold and the Evolution of an Ecological Attitude toward Deer, Wolves, and Forests.* Columbia: University of Missouri Press, 1974.

Foster, Edward Halsey. *The Civilized Wilderness: Backgrounds to American Romantic Literature, 1817–1860.* New York: Free Press, 1975.

Frome, Michael. *Battle for the Wildnerness.* New York: Praeger, 1974.

Gibbons, Felton, and Deborah Strom, *Neighbors to the Birds: A History of Birdwatching in America.* New York: Norton, 1988.

Gill, Brendan, and Dudley Witney. *Summer Places.* New York: Methuen, 1978.

Gowans, Alan. *The Comfortable House: North American Suburban Architecture, 1890–1930.* Cambridge: MIT Press, 1986.

Graber, Linda. *Wilderness as Sacred Space.* Washington: Association of American Geographers, 1976.

Hammond, John. "Wilderness and Heritage Values." *Environmental Ethics* 7, no. 2 (1985): 165–70.

Hanley, Wayne. *Natural History in America: From Mark Catesby to Rachel Carson.* New York: Quadrangle Books, 1977.

Hay, John. *The Immortal Wilderness.* New York: Norton, 1987.

Jackson, John Brinckerhoff. *Landscapes: Selected Writings of J. B. Jackson.* Edited by Ervin H. Zube. Amherst: University of Massachusetts Press, 1970.

Kazin, Alfred. *A Writer's America: Landscape in Literature.* New York: Knopf, 1988.

Kolodny, Annette. *The Lay of the Land: Metaphor as Experience and History in American Life and Letters.* Chapel Hill: University of North Carolina Press, 1975.

Krieger, Martin H. "What's Wrong with Plastic Trees?" *Science* 179 (no. 4072): 446–55.

Labastille, Anne. *Women and Wilderness.* San Francisco: Sierra Club Books, 1980.

Leighton, Ann. *American Gardens of the Nineteenth Century.* Amherst: University of Massachusetts Press, 1987.

Lopez, Barry. *Arctic Dreams: Imagination and Desire in a Northern Landscape.* New York: Scribner, 1986.

Lyon, Thomas J. "American Nature Writing: A Selective Booklist on Nature and Man-and-Nature." *Antaeus,* no. 57 (Autumn 1986): 302–17.

————, ed. *This Incomperable Lande: A Book of American Nature Writing.* Boston: Houghton Mifflin, 1989.

Machor, James L. *Pastoral Cities: Urban Ideals and the Symbolic Landscape of America.* Madison: University of Wisconsin Press, 1987.

McLaughlin, Andrew. "Images and Ethics of Nature." *Environmental Ethics* 7 (Winter 1985): 293–319.

Marx, Leo. *The Pilot and the Passenger: Essays on Literature, Technology, and Culture in the United States.* New York: Oxford University Press, 1988.

Meinig, Donald W., ed. *The Interpretation of Ordinary Landscapes.* New York: Oxford University Press, 1979.

Merchant, Carolyn. *The Death of Nature: Women, Ecology, and the Scientific Revolution.* San Francisco: Harper & Row, 1980.

Merton, Thomas. "The Wild Places." In *The Ecological Conscience: Values for Survival,* edited by Robert Disch. Englewood Cliffs, N.J.: Prentice-Hall, 1970.

Muir, Richard. *Shell Guide to Reading the Landscape.* London: Michael Joseph, 1981.

Nash, Roderick F. "The American Invention of National Parks." *American Quarterly* 22, no. 3 (1970): 726–35.
———. *Environment and Americans*. Huntington, N.Y.: Robert Krieger, 1972.
———. *The Rights of Nature: A History of Environmental Ethics*. Madison: University of Wisconsin Press, 1989.
Nichols, John. *A Fragile Beauty*. Salt Lake City: Gibbs M. Smith, 1987.
Niemi, Judith, and Barbara Wieser, eds. *Rivers Running Free: Stories of Adventurous Women*. Minneapolis: Bergamot Books, 1987.
Novak, Barbara. *Nature and Culture: American Landscape and Painting, 1825–1875*. New York: Oxford University Press, 1980.
Olds, Elizabeth Fagg. *Women of the Four Winds: The Adventures of Four of America's First Women Explorers*. Boston: Houghton Mifflin, 1985.
Owings, Loren C. *Environmental Values, 1860–1972: A Guide to Information Sources*. Detroit: Gale Research, 1976.
Passmore, John. *Man's Responsibility for Nature*. New York: Scribner, 1974.
Perrin, Noel. "Forever Virgin: The American View of America." *Antaeus*, no. 57 (Autumn 1986): 13–22.
Reiger, John F. *American Sportsmen and the Origins of Conservation*. New York: Winchester Press, 1975.
Relph, Edward. *The Modern Urban Landscape: 1880 to the Present*. Baltimore: Johns Hopkins University Press, 1987.
Rosenkrantz, Barbara G., and William A. Koelsch, eds. *American Habitat: A Historical Perspective*. New York: Free Press, 1973.
Rosenthal, Bernard. *City of Nature: Journeys to Nature in the Age of American Romanticism*. Newark: University of Delaware Press, 1980.
Roszak, Theodore. *Where the Wasteland Ends: Politics and Transcendence in Postindustrial Society*. Garden City, N.Y.: Doubleday, 1972.
Santmire, H. Paul. *Brother Earth: Nature, God, and Ecology in Time of Crisis*. New York: Thomas Nelson, 1970.
Schmitt, Amy L. "We Took to the Woods: Women in the Wilderness in the Twentieth Century." Senior thesis. Wooster, Ohio: College of Wooster, 1989.
Schneider, Stephen H., and Lynne Morton. *The Primordial Bond: Exploring Connections between Man and Nature through the Humanities and Sciences*. New York: Plenum, 1981.
Schuyler, David. *The New Urban Landscape: The Redefinition of City*

Form in Nineteenth-Century America. Baltimore: Johns Hopkins University Press, 1986.

Shelton, Peter. "Growing Up in the High Country." *Backpacker* 17, no. 4 (1989): 20–25.

Shepard, Paul. *Nature and Madness.* San Francisco: Sierra Club Books, 1982.

Sipchen, Robert. "The New Naturalists." *Orion Nature Quarterly* 7, no. 4 (1988): 61–64.

Snyder, Gary. *The Old Ways.* San Francisco: City Lights Books, 1977.

Steinhart, Peter. "Place as Purpose: Muir's Sierra." *Orion Nature Quarterly* 7, no. 4 (1988): 42–49.

Stilgoe, John R. "Bikinis, Beaches, and Bombs: Human Nature on the Sand." *Orion Nature Quarterly* 3, no. 3 (1984): 4–15.

———. *Borderland: Origins of the American Suburb, 1820–1939.* New Haven: Yale University Press, 1988.

———. *Common Landscape of America, 1580 to 1845.* New Haven: Yale University Press, 1982.

Thomas, Keith. *Man and the Natural World: A History of the Modern Sensibility.* New York: Pantheon Books, 1983.

Todd, Nancy Jack, and John Todd. *Bioshelters, Ocean Arks, City Farming.* San Francisco: Sierra Club Books, 1984.

Trimble, Stephen, ed. *Words from the Land: Encounters with Natural History Writing.* Salt Lake City: Gibbs M. Smith, 1988.

Tunnard, Christopher. *A World with a View: An Inquiry into the Nature of Scenic Values.* New Haven: Yale University Press, 1978.

Vest, Jay Hansford C. "The Philosophical Significance of Wilderness Solitude." *Environmental Ethics* 9 no. 4 (1987): 303–30.

Wadland, John Henry. *Ernest Thompson Seton: Man in Nature and the Progressive Era, 1880–1915.* New York: Arno Press, 1978.

Whisenhunt, Donald W. *The Environment and the American Experience: A Historian Looks at the Ecological Crisis.* Port Washington, N.Y.: Kennikat, 1974.

Williams, Raymond. *The Country and the City.* New York: Oxford University Press, 1973.

Worster, Donald. *American Environmentalism: The Formative Period, 1860–1915.* New York: Wiley, 1973.

———, ed. *The Ends of the Earth: Perspectives on Modern Environmental History.* New York: Cambridge University Press, 1988.

Index

Abbott, Charles, 109

Abbott, Lyman, 55, 141; attacks nature movement, 31

Adams, Charles C., 174

Addams, Jane, 74

Adirondacks, 7

Agrarian myth, 5, 6, 188; definition of, 4

Alexander, John, 109, 113

Alvord, Dean, 18

Anderson, Nels, 182

Arcadian myth, 11, 15, 16, 36, 60, 62, 65, 77, 83, 101, 105, 114, 136, 184, 188; and camping, 8; and cemeteries, 67; and children, 86, 93, 94; and country life, 5, 6, 7, 18, 22, 182; definition of, xvi–xvii, 17, 56, 94, 188; and fiction, 118, 124, 126, 140; and nature writing, 45, 53, 54, 55; origin of, xvii; popularity of, 32; psychology of, 18, 79; and regional planning, 183; and sportsmen, 9; *see* Nature movement

Art Nouveau, 15, 135

Atlantic Monthly, 22, 23, 24, 49, 125, 146

Audubon, John J., 34

Audubon Societies, 42

Automobiles, and parks, 72, 153, 155, 160–62, 163, 166, 171; and suburbs, 16; and traffic congestion, 178; and wilderness, 173

Bacheller, Irving, 126

Badé, William, 144

Baden-Powell, Sir Robert, 106, 108, 110, 111, 112

Bailey, Liberty Hyde, 4, 5, 17, 30, 84, 94, 96, 144, 171, 174; on children, xx; on farm problems, xxi; on problems of nature movement, xxiii; on suburbs, xxi

Baker, Ray Stannard, 21, 31; as David Grayson, 26

Balch, Ernest, and Camp Chocorua, 99

Baldwin, Charles, 139

Ballinger, Richard A., 159

Barrows, Walter, on English sparrow, 39

Barrus, Clara, 24

Barton, Bruce, 144, 145

Bates, Katherine Lee, 142

Beach, Rex, 173

Beard, Daniel C., and boys clubs, 106, 107, 108, 109, 110, 112; and summer camps, 99–100

Bierstadt, Albert, 155

Bigelow, Maurice, 87

Bird-watching, and Christian ornithology, 36–38; and English sparrows, 38–40; literature on, 35, 36; and nature writers, 35; and ornithology, 34–35; and photography, 149; and school children, 42, 82

Blanchan, Neltje, 30, 35

Bogardus, Emory, 102

Bok, Edward, 68, 107

Boston, Massachusetts, 11, 23, 59, 61, 63, 78; and Fresh-air charity, 97–98; and nature-study, 77; and

Torrey, Bradford, 185
Trafton, Gilbert, 35, 40
Transcendentalism, 22, 24, 63, 188
Turner, Frederick Jackson, xv
Tynan, James J., 132

United States Government, and
    Hetch-Hetchy, 156–58; and Park
    Service, 159; and parks, 154–56;
    and wilderness areas, 174
Urban sociology, 179–81
Urbanism, 74, 180
Urbanization, conveniences of, 3, 31;
    fear of, 179–81, 186; lure of, 180;
    problems of, 3, 13, 133, 178

Vandergrift, Joseph, 30
Van Dyke, Henry, 38, 109, 142, 144,
    145
Van Dyke, Theodore, 8
Vaux, Calvert, 20, 59

Wallace, Dillon, 121–24, 137, 170
Waller, Mary, 126, 131, 135
Ward, Carlos, 103, 105, 113
Warner, Charles D., 8
Washington, D.C., 23, 59, 71, 99
Waugh, Frank A., 60; on preserva-
    tion, 15
West, James E., 109
Wheeler, Andrew, 7
Whipple, T. K., 177
White, Gilbert, 148
White, Stewart Edward, 126, 127,
    137, 138, 171, 176, 185; and *The
    Cabin*, 169, 170; and Yosemite,
    167
Whitney, Caspar, 29
Wiggin, Kate D., 94
Wilderness, 4, 7, 14, 16, 53, 181,
    186; and Appalachian Trail, 184;

and children's fiction, 119, 120;
    criticism of, 135; films, 149–53;
    and government, 174; meaning of,
    169, 174, 175–76, 177; and parks,
    155, 166; publicity, 170, 172; and
    solitude, 167–76; and summer
    camps, 101; and vacations, 168,
    172–73; and wilderness areas,
    173; and Wilderness Society, 175,
    176; *see also* Wilderness novel.
Wilderness novel, 125–40, 147; char-
    acterization, 129–33; and cities,
    133; compared to Western novels,
    130; criticism of, 138–40; and
    culture, 131; and logging, 126;
    and religion, 142, 143; and scen-
    ery, 128
Williams, James M., defines "myth,"
    xv
Wilson, Alexander, 34
Wilson, John, 83
Wister, Owen, 125
Wood, J. G., 81
Wright, Harold Bell, xix, 125, 126,
    133, 134, 137, 138; characteriza-
    tion, 129–30; criticism of, 139; on
    nature worship, 142
Wright, Mabel Osgood, 35, 44, 54

Yard, Robert S., 161, 163, 164, 166;
    and Wilderness Society, 175
Yellowstone National Park, 154, 155,
    161, 162, 176
Yosemite National Park, 59, 154, 155,
    160, 161, 163, 164, 171, 176
Yukon, 170, 171

Zorbaugh, Harvey, 180